MW00356394

"My friend Larry Katzen is just as evocative with words as he is with numbers—a rare gift. This beautiful story shows that the road warrior can also be a spiritual warrior."

—Deepak Chopra, M.D. and author

"A person who always tried to do what was right and lived by the firm's culture of think straight—talk straight."

—David Maxwell, Chancellor of Drake University

"Larry's exceptional and personal candor will arm readers with very valuable leadership insights."

—WR Howell, former CEO and Chairman of JC Penney

"You will enjoy reading this adventure. I guarantee it."

—George Zimmer, Chairman of The Mens Wearhouse

"Katzen illuminates how one can engage in their work, develop meaningful relationships and be involved in continuous learning. This is a must read for anyone interested in maximizing their career growth."

—Jan Torrisi-Mokwa, CEO and founder of Congruence-Inc.

AND YOU THOUGHT ACCOUNTANTS WERE BORING

My Life Inside Arthur Andersen

LARRY R. KATZEN

to Susan

My wife, my love,
the woman who
sacrificed so much
to support my career

Contents

Contents

Acknowledgments

Before Arthur Andersen's demise, I met so many interesting and great people who helped me prepare for my next stage in life. I would like to acknowledge just a few, while hopefully not insulting any whom I have left out. So many people have made an impact in my life that it would be impossible to acknowledge them all. I present the following list in no particular order.

Al Winick: A partner in the Chicago office, Al had the courage to hire someone with only a "B" average to join the firm. He was confident that I would fit in well with the Andersen culture. He took a gamble, and he was right.

David Schwartz: David was the first person I worked for when he was a manager in the retail division of our Chicago Office. We worked on so many different and difficult assignments together that he undoubtedly served as one of my strongest mentors. He guided my career and made sure I didn't step on any landmines—sometimes a very difficult task. Without him, I wouldn't be where I am or who I am today.

Jim Brice: The managing partner of our Chicago office when my wife gave birth to quadruplets, Jim supported me and my family through everything. I will never forget his kindness and understanding during those hard times.

Van E. Wells: Van taught me so much while I worked in the Chicago Office. He taught me everything from how to maintain client relations in times of sensitivity and controversy to the true meaning of quality service.

Frank Rossi: Frank transferred me to Dallas and gave me the freedom to develop and grow a retail practice in Texas. I learned so much just watching Frank in action. He threw me into a very difficult new client situation and let me have the flexibility to handle it on my own.

Terry Lengfelder: When I was assigned to be managing partner of the St. Louis office, I reported to Terry Lengfelder, the regional managing partner. Terry gave me the encouragement and financial support I needed to turn the office around. Without his support, it would not have been possible.

Tom Kelly and Dick Measelle: I worked with Tom, managing partner of the Western Region, and Dick, managing partner of our business unit, to help develop a process to design and implement an international strategy for the firm. It was a joy to work with both and see how they each thought outside of the box. I appreciate the opportunity they gave me—this most interesting, professional experience.

Jim Kackley: Jim showed me how important it was to support the organization and how to encourage others to perform beyond their own expectations. He taught me how to lead.

Jerry Loeb: The CFO for the May Company, Loeb probably taught me more than any other individual. He taught me how to view things from so many different perspectives and to focus on what is most important. Jerry was the toughest person I ever worked with, but he was also the smartest.

Donald Zale and Bruce Lipshy: Together, they ran the Zale Corporation when it went through some very difficult times. Both of these individuals worked under severe personal and professional pressures as they led the company through one crisis after another. For a number of years I spent a good portion of my life working by their side. They taught me how to remain calm under the most difficult of circumstances.

W.R. Howell: He was the one who made the tough decision to move JC Penney and their executive team from New York City to Dallas, Texas. It was an absolute pleasure to work with W.R. and his executive team. He was a person who lived by his values and respected and honored all of those around him. W.R. lived and breathed the JC Penney culture. He was an amazing man to watch.

All of these people taught me so much. I can only hope you learn some of what they taught me. At Arthur Andersen, we worked hard and played hard. We laughed together and cried together. We were a family, and I would not trade that for anything.

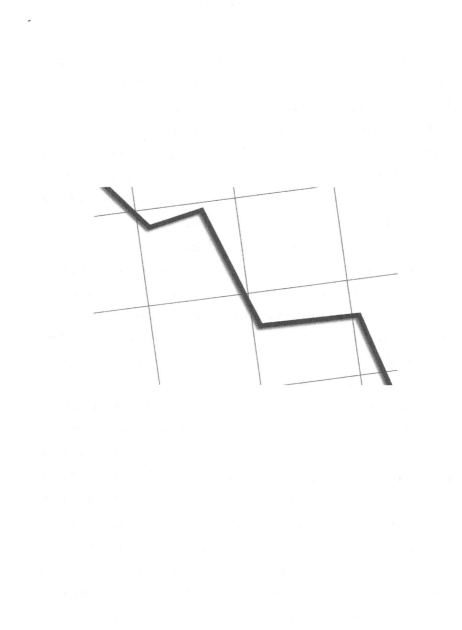

Preface

Background Information[1]
Who Was Arthur Andersen?

On December 1, 1913, the firm of Andersen, DeLany & Co. was started in Chicago, Illinois. It was founded by Arthur Andersen and Clarence DeLany, who acquired a company named the Audit Company of Illinois following the death of the founder. When DeLany left the firm in 1918, its name was changed to Arthur Andersen.

In the beginning, Arthur Andersen specialized in serving public utilities. But by the 1920s, the company had acquired a number of commercial clients, including Colgate-Palmolive, Parker Pen, and Joseph Schlitz Brewing Company. The firm quickly earned a reputation for its quality work and principled approach. In those days, there were no accounting rules. Each firm used its best judgment to certify the financial statements, and Arthur Andersen

---

1 For additional background information and explanatory diagrams, please see the references and exhibits at the end of the book.

quickly developed a reputation for improving the integrity of financial reporting to the public.

In 1947, Arthur Andersen unexpectedly passed away, and the remaining partners were considering liquidating the firm. After some difficult debate, the partners agreed to buy the family interests out for $1 million, a significant amount of money in those days. Leonard Spacek became head of the firm.

At this time, there were seven large auditing firms followed by the up and coming Arthur Andersen. Leonard Spacek was invited to work with the other major accounting firms to discuss the establishment of universal accounting principles. At that meeting, the head of Price Waterhouse, one of the largest auditing firms, extolled the idea that these decisions should be made by the larger firms alone. To him, the smaller firms, such as Arthur Andersen, should not have a voice.

This meeting so riled Leonard Spacek that, as the story is told, he said, "If size is necessary to have a voice at the table, then Andersen is going to be much larger." From then on, Leonard Spacek pursued an aggressive strategy of hiring the best people, providing them with the best training, and enthusiastically serving our clients. This emphasis on attracting and developing the best talent enabled the firm to grow rapidly.

Arthur Andersen was the first firm to do campus recruiting. At the same time, they developed central training so that new people who joined the organization were all trained in the same processes and procedures. They had a universal knowledge base. Partners were required to be instructors, and soon the company's training programs became the envy of the profession. In the 1970s, Arthur Andersen further demonstrated its commitment to training with the purchase of St. Dominic College in St. Charles, Illinois. The company subsequently made significant investments in the facility that resulted in its expansion from 45 to 145 acres, thereby increasing the company's investment in the venture to somewhere in excess of $140 million. This facility became one of the most highly regarded training facilities in the world.

Leonard quickly became a powerful voice in the accounting profession. He emphasized that accounting principles were far too loose in the United States and introduced the concept of an "accounting court." According to Leonard's vision, this decision-making body would reach conclusions as to the acceptable accounting principles. Although this accounting court never materialized, it was the impetus for the establishment in 1959 of the Accounting Principles Board.

Leonard also believed that the financial statements of the United States of America should be prepared like those of a corporation. He volunteered the firm to compile and publish the first ever consolidated financial statements for the United States prepared on an accrual basis. This demonstrated the need to be more fiscally responsible and to recognize the cost of future promises that were being made, but not reflected in the cash basis U.S. financial statements. His vision attempted to provide governmental accountability.

The firm was unique in many ways. Arthur Andersen established what was known as "Subject Files," where the audit team wrote up its experiences and reasons for coming to certain conclusions in order to share them with all other members of the firm. In this manner, the company gave a consistent answer to an accounting issue no matter where they were located. The firm was truly unified. They developed the "One Firm" concept with each office following the same policies and procedures and sharing equally in the success of the firm based on worldwide results. Most other firms shared earnings based on their office or country results, promoting cutthroat competition and sabotage. This "One Firm" concept influenced everything that the company did, from recruiting, to training, to serving clients, and to the way each office was administered. One could walk into any Arthur Andersen office throughout the world and feel comfortable working there.

This strong culture resulted in strong bonds within the organization. Members of the organization called Arthur Andersen "the firm," as if there were no others. The younger people would call the firm "Arthur," as everyone called each other by their first names. There was no such thing as "Mr." or "Mrs." Everyone was treated equally. When people left the firm, they always referred to themselves as "we," even if they left the firm years ago.

Arthur Andersen also believed in stewardship, whereby everyone was committed to leaving the firm in a better position than when they had joined it. This made it easy to continually invest in the future rather than simply put more money in the partners' pockets. It enabled the company to do things like investing hundreds of millions of dollars into a training facility.

Up until 1955, Arthur Andersen primarily operated in the U.S. However, in order to serve international clients, from 1957 to 1963 the company opened 25 international offices, and from 1963 through 1973, another 25. In order to maintain the "One Firm" concept, they transferred core personnel to overseas offices in order to hire, train, and develop the people. Local staff were all recruited in the same fashion as in the U.S. They were trained in the same firm schools and learned the "One Firm" concept. This was quite different than all the other firms, which operated similarly to a confederation of offices, whereby each office or country operated independently of one another.

By growing in this manner, most of the Andersen offices outside the U.S. were much smaller than the competition's. Many of the other firms started their practices in the UK and then expanded to the U.S. Arthur Andersen did it the opposite way. Similar to what happened in the U.S., however, Arthur Andersen eventually grew rapidly overseas and dominated the market in many countries.

Arthur Andersen always felt clients needed their assistance in designing and installing systems for reporting financial data and believed the firm had the skills to do so. In the mid-1950s, they handled the first consulting project of its kind with the installation of a computer payroll system for General Electric. Later, Arthur Andersen developed a modular system for designing computer installations. This resulted in their being a leader in systems integration, whereby they helped clients design disparate hardware and software to work together. This practice eventually grew into Andersen Consulting ("Accenture").

In 1974, Arthur Andersen instituted the "Public Review Board," composed of senior people who held major positions in business, politics, and government. Its mission was to provide oversight on Andersen's responsibility for acting in the public interest and to review the organization's effectiveness, just as an independent board of directors does for a public company. In the 1980s, the company published its own financial statements and shared them with the public. They were the only firm that was so transparent.

In the 1980s, Andersen saw tremendous growth opportunities in Asia Pacific. Virtually all firms were represented by a firm in Southeast Asia known as SGV. SGV admired Arthur Andersen and in 1983, it merged with Arthur Andersen. It was one of the few acquisitions that the company made, and it helped them become a major player in that part of the world.

Arthur Andersen was a leader and pioneer in the accounting profession. Its growth and success was the envy of the accounting profession, as shown by the following results, which occurred since the time I, Larry R. Katzen, joined the firm:

Year	Revenue in Millions
1967	$ 96.8
1970	190.2
1975	386.3
1980	805.5
1985	1,573.8

By 1995, Andersen grew its revenues to over $8 billion and to over $14 billion at the time of its separation from Andersen Consulting in 2001. Its profitability per partner was the highest in the profession. During my career, I saw the firm grow from 5,800 people to more than 135,000.

By the 1990s, the once infamous Big 8 became the Big 5, with the merger of several large firms. In 2002, the Big 5 became the Big 4 when Arthur Andersen went out of business as a result of the U.S. government's indictment against the company for obstruction of justice in connection to the federal investigation of the Enron audit. Later, the Supreme Court reached a unanimous decision that the previous verdict was incorrect and reversed the decision of the lower federal appellate court; however, it was too late. A great firm went away and will be missed by many: clients, employees, Andersen alum, and even the profession.

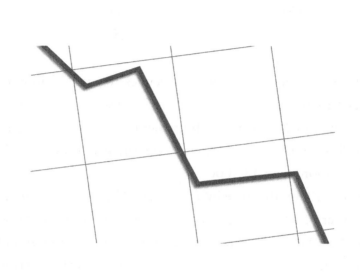

Prologue

The End – 2002

Friday, August 2, 2002. Hot, humid. One of those days when you can feel the sweat pooling in your wrinkles. I looked out of my window at 1010 Market Street in St. Louis, Missouri. Just a few blocks from the Cardinals stadium, it was normally bustling with people, but today both the streets and the office behind me were empty. The Cardinals were out of town, and everyone else had already packed up and moved on weeks before. I was the only one left.

Maybe I should have retired earlier. Technically, I had. But I couldn't leave during the Enron crisis. Nobody—certainly not any of my clients, employees, or friends—would have ever believed that the managing partner of the St. Louis office would leave in the middle of that mess. I'd had to keep coming to the office, making sure our people were taken care of while I negotiated with my former competitors to buy our offices.

In a way, I felt like Schindler from *Schindler's List*. I wanted every person to land somewhere new and restart their careers, wherever they might be. So when I negotiated deals to sell our offices, I tried to convince the other companies to hire as many of our people as possible.

As Finance Chairman of the St. Louis Regional Commerce and Growth Association (RCGA), when I attended board meetings, I bragged about the quality of our people and encouraged the other members to hire even just one person. I knew St. Louis was concerned about losing talent. If each member hired just one person, all of our people could remain employed in St. Louis.

I sighed. My lifelong journey with Arthur Andersen was over. I picked up my last box, turned out the lights, and walked to my car. As I opened up the trunk and placed the box inside, I paused. A trunk full of boxes was all I had left of my 35 years with Arthur Andersen. There was no party or celebration. No excitement or jubilation. Just boxes. I closed the trunk and drove home.

CHAPTER 1

The Beginning – 1967

Interview Season, 1967. Each week, I boarded a plane and went to another city, interviewing for everyone from Chrysler to governmental agencies to the "Big 8" accounting firms. In those days, it was not uncommon to have a drink or two for lunch, and I quickly noticed the most common drink ordered was a martini. So after a few interviews, I ordered a martini on the plane. I was determined to be like everyone else. There was no question in my mind that the Big 8 was for me.

As a senior at Drake University, this was one of the most exciting periods of my life, being able to leave campus. I'd always wanted to travel more. I'd even dreamed of going to UCLA most of my life, until my senior year of high school, when my parents suddenly told me I had to stay in the Midwest. The next day I was sitting in the cafeteria, dejectedly staring at my food when a classmate walked by. He asked me where I was going to college, and I told him I had absolutely no idea. Because I didn't. He suggested Drake

University, said it had a great accounting school. I had nothing to lose, so I applied. I got in. This classmate didn't.

But now, I got to live my dreams. Each weekend, I boarded a plane and met with new people in new places. One of my most unusual visits was my trip to Detroit to meet with Chrysler. I was supposed to meet with the CFO and some other executives at the corporate headquarters before taking a helicopter to one of the factories. When I arrived, I gave the receptionist my name and then waited for the first interview to begin.

I waited....

And waited....

And waited.

Finally, one of the executives came up to me and asked if he could help me. I told him who I was waiting for and he looked at me confused. That man wasn't there that day. This other executive then introduced himself as the head economist for Chrysler and was kind enough to take me into his office to talk.

I had a most fascinating discussion with him as he explained to me the economics of the auto industry and how they were trying to increase their market share. I spent a few hours with him before going back to the airport to return to Drake University. Thinking the interview was a complete failure, I was relieved the day was done. I figured there was no way I would receive an offer from this company, and, if by chance I did get an offer, there was no way I could accept it.

However, a few weeks later, I received an offer in the mail

saying they apologized for the mix-up, but the letter continued by saying that I impressed the people I talked with so much that they offered me a starting salary of $11,700 a year plus a car and tuition at the University of Michigan graduate school. To put things in perspective, the Big 8 offers were coming in at around $8,400 with no comparable fringe benefits.

I was in total disbelief. At first, I thought this had to be a mistake, but I kept rereading the letter. It was definitely addressed to me. I called my Uncle Sidney to get some advice. Uncle Sidney was my biological father's brother. I never really knew my father, Jack Rosen. He'd died of kidney disease on October 4, 1946, when I was just a baby. Uncle Sidney and his sister, Lillian, were my only ties to him. Sydney was the man who provided for my college, as the trustee of the small inheritance I received from my grandfather, Louis Rosen, who died one week before I was born as Louis William. After my mom later remarried, my name was legally changed to Larry Rosen Katzen. Thus, my uncle was my main connection to the Rosen heritage. Uncle Sidney was also one of my closest confidantes. I talked to him about almost everything, so naturally I wanted his advice now, especially since he was a partner in a local accounting firm in Chicago called Katz Wagner. He knew the industry, and since I had previously interned at his firm, he also knew me and my capabilities.

My uncle gave me some great advice. He said, "You should take your first job offer based on where you think you will be the happiest and not based on money. You will have plenty of years ahead of you to earn money and you should not select your first job based purely on the financial reward." It seemed wise to me, but I decided I should seek a second opinion just in case.

So, I decided to share my thinking with Professor Dilley, the head of the accounting department at Drake. Professor Dilley was the most boring accounting professor ever. An extreme introvert, he was far from popular with the students. No one got close to him or liked him, but I knew he loved the Big 8 accounting firms. He even made sure one of the first tests in the department was a simple spelling test. Spell the names of the Big 8. Get any wrong and you weren't going to be an accountant. If anyone at Drake could help me in this crisis, it would be him. The man with so much knowledge of and passion for accounting.

When I told him, he was so proud that I had received an offer that was so much higher than that of any other person in the class. He said that would increase the average starting salary of a Drake accounting grad and would be great publicity for the school. However, when I told him what my Uncle Sidney said, he strongly disagreed. He explained how many years I would have to work before I reached that level. He further mentioned that Chrysler was beefing up the quality of its financial organization and that I would undoubtedly have a tremendous future there.

I was now totally confused. I decided to defer my decision until I finished all my interviews. I interviewed with seven of the Big 8 accounting firms: Deloitte Haskins & Sells in New York; Ernst & Whinney in Minneapolis; and Peat Marwick Mitchell,

Price Waterhouse, Touche, Ross Bailey & Smart, Arthur Young, and Coopers & Lybrand in Chicago. Out of this bunch, I felt most comfortable with Peat Marwick Mitchell.

Arthur Andersen was my last visit, and I had already heard a consistent story from the other seven firms: If you go with a Big 8 firm, do NOT go with Arthur Andersen. Andersen, they said, was too rigid. You had to wear white shirts, hats, and bring an umbrella. They were arrogant. They worked you too hard. I would not be happy at Arthur Andersen.

Not to mention the pervasive stereotype that Arthur Andersen was an anti-Semitic firm. I once met a man who'd worked for Arthur Andersen before becoming a cattle rancher. He told me about how he had to change his name to work there. No one knew he was Jewish, and he never told them. He would have been a leper. The only Jew in the New York office.

The messages were so consistent, I figured they had to be true. So, I went back to Professor Dilley and told him of my desire to go with a Big 8 firm and that the one I wanted was Peat Marwick Mitchell (now called KPMG). Professor Dilley tried one more time to convince me to go with Chrysler, but the only reason I was even considering Chrysler was because of the money. I told him if it were not for that, I wouldn't even give them a second's worth of thought. I could not accept their offer.

I then informed him that I was going to skip my visit with Arthur Andersen and accept the offer from Peat Marwick Mitchell. Professor Dilley's face turned bright red and he said with no uncertain terms, "My son, you signed up for that interview with Arthur Andersen, and it is your responsibility to follow through on your commitment." He would not tolerate anything else. Since he did not pressure me anymore on Chrysler, I decided to placate him about this. So off to Chicago I went to interview for Arthur Andersen with my letter of acceptance from Peat Marwick Mitchell in my pocket.

I visited Arthur Andersen on March 21, 1967. I arrived the night before and stayed with my parents, my mom, Marion, and my dad, Rube Katzen. Ignorant to the fact that Rube wasn't my biological father until I was about five or six, I idolized him. He was everything I wanted to be: honest, caring, and smart. Not to mention athletic. He was a jock in high school, part of the Roosevelt High basketball team that won the city championship. He was an amazing man albeit an introverted one. Marion was the opposite. Reminiscent of Lucille Ball in looks and personality, she was a hoot. An extrovert, she had a lot of friends and loved to go out and do things, always dragging my dad around with her. My mom was quite a character. If she didn't like you, she'd let you know. She was the most influential woman in my life.

Because of my close relationship with my parents, I shared with them that my interviews were just about complete and that I was going with Peat Marwick Mitchell. We celebrated together with a nice home-cooked dinner. I was totally relaxed, as I thought my interview the next day was a mere formality. After all, my decision was already made.

But my interview with Arthur Andersen was nothing like I'd expected. Unlike the other firms, these partners were young and aggressive. I interviewed with Bob Mednick who, after four years with the firm, was the audit manager on Brunswick Corporation. He was full of energy and enthusiasm and later would become one of our senior partners. I also interviewed with Gene Delves, a consulting partner, who shared with me how this was a full service organization that did more than just auditing. In those days, consultants worked on audits and auditors also did consulting. I would get an experience that I could not get anywhere else. I would work on a little of everything. Then there was Al Winick, a Jewish partner, who interviewed me on campus and convinced me that contrary to what I had heard, Arthur Andersen was not anti-Semitic or militaristic. This firm simply had strong values and beliefs. If they disagreed with a client, they'd stick up for what was right and they were proud of it. They shared stories of how they walked away from major clients and industries because they thought the accounting was too aggressive or morally ambiguous.

Andersen was also the fastest growing of the firms even though they were the smallest. It became clear to me why these other firms were all jealous and, in fact, scared of Andersen. This was the culture I was looking for. This was the organization I wanted to be a part of. This was where I wanted to be a partner one day.

At the end of the day, Al Winick brought me into his office and, with a cigarette in his mouth, proceeded to offer me a job starting at $680 per month. All the other Big 8 firms offered me a salary between $700 and $725 per month. I told Al this was the lowest salary of all my offers, but said I was very impressed with the firm and its culture and would be making my decision shortly. Al said he could see if they could raise my salary to match the others, and I said he did not have to. I was in this thing for the long haul and would not be making my decision based solely on money. I left that interview feeling great. As I walked out of the office, I took out my letter of acceptance to Peat Marwick Mitchell, ripped it up, and dumped it in the Arthur Andersen trash can. I knew this was the firm for me.

When I came home that night, my father greeted me with a smile and said that he hoped I would have a great career with Peat Marwick Mitchell. I told him I was joining Arthur Andersen instead.

At first, my dad thought I was joking. Then he looked concerned. Based on its reputation, he questioned whether a Jewish person could survive at Arthur Andersen. I told him I had no doubts. My gut told me that this was the firm for me. It was the only one that I felt comfortable with. All he could say was, "Good luck. I hope it is the right decision."

On April 3, 1967, I received my offer in writing. My career at Arthur Andersen was beginning.

CHAPTER 2

No Graduation

As graduation loomed, the war in Vietnam was going strong. I'd seen the pictures and the news segments. I certainly did not want to go from the classroom to the battlefield. The alternatives were simple. My first choice was to join a National Guard unit and start my career with Andersen. Me second choice was to enroll in graduate school and defer my employment with Andersen.

In the winter of 1966, I visited as many Guard units as I could find in the Chicago area, but in each case there was a long waiting list. That would leave me too vulnerable. So, I decided to take the graduate school exams and begin preparing my applications.

My last year at Drake University was a very busy and stressful one. Not only was I taking a full course load in order to graduate on time, but I was also taking a CPA review course to prepare for the exam. The pressure was on. Graduation, the CPA exam, and Vietnam.

Luckily, in April, I ran into a fellow classmate named John Joseph Jenkins III from Oskaloosa, Iowa, whom I'd met as a freshman. John said he had just returned from enlisting in a local National Guard unit in Des Moines, Iowa. He was so excited and I was so jealous, until John said there was room for some 20 other recruits. John offered to take me there the next day. I was thrilled. This was the perfect solution. I could take the CPA exam, finish my semester, graduate from Drake, go to boot camp, and then start at Andersen. I told the Sergeant of my plans, and he assured me this would be no problem. They always accommodated graduating seniors.

Two weeks later, I got my orders from Minneapolis that I needed to report to Ft. Leonard Wood, Missouri to start boot camp the week before the CPA exam. I was in total shock. After all, the Sergeant promised that I would not go away to boot camp until after I graduated. I went to ask Professor Dilley to get some advice. I told him that I had not yet notified my parents, since they were looking forward to attending my graduation, particularly since they never went past high school themselves. Professor Dilley tried to calm me down. He said he knew a Major in the Army and would talk to him. I dared to hope, but I knew I still had to break the news to my parents.

Since my dad was the calm one of the family, I broke the news to him first. He was the reassuring type. He gave me the comfort and encouragement I needed. He told me he would immediately try to contact Congressman Charles Percy of Illinois to seek his help. Despite my dad's best efforts, I still felt helpless.

There was nothing I personally could do. I was relying on Professor Dilley and my dad to get an influential person to help me. I decided to take matters into my own hands. So with the CPA exam just a few weeks away, I contacted the Minneapolis U.S. Army recruiting office where I got my orders and asked for their help. They were not very sympathetic and hung up on me.

I was not so easily discouraged. I'm persistent. Minneapolis was not too far from Des Moines, and I thought a personal visit would be more productive than a talk with a stranger over the phone. So, I flew to Minneapolis and presented them with my counter offer. Forget graduation. I just needed to defer my boot camp to the day after the CPA exam. Fortunately the enlistment officer agreed but left me with very little wiggle room. He said I needed to report for active duty the day after I took the CPA exam. I eagerly accepted his offer, but until I had the revised orders in hand, I could not sleep.

My weight was now down to 115 pounds thanks to the stress and studying, much less than my normal 145 pounds. I continued studying day and night for my CPA exam and running to the mailbox to see if I got the revised orders. Finally, they came. I nervously opened the envelope to see the revised orders. Not only was the date revised, but instead of going to Ft. Leonard Wood, Missouri, my orders were to report to Ft. Ord, in beautiful Monterey, California. I could take the exam, finish up my military duties, and be done in time to work for Andersen.

I immediately called my dad to tell him we didn't need Senator Percy's help anymore. Then I ran over to the business school to break the news to Professor Dilley. He would be elated that I could take the CPA exam.

Professor Dilley was glad to hear the news but told me I still would not be able to graduate. If I left school in April, I would not be there to take my final exams in May and complete my courses. Professor Dilley sternly pointed out that I had to complete my finals before I could graduate. My limbs went numb as tears rolled down my cheeks. I was in shock. As I stared at Professor Dilley in disbelief, he finally expressed some empathy. He asked to give him some time. He would see what he could do. I knew Professor Dilley wanted all his students to excel in life, and for some reason I had confidence that he would come up with a workable solution.

A few nerve-racking days later, he told me the good news. I could take my finals in solo with a proctor one month early on the Monday and Tuesday before the CPA exam. Then on Wednesday, Thursday, and Friday, I could take the CPA exam. On Saturday morning at 6:50 a.m., I would be on a United Airlines flight to San Francisco, so I could report to Ft. Ord.

It was not my preferred solution, but it was a solution, a viable one that would enable me to accomplish all my objectives. Professor Dilley and I shook hands on the deal. Now I just needed to study.

Soon after talking to Dilley, I called my parents. My mom was disappointed that she would not get to see her son walk across that stage at graduation, but she offered to help in any way she could. So, my parents drove from Chicago to pack up my belongings while I was taking the CPA exam. When I flew to California, they drove back to Chicago. It wasn't an ideal situation for any of us. But it worked. I ended my life at Drake without jubilation. Just anxiety and stress, as I made my way to Ft. Ord.

The Army was quite a shock. Being relatively ignorant of California geography, I thought it would be sunny and warm in Monterey in May. It was far from it. It was freezing cold, and all I had was my short-sleeve khaki uniform. When I arrived at Ft. Ord, I was told to wait outside until given further orders. I tried, but soon I was shivering from my teeth to my toes, so I went inside. Bad choice. The soldiers were not too happy to find me inside, luxuriating in the warmth when I should have been outside waiting for them. I was already off to a bad start.

To make things worse, Ft. Ord had only recently been re-opened following an outbreak of spinal meningitis. According to the health codes at the time, we had to sleep with our windows open. You'd wake up at 4:30 a.m. to the sound of garbage cans being banged against the floor and finding snow flurries on your blanket. I could tell from day one that this was not going to be an easy time.

It didn't help that I was also the weakest I'd ever been after months and months of stressful studying. On Day One, we were asked to go through the monkey bars before dinner. If you made it through, you had to do 25 push-ups. If you didn't, you had to do

50. I only made it through three or four bars before I fell, but the push-ups were not any easier. I only did 10 or so before I started shaking. I stood up and told the Sergeant I would do better next time. His response was to slap me so hard, I saw stars. I was in so much shock afterwards that when we were eating dinner, I couldn't keep my spaghetti on my fork. I eventually gave up, electing to eat the pasta with my hands.

I still had six months to go.

CHAPTER 3

The Start

I was discharged from Ft. Ord in September 1967 and stopped in Des Moines to see my college sweetheart, Susan Nieder. The two of us had met at a Des Moines synagogue in 1964 during Rosh Hashanah services. I saw her from across the balcony and she immediately caught my eye. Unfortunately, she was in the middle of rushing a sorority, and as part of her initiation dues, she wasn't allowed to talk to any boys that day. Luckily, they didn't say anything about writing. She gave me her number, and I called her a couple days later to ask her out for a Coke date.

It was fairly normal. You'd ask a girl to get a soda with you at 9:30 p.m. If she was a dud, it wasn't too much of a time commitment, since girls had to be in their dorms by 10 p.m. Susan definitely wasn't a dud. Half an hour wasn't nearly long enough. She was a caring, sweet gal with an outgoing personality. She liked to dance. She liked to party, and the two of us were pretty much inseparable throughout my college career.

When I went to Ft. Ord, I realized just how much I loved her. After all, absence makes the heart grow fonder. So, on my way back to my parents, I stopped to see her in Des Moines, Iowa. We went out for dinner and I asked her to marry me. Perhaps I should have asked for her parents' permission, but I never did. I knew she was the one for me. Luckily, she said yes.

Not too long after that, I drained my bank account to declare my love for her. I took her to Lee and Kay Jewelers with my mom to pick out the perfect engagement ring, draining my $1,700 in savings for the purchase. It was worth it, though. Susan was worth that and much, much more.

Soon I was back in high spirits. I was now back to 150 pounds and in a lot better shape than when I'd left. I'd also learned that I had passed two parts of the CPA exam—fortunately, the two hardest parts—Accounting Theory and Accounting Practice, while Law and Auditing did me in. The next sitting for the CPA exam was in November 1967, so I registered to take it, planning on starting with the firm on the following Monday. It seems I was destined to follow the CPA with militarism. The first time I sat for the exam, I was in the Army the next day. This time I would go from the exam to the "Marine Corps" of the accounting profession. Andersen was "tough."

Yes, the firm was demanding, but it also had a soft side to it. The partners expected your best and for you to have total dedication to client service, but they were also there if you needed help. I remember passing the CPA exam and being greeted by Leonard

Spacek, our CEO, who came down to shake the hand of any new employee to congratulate him on passing the exam.

I started with the firm at a good time. The accounting profession was starting a long ride up. Arthur Andersen was the first accounting firm to start a consulting practice, and it was about to take off. From 1966 to 1971, the firm doubled in size to become the largest accounting firm in the world. From 1966 to 1976, it tripled in size! There was no shortage of opportunities in the firm for those who were dedicated to success.

Just like the Army, when I joined the firm, I went to "boot camp." But instead of six months, I only had three weeks. This was three weeks of 12-hour days, seven days a week. At the end of these 21 days, the Andersen culture had been engrained into my brain. I knew how to conduct myself when I visited a client.

I learned about the major tenets of the company. The firm believed in "stewardship"—leaving the firm in better condition than when you had arrived. They talked about the "One Firm" concept, whereby the quality of our work was the same throughout the world and all offices followed the same procedures, policies, and standards. They taught their employees how to "think straight and talk straight" with clients and how "training" was a lifelong exercise. You never stopped learning. Stop learning and you stopped innovating.

In my training, I worked on an actual audit of a fictitious company, learning all facets of an audit. I was taught by partners and managers who questioned and challenged me all day. They were the ones who reviewed me and evaluated my strengths and weaknesses, before I set foot at a client. My instructors included a partner from our San Francisco office and Jim Kackley, a manager from our Chicago office, who eventually became my future boss.

Since this was prior to the firm having its own training facility, the school was held at a Marriott hotel. It was a new Marriott, located near O'Hare Airport in Chicago, and we were there at the grand opening, inaugurated by the later imprisoned Governor Otto Kerner. It was exciting and different. All other sessions were held at Northwestern University; however, since this was the first historic December session, we had to have it at a hotel.

My roommate was from our Tampa office and hailed from the Deep South. We certainly had very different backgrounds and personalities, but this was all part of our education at the firm.

The most difficult part of the three weeks came when we audited inventories. We were given a homework assignment on a Friday night, which had to be completed by Sunday night. We presented the results first thing Monday morning.

Although I enjoyed the school and meeting all these new Andersen people, the inventory section and a bad tooth did me in. It was more than 10 years since I'd last visited a dentist. I was afraid of them. When I was 11 years old, I was playing with a close friend, Carl La Mell, when I fell and cracked my top right front tooth. My nerve was exposed and, unfortunately, I was treated by a quack dentist. My parents thought he was great because he was cheap, but, little did we know, he was also totally incompetent.

Later, I would get my front tooth capped, but the process turned me off of dentists, so I avoided them for a long time. Now, I was at the Marriott hotel trying to impress these Andersen partners only to be in pain again. This time I needed a root canal on another tooth. So I called my dad, who picked me up and drove me to the dentist to have a root canal.

My dad saw the pain I was going through and encouraged me to stay at home and skip the Andersen school, but I didn't want to miss any training. When I returned, my roommate was working hard on the inventory case study and offered to work with me, so I could catch up. We tried, but my pain was not cooperating, so he offered me some advice—you need to drink some bourbon!

At first, I didn't take his advice, but after a while, I just needed to get rid of the pain. The drinking began. The next morning the two of us woke up with splitting headaches and inventory work papers all over our bodies. I don't know how we managed to finish the assignment.

At the end of the session, Mr. Kackley critiqued my performance. He said, "Larry, you performed well and have a bright future, but what happened to you during inventories? That work was just terrible!" I laughed. Little did he know I'd been drunk as a skunk during that portion. Nevertheless, I passed the FASTS (Firm-wide Audit Staff Training School) and was now qualified to work with clients, some of whom were the biggest and most complex in the world. I was now eager, ready, and willing to serve!

CHAPTER 4

A Cold Beginning

One of my first audit engagements was a small retailer in Chicago called Foyers, a local chain of women's specialty stores located on Randolph Street in downtown Chicago.

At the time, I lived with my parents in an old apartment building on the northwest side of the city. We had two bedrooms and a porch off the kitchen, which my parents converted to a third bedroom. Fortunately, my brother, Bob, got married a few years later, so I was able to have the bedroom to myself. The only difficult part was that I still had Sandra, my sister, living at home, and one bathroom for four people was tight. But it was certainly better than sharing it with five, which I had done for most of my life.

To get downtown, I would walk four blocks and then catch the Devon Avenue bus to the Howard Street subway. From there, I only had a few blocks to walk to Foyers.

One day, my senior supervisor on the project suggested we get a quick bite to eat at the nearby Greyhound bus depot. It was a cold winter day and I was enjoying my new cashmere top coat, which I had recently purchased at Sears Roebuck on State Street. It was expensive starting work at Andersen as you had to buy suits, ties, shoes, and in Chicago, a top coat. But with my starting annual salary of $8,100, I felt I could get out of debt quickly. On this cold wintery day, I made the mistake of hanging my new cashmere top coat on the coat rack near our table. When we finished our quick lunch, I went over to the rack to find every kind of coat, except a cashmere top coat. It was gone!

The senior seemed even more concerned than I was, but there was nothing we could do other than to walk back to Foyers in the snow. That night I walked to the subway to return home, and the snow started coming down harder. I was okay until I got off the subway to wait for the Devon Avenue bus to take me home. I was cold and wet, and it didn't get any better when I got off the bus and walked the four blocks home.

When I walked in the door, my mother was shocked to see me enter with my new suit full of snow and no top coat in sight. When I told her what had happened, she looked at me in amazement and said, "How in the world am I going to afford a new coat?"

I quickly calmed her by saying that she never ever had to worry about giving me any money again. As a professional with Arthur Andersen, I would be able to take care of it myself.

The expenses continued to pile up when I got my new audit assignment and asked how to get there. The answer was given in the form of driving instructions. There was one problem. I did not own a car. Despite my parents' protestations and concerns about my spending, I went out that night to buy a car. My dad and I went to a neighborhood car dealer and bought a gold 1968 Pontiac Firebird for $3,600. It was a shame that I had to drive this new shiny car out of the dealership on a snowy night. Luckily, my dad was nice enough to lend me the garage. At least my first car would be clean for one night.

I loved this car and was sometimes concerned about driving it in certain neighborhoods. I had two clients on the South Side, and it seemed I was always surrounded by trucks. At one company, we had to park our cars on the street, and I worried about whether it would be there when I was finished with work late at night.

Sure enough, one night I walked to my car and was suddenly sick to my stomach. Yes, my car was there, but the whole left side was indented with a large tire mark. There was my new 1968 gold Firebird no longer looking new. I was heartbroken. I drove home, concerned again about how I was going to explain this to my parents. I remember my mom saying, "I don't know if you can afford this job."

The next day I went to see the client to talk about it and was approached by someone who had seen the accident. He gave me the name of the trucking company and the truck's license plate. I was determined to find out who hit my new car. When I approached someone from the company, I was informed that the company was in the same building as my client. I was confused. How was that possible? So I went over there, only to learn that my client actually owned this company as well!

It was now time to call the partner on the account, Dick Starkey, and get some advice. However, when I talked to Dick, he insisted that I was mistaken. He said his client did not own any trucking company. None of his records indicated he did, so I went back to see if I heard things right. I had. With my story confirmed, I called Dick back to tell him the news. That afternoon, Dick brought me with him to the client's CEO's office to hear my story. When I was done, the CEO confirmed that it was his company. Dick then made it really clear that their financial statements needed to reflect this entity!

This was the first accounting issue I was exposed to in my career at Andersen, and it was discovered entirely by accident (no pun intended). The experience taught me a lesson. You always had to keep your eyes and ears open and take nothing for granted. You just might learn something that could dramatically affect your work and your client, such as the apparent existence of an entire company.

CHAPTER 5

Work Hard, Play Hard

When I started at Arthur Andersen, we were a relatively small firm. We ranked eighth among the Big 8, and our international practice was also relatively small. Our philosophy was to open offices in each country by having a U.S. partner transfer overseas to start an office from scratch versus buying another firm. In this manner, Andersen protected its culture and its "One Firm" concept. We truly operated as one firm and shared the profits on an international basis. Each office was equal, no matter where it was located or when it was started.

Another unique aspect of the firm was that we were the only firm with a consulting practice, known as the "administrative services" division. This tiny division was started by some audit partners. In those days, many of the audit people were assigned to work on some of the administrative services jobs and vice versa. In this regard we were truly one firm. Among my first administrative services assignments was to be the assistant at one of the administrative services division two-week training sessions. Like the audit division, each staff person in the administrative services division was required to attend a two-week program before they were assigned to a client engagement. So, another administrative services staff person and I were assigned the grunt work for this school. The person I worked with was George Shaheen, a good-looking, cocky, and egotistical, tech-savvy guy.

This was the same George Shaheen who 25 years later was in charge of the entire division eventually known as "Andersen Consulting." He was also the man who eventually led the consulting practice's split from the firm to form Andersen Consulting. At the time though, I had no inkling of things to come. George and I were just two guys working as gofers for those two weeks.

We were placed in a large room at the Knickerbocker Hotel in downtown Chicago with one tiny Xerox machine. Our job was to do the duplicating and pass out the material to the students. In those days, a copier only made 10 or so copies a minute. You had to do something to kill the mind-numbing boredom. George and I soon started a game. George had played basketball at Bradley University, so he was a better basketball player than I, but he was not a better baseball player. With our ingenuity, we found a big stick and rolled up some Xerox paper into a ball and played stick ball in this large room. It was far better than doing nothing or watching the Xerox machine slowly duplicate a sheet of paper. We had some great games, and it helped work up our appetite for lunch, where we were able to taste the finer cuisine of the day, whether it was filet mignon, lobster, lamb chops, or other meals normally saved for special occasions. I now began to understand the role of being a professional. Finding joy in the mundane.

This was my first summer with the firm and I was already able to take my first vacation, my honeymoon. Susan and I got married on June 9, 1968, and traveled to Acapulco to celebrate. Susan and I loved lying about in the sun, so we figured Acapulco would be the perfect locale. Too bad it was so hot and humid that you could barely stand in the sun, let alone laze about in it for hours.

Despite these setbacks, it was still memorable and fun. It was our first time out of the country and we met some great people, all of whom were also on their honeymoons. Getting away with Susan reinforced the importance of rest and rejuvenation. Sometimes, you just needed to recharge your batteries.

I followed my own advice the next year when Susan and I took our first "normal vacation" after my busy season. This was just a short trip to Las Vegas, but it was fun. We had a reservation at the Hilton Hotel and our taxi driver dropped us off with our luggage at the front door. I told Susan to watch the luggage while I went in to get some help and check in. Instantly, I turned around. I said we must be at the wrong entrance. This is the casino!

I asked for help, only to be laughed at. The bellhop informed me that this was the main entrance, and if I turned right I would see the registration desk, just past the slot machines. Boy, was I surprised! I'd never been to Las Vegas before. It was an entirely different culture. This certainly wasn't Chicago.

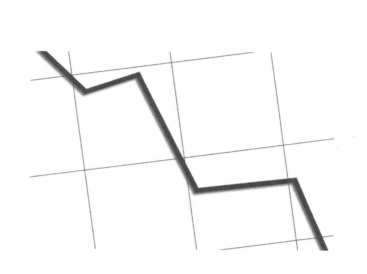

CHAPTER 6

DOWN UNDER AND AWAY

My busy season in 1970–71 was everything I was promised. I was given more responsibility. I was starting to run audit engagements: small ones like Foyers and the Chicago Botanical Garden, where I was in charge of the day-to-day experience, and large ones like Montgomery Ward, where I was a part of a larger team and reported to a senior accountant.

Montgomery Ward was located on Chicago Avenue, just south of the Cabrini Green development, one of the more dangerous areas of Chicago. It was just a few blocks from where my dad once owned a men's clothing store at 414 West Chicago Avenue. I remember visiting the store and playing next door with the Italian kids, whose parents owned a grocery store. After returning from World War II, my dad took over the store from his dad. He liked the men's clothing business, but my mom did not. Every once in a while, my dad would show up at work on Monday morning to find a dead body in front of the store. Yes, Mack the Knife had been busy.

After my dad was robbed at gunpoint one too many times, my mom made him sell the business, and he became a salesman at a shoe store in downtown Chicago. How ironic, now 20 years later, I was working for a client located just down the street from my dad's store.

Montgomery Ward was one of the firm's oldest and largest clients, and some of the most senior partners worked on the engagement. On this account, I worked for a number of seasoned senior partners of the firm including David Schwartz, Van Wells, Jim Brice, and Leonard Spacek. I had to be on my toes working for these guys. They were all tough. They made me and my fellow newbies learn and develop our careers. In turn we worked hard—very hard. It was not uncommon to work seven days a week and get home in the wee hours of the morning, only to get a few hours' sleep and return for more.

One day, everything changed when I was asked to come into the office and meet with our division head, Jack Boyle. Jack asked if I had a passport with me. When I told him no, he immediately went into his suit pocket to pull out his own. He could not believe that anyone who worked at an international accounting firm would not carry a passport. He then said not to worry. The firm had connections and would be able to get a visa for Susan and me within a few weeks. We would be moving to Australia for less than a year to help supervise the audit of the Myer Emporium, the largest retailer in the Southern Hemisphere. The Melbourne office needed a senior accountant with retail experience. I was to complete the audit, train their people, and then come back the next busy season to rejoin the Montgomery Ward team.

I was shocked. I probably had a million questions, but none came to mind at the time. I felt excited and thrilled that I was considered for this major assignment so early in my career but could not comprehend all the things that I would need to do before I left. After all, I was right in the middle of finishing the audit for Montgomery Ward. I also had no idea how Susan would react to this. I collected all the forms I needed for a visa and then mentally prepared myself for how I would break the news to Susan.

When I returned home that night, I was so excited to tell Susan that I barely let her give me a kiss before I shared the news. The firm wants me to move to AUSTRIA! In my shock listening to Jack Boyle, I'd misheard him. I thought he said he was sending me to Austria.

"Austria?" Susan asked. "How are we going to live in Austria? We don't even know the language."

The next day I went to Jack's office and told him that Susan and I were concerned about the move, since we didn't know the language. Jack asked, "What language?"

"Austrian or German or whatever it is Austrians speak!" I told him.

Jack laughed and then corrected me; it was Australia not Austria. Most guys in the firm would have made me feel like a real jerk for my mistake, but Jack was a real gentleman. He had a good laugh but made me feel special. That night I came home and shared the story with Susan. We shared a good laugh, but mostly we were just relieved. The next day, Susan borrowed some books on Australia from the school library where she worked. Long before the Internet, these books were all we had, and they made Australia sound so primitive. They talked about Aborigines, koala bears, and kangaroos. We had no idea what we were getting into.

The days of March 1971 were similar to my final days at Drake: stressful and somewhat painful. I had to work long days and nights to complete the audit in time for Susan and me to catch our plane to Australia. Fortunately, the visas came in time.

My parents would live in our apartment temporarily. They were in process of retiring and moving to Florida with Sandra, my younger sister. My dad was recovering from his second heart attack and my mom was recovering from breast cancer. With our move to Australia, they could all live in our apartment and move to Florida at their leisure.

The firm had us booked on first-class flights from Chicago to Los Angeles to Honolulu to Sydney to Melbourne. All told, the flight was 26 hours. When we got on the United flight, a Boeing 707, the service was amazing. It was our first experience flying first class. They started with cocktails, then a carving station of prime rib or lamb chops, then dessert, then cordials. We were in heaven and excited about our new journey. First class made flying seem easy.

When we caught our plane in Los Angeles to Hawaii, the

service started all over again. Most people were going on their Hawaiian vacation. Once again came the drinks, the carving stations, the desserts, and the cordials. Only this time, we could only nibble. We were so tired, that we slept most of the way to Hawaii. Then we had a long layover in Hawaii before our plane left at midnight to Sydney.

Finally, we boarded the Pan Am flight to Sydney. All we wanted to do was sleep, but first came the drinks, then the carving station, then the desserts, and then the cordials. This time we passed on them all so we could do nothing but sleep. This was important not only because we were tired, but also because Susan does not like to travel. All her life she suffered from motion sickness. She was doing well up until then and sleeping would help, but halfway through that flight, we both woke up and could not go back to sleep. In those days there were no movies or entertainment. The only thing Susan could do was stare at the ceiling and think about her mounting nausea. Needless to say, it was a very long flight.

Unfortunately, as we got closer to Australia, the air got rougher. The flight coming in was turbulent. Susan could not handle the last hour and had to use the disposable bags. We got off the plane and had to change terminals for our next flight to Melbourne. By this point, Susan was so sick she could not move. It took all my persuasion to get her on the last leg to Melbourne.

Luckily, the flight to Melbourne was relatively short. By the time we landed, all Susan wanted to do was get to our new cozy apartment and climb into bed. Unfortunately, the manager on the

Myer account, John Kolasche, had other plans. John was a great guy. He met us at the airport in his Volkswagen Beetle, but he had no idea that we were bringing so much "stuff." Fortunately, a lot of our "stuff" got lost in transit; otherwise we would have really been in trouble. After somehow cramming all this "stuff" into his Volkswagen Beetle, John asked us if he could show us around Melbourne. I took one look at Susan's face and thought she would throw up right then and there, but I didn't want to get off on the wrong foot with John, so I said, "Great! Show us around!"

The city was beautiful and quite different from Chicago. I couldn't wait to see where we'd be living. After all, the firm treats you first class all the way. That is except in Melbourne. John showed us our new rental. The furniture was cheap and uncomfortable. We were situated next to, what I thought was, a restaurant. We were disappointed, but we just wanted to unpack and get settled.

We both felt we could not live here and that I needed to say something to the partner when I showed up for work the next day, but we were so tired that we just jumped into our two single beds and went to sleep. That is, for three hours. We were soon awakened by a rock band playing loud music. What we thought was a restaurant was actually a nightclub. I was furious and started to second guess my decision to move to Australia. My stomach was rumbling with acid indigestion. I couldn't sleep. We were not off to a great start.

CHAPTER 7

My Way or the Highway

Having survived the trip from Chicago to Melbourne, I made it to the office on day one only to be told to take it easy during my first week and to spend some time getting acclimated to Australia. However, I was eager to start the Myer Emporium audit. After all, we had come here as fast as we could to get started on the job. But in Australia, leisure time is as important as work time, and our office management wanted me to first meet the people in our office, learn about Australian accounting rules, and get used to the new time zone.

I met with the office managing partner, Geoffrey Cohen, who was also the partner on the Myer Emporium account. I assumed he would be interested in making our adjustment a smooth one, so I told him what I thought of the apartment they had rented for us and that I needed to rent a better place. Geoffrey was shocked, as he said this was one of the nicer places to rent and was a great location. I told him we could not live there and asked if we could look on our own to find a more suitable apartment at roughly the same price. He approved the plan.

The next day, Susan and I saw our real estate broker, Rhea Castle of the Williams Companies, who showed us a beautiful, cozy, second-floor "own your own," or as we say in the U.S., a "condo," that was available for rent during our stay. It was located just a block from where the firm had put us up. The owner was leaving the country for nine months and wanted to rent it out while she was gone. This was perfect for us! So, we signed up and immediately moved out of our first apartment. It was the best thing we did. We loved our little two-bedroom Flat #4 at 97 Caroline Street in South Yarra. It was tiny, but we didn't need much room.

My joy was short-lived, though. After Geoff got my bill for $450 to cover the cost of shipping our luggage from the U.S., he was furious. He made me write United Airlines a letter requesting a waiver of these costs since our luggage was originally lost. After the airline refused, he reluctantly reimbursed us for our expenses.

By the end of the week, I was eager to get out of the office to meet with Myer Emporium and the staff. They had already started the audit without much supervision. Gary Hershan was in charge. Although I enjoyed Gary and we later became dear friends, his standards were not the same as mine. Gary felt it was more important to get the work done efficiently than it was to do it right. Several days passed before Gary was willing to introduce me to the financial management and to explain who I was and what I was doing there. Most of his employees were working without any audit program and without much supervision.

After getting the lay of the land, I spent time trying to plan the audit engagement. I now knew what a significant effort the job would require and laid out a detailed plan for how to get this audit done the correct way. I then met with the staff to tell them what they were responsible for and the commitment I needed from each person. I sat down with the first staff person and told him that based on my estimate, he would need to work every night for the next month in order to finish on time. At first he seemed to have no problem, until he told me that he played "footy" and needed to leave at 5 p.m. every night. Footy is the term used for Australian Rules football. So I thought he was a professional football player. I later learned that his "footy" was an informal group of guys who got together after work. This certainly wouldn't be tolerated by Arthur Andersen in America. After all, clients come first!

I then sat down with staff member #2 and went through the same ritual. Like the first staff member, he told me about his conflict. He played bridge on several nights during the week and had to leave by 5 p.m. on those nights.

This process was repeated in meetings with all eight staff members. I soon found out that after 5 p.m., I was working all by myself! I was frustrated but determined to complete the audit on time and not disappoint the manager or partner. So, I started staying late on my own. We worked in a partitioned section of this huge old department store in downtown Melbourne. One night while I was working, I heard dogs growling and trying to jump over the partition. I was scared to death. I tried to explain to the security guard why I was still in the store and what I was doing, but he didn't quite understand. Finally, he told me I needed to leave and escorted me out.

The next day, I had my second encounter with Geoffrey Cohen. I asked him how important it was for us to meet the deadline, and he responded that there was absolutely no leeway. I then told him about staff member #1, wanting to play footy. Geoffrey responded that you can't stop someone from playing footy. Not understanding his reasoning, I then told him about staff member #2, playing bridge. Once again, Geoffrey said you can't deprive staff of those commitments. I was astonished! In the States, whatever I would say, the staff would do. It was my way or the highway. In Australia, it was the opposite. Here you had to adjust the work to fit the personal schedule of the staff.

Having gone through the episode in the office, then with the staff, then with dogs, and then again with the office managing partner, I realized that I was not going to change the Australian culture. I would have to adapt. As soon as I accepted that reality, my time in Australia was heavenly.

My job took me to some distant places like Ballarat or Bendigo, which were old mining towns, and Tasmania, an island state off the coast of Australia. It was great meeting all these new people and learning about their culture. It also helped that I was working and traveling with Gary Scott, a staff member who became a good friend. He could help me understand and process the things I saw.

I will always remember the wonderful dinner that Gary and his wife, Ann, made for us. We had been traveling to Ballarat and Bendigo to complete the audits of these stores for weeks. To get a break from it all, Gary invited Susan and me over for dinner with another couple. They had a lovely little house, but without indoor wash rooms. If you needed to use one, you went to an outdoor bathroom. Yet his wife, Ann, went out of her way to make this beautiful rack of lamb and then apologized to us, as, "This was all we could afford." Susan and I were amazed. We both loved rack of lamb and viewed it as a luxury. But in Australia, it was like serving hamburgers.

Not too long after this, I had another confrontation with Geoff Cohen on expense reimbursements. It was the firm's policy to pay for meal allowances if we worked 10 hours or more. We were all working at least that much, and I encouraged the staff to report that expense so they could get reimbursed. Gary and others warned me that the managing partner reviewed these expense reports carefully and would not accept those charges. I reassured them that this was firm policy and it would be okay to do so.

Sure enough, Geoff soon called me to his office and asked what the heck was going on. He had been examining my time report as well as those of the other staff on the engagement and saw meal charges. He wanted to know where I ate dinner. I replied that I ate at home. With that, Geoffrey went ballistic. He issued a memo to all office personnel stating that they would only get reimbursed for meals if they stopped working after eight hours, then went to dinner, and then returned to work at least two more hours. The memo reinforced the view of how "cheap" the office was, and frustrated Gary and the other staff even more.

But it didn't stop there. When we needed to drive out of town, Geoff Cohen would make me drive the other staff. I wasn't the best at driving on the other side of the road and dealing with turnabouts, but Geoff realized that making me drive was the cheapest option, since he was already paying for my rental car on a monthly basis. If I drove, then he wouldn't have to reimburse other staff members for mileage.

On the way out of town on one of these trips, Gary and the others told me that I would not like where we would be staying. When we got to the hotel, I immediately found out why. The place was a dump. However, a few blocks away, there was a little nicer place that cost a few more bucks a day. I told Gary we were changing hotels. When I registered for four rooms, Gary said the office usually requires staff to share a room. I told him this was unprofessional. We were all going to get private rooms. I became their hero for making this decision, but they were all anxious to see how Geoff would react. A few days later, Geoff Cohen came to review our work and almost had a heart attack when I told him where we were staying and that we each had our own room.

I must admit, that despite his severe cost consciousness, Geoff really was a great guy. After seeing how the staff was treated in the

U.S. compared to Melbourne, Geoff even eventually recognized that what he was doing was not in the best interest of morale. Deep down, he was concerned about our staff and recognized that he needed to be more flexible in how he treated them, particularly if he wanted to keep the better performers. Plus, while he faltered in his relationships with employees, he excelled in his conduct with clients. Geoff was a great client service partner and was greatly admired by the executive team at Myer and the other partners in the office. Geoff and his wife, Ola, were wonderful to Susan and me. They invited us to celebrate the Jewish holidays and on several occasions invited us to their home for dinner. Both Susan and I admired them.

Life in Australia was often quiet. In 1971, retail stores in Melbourne closed at noon on Saturdays and all day on Sundays. As a result, Susan and I got to spend a lot of time together. Susan would meet me downtown on Saturdays for lunch, and then we would go home to watch movies on TV. Television was in black and white and celebrating its 15th anniversary. We loved all the time we spent with each other.

Susan also enjoyed her time. She volunteered at the hospital with Ruth Garner. Ruth was the wife of Howard Garner, another expatriate who came from our St. Louis office. Susan would come home from work and tell me all about the wonderful people she and Ruth met and how much they enjoyed their work. Our life together couldn't be much better for two people who were just 25 years old, earning a living and developing a career.

Every Friday, our office would congregate at the local pub next to the office to catch up on what happened in our professional lives during the preceding week. Once we got in this place, we could never leave. Beers were sold in small glasses but were only 25 cents. At any time, there were at least three lined up in front of you, and without knowing who was buying. Although I enjoyed those Friday evenings, Susan did not. She would work on preparing our Friday night dinner, only to see me come in at 8 p.m. or later. Finally, she said no more Friday night meals. I could not blame her. I had adapted to the Australian culture.

Our time in Australia only got better each week we were there. After we signed off on the first audit, Susan and I would go on excursions over the weekends and explore. We saw Phillips Island, where penguins come out of the ocean at a precise time every night. We visited the nearby Dandydong Mountains. We drove to the southern coast to see the amazing 12 apostles. When we had longer weekends, we travelled to Canberra, the country's capital, or Sydney. Many of our trips were with the Garners. Sometimes we had the occasional visitor, such as when Susan's folks came to visit. The time flew by. We made some great friends. It was an experience we shall never forget.

We left Australia in October 1971, taking vacation time to stop in Fiji and the French Polynesian Islands of Tahiti, Bora Bora, and Moorea, where they filmed the movie *South Pacific*. In those days, Susan and I were content to just sit in the sun, do some snorkeling, feed the fish, and read books. This was heaven to us, until something didn't agree with Susan the night before we were to catch a plane back to the States. Susan could hardly move without my assistance. The thought of getting on a long plane ride was the last thing she wanted to do. It took a lot of persuasion to get her on board. As we were flying to Los Angeles, whatever Susan had, soon got to me. It was a good thing we were going first class so that we didn't have a long journey to the restroom.

The next day, we headed to Chicago to be greeted by family and friends. In those days, you could be greeted at the gate and we certainly surprised everyone. Here were two strangers with dark tans coming off a plane. I certainly didn't look like I had spent the past year working long hours on a difficult assignment. Feeling more relaxed than ever, I was ready to get back to the home office and Chicago and do my third consecutive busy season with the firm.

CHAPTER 8

Back to the Marines

On my first day back in the Chicago office, I was never so relaxed. My time in Australia taught me how to enjoy a balanced life, and I was determined to continue this high quality of life in Chicago. I did not want to fall into the old trap of 60-70-hour workweeks. Too bad I didn't really have a choice. I got off the elevator on the fifth floor of the Brunswick building at 69 West Washington Street, only to be greeted by Van Wells, the partner on the Ward's account.

At first, I thought they must have really missed me, but I could soon tell from the look on Van's face that he was under stress. Van greeted me with a curt, "So did you have a good time?" No sooner had I replied, "Yes," than he handed me a ticket to Minneapolis, where I was to work with our administrative services division at the Montgomery Ward catalogue house doing time and motion studies to determine the incremental cost of servicing a credit customer versus a cash customer.

Evidently, the U.S. government was claiming that the retailers were charging usurious rates to credit card customers. The retailers were saying this was not an interest charge, but a service charge to reimburse them for the extra cost of offering credit. So, each of the major retailers was studying what the cost of their credit was, in order to justify the finance (not interest) charge to the customer. Our job was to support the cost of processing a charge order through the catalogue house versus a cash order. We did this by doing time and motion studies on each process where we thought it took longer to process a credit order than a cash order. As an example, if someone had to staple an extra piece of paper to a credit order when they did not have to do this for a cash order, we would do time studies using a stopwatch to calculate the incremental cost of processing a credit order.

We lived in the Minneapolis catalogue house on and off for the next several months during a very cold winter. Each day we would get up early, clean another six inches of snow off the car, warm it up, and head from our dumpy hotel room to the Montgomery Ward catalogue house. In between these assignments, I worked on the Montgomery Ward audit, taking on a new and different role than I had the year before. Now I was at the corporate office and being trained to run the entire audit the following year.

I was fully immersed in work again. My plan to lead a balanced life lasted all of a minute. In a short time, I was totally consumed by work and Australia was a distant memory. Despite being thrown to the wolves, we did make time for some fun.

In 1967, Chicago finally got an NBA basketball team. To encourage people to support their Chicago Bulls, management introduced various marketing promotions. We took advantage of a 15-game package by selecting any 15 games we wanted and getting a guarantee for the same seats should they make the playoffs. Our courtside mezzanine seats cost $5 each.

The Bulls soon assembled a team of very talented players who, under Coach Dick Motta, were always entertaining. Soon, the Bulls filled their roster with the likes of Chet "The Jet" Walker, Bob Love, Jerry Sloan, Bobby Weiss, and Norm Van Lier. They had Tom Boerwinkle to clog the middle. This team was exciting to watch, and soon, more than 6,000 people attended each game. Susan and I went to the games with my closest friend, Carl La Mell, and his wife, Randy. We picked the top opponents to watch, like the Los Angeles Lakers, the Boston Celtics, the Philadelphia 76ers, and the Milwaukee Bucks, who then had Lew Alcindor (Kareem Abdul-Jabbar) at center. Going to these games was great entertainment. The only problem was when there was a game on Saturday night; it interfered with the TV show, *All in the Family.* Luckily, in those days, Carl owned a photography and electronic store in the Loop called Mercury Photo, and he brought a portable TV with him that could be plugged into his car. We got to the games early, sat in the parking lot, and watched the antics of Archie Bunker, before rushing to our seats for tip off.

The Bulls eventually made the playoffs and went to the Western Conference Finals, but they could never get past the Lakers.

The seventh game always did them in. The Lakers were our source of frustration, similar to Chicago baseball, where the New York Yankees always frustrated the White Sox. We could come close, but no cigar.

During this time I continued to serve a number of clients, but most of my time was focused on Montgomery Ward. Later that year, Montgomery Ward bought a retailer in Florida called Jefferson Stores. The purchase price was based on the closing balance sheet, so our job was to audit that balance sheet to make sure Ward's was not overpaying. David Schwartz was the manager and I was the senior. Since we did this work in January 1973, we did not have enough available people in one office to support my efforts. So, we solicited help from every office that could find a staff person for at least a week or two.

I went to Florida to meet with a new crew every few days to explain the assignment, in order to make sure nothing was lost in transition. At first, I thought this would be great. The job had high visibility and I could see my folks, who now lived in North Miami Beach. However, the Jefferson organization was made up of entrepreneurs who used to nickel and dime everyone—customers, vendors, employees, etc. Frequently, they would pay their invoices by taking a discount, whether or not it was deserved. So, as we found questionable items, they would always come back with some innocent reason why they did what they did. Because we were encountering issues, we expanded our scope and extended the assignment. As we found more abnormalities, Jefferson would take more time trying to defend its position. Finally, we gave them a deadline to prove us wrong.

The more we worked together, the more laughs we had. Jefferson management began to realize that we weren't as easy to control as their previous auditors had been. We started to make fun of their delay tactics and kibitz with them. I will never forget when David Schwartz came down to review our work, and we ended up laughing hysterically when we found the chief executive officer (CEO) on his hands and knees behind a desk trying to find shipping documents to support his position. Eventually, the deal closed, the price was adjusted, and Ward management was thrilled with our work. Despite our playing hardball, Jefferson management also really enjoyed working with us and took David and me out for cocktails and dinner to celebrate the conclusion of the project. I learned from David how humor could calm almost any situation.

David and I worked many hours together on Montgomery Ward. The work kept growing, and we developed close working relationships with Ward management. The controller, Jim Reins, was one of the most honest and nicest people you would ever want to meet. Jim would always share with us what was going on, making our ability to audit the company that much more effective. Just to make sure Jim was sharing all, David sometimes went into his office with me and asked, "Have you heard?" Jim, who was always nervous around executive management, responded by saying, "Heard what?" David then turned to me and said, "Oh, he knows," and we would both walk out, with Jim following us out of his office saying, "Tell me, tell me, I have not heard." David employed this tactic to make sure Jim was telling us everything we needed to know. David had nothing to tell Jim but wanted to get him to start talking. Because when Jim started, he could not stop.

One day, David and I walked in and David started with, "Have you heard?"

Jim replied, "Yes, how did you guys find out?" David looked at me and I looked at David, and we both thought Jim was getting even with us for all those times we had pulled his leg. But he was serious and replied, "What a pisser, who would ever think that Mobil Oil would be buying us." David and I were both in shock!

Only a little time had passed since Montgomery Ward had last merged with another public company called Container Corp. to form a new entity called Marcor. Both companies felt they could be takeover targets. They agreed to merge into a combined company, so large that no one could or would want to buy them. They were two different companies (one a retailer, the other a producer of container boards and corrugated boxes) with different business cycles. Now, an oil giant was disregarding these obstacles and was willing to spend a premium to buy Marcor.

Even before this confusion, the audit of Marcor was extremely difficult. Everything was so complex. And, our deadlines were never softened. We literally worked around the clock. When we finished the audit, our firm made a presentation to the audit committee of the board of directors. I worked on putting that presentation together and literally finished around 2 a.m., after not going home at all the night before. I went home for a few hours sleep, got dressed, and went to the Marcor headquarters. I was honored to go, as, in those days, it was only the partners or managers who attended such meetings. My purpose was to pass out the presentation books and not to open my mouth. That was left to partners Spacek, Brice, Wells, Bucholtz, and Schwartz. They were the ones in charge.

The Marcor audit committee consisted of CEOs of major companies, such as Charles Brown, the former CEO of AT&T. I sat next to him in the meeting, which was conducted in the Montgomery Ward boardroom around the largest conference table I had ever seen. The table seemed to be at least six feet wide, and I couldn't venture to guess the length. Now it was time for me to pass out the books. As soon as I got the signal, I was ready to do my job. But instead of going around the large table to hand the book to everyone, I slid it across, only to have it stop in the middle. I got menacing looks from the Andersen partners when they saw one of the audit committee members get up and lay across the table to reach for the book. I was totally embarrassed. How could I screw up my all-important role?

After the meeting, Brown asked me if I was scared. I quickly replied, "No, of course not."

He then asked, "Then, why did you lose your stripes?"

I didn't understand his comment until later when I saw in more vivid light that I dressed that morning with a navy blue pinstripe jacket from one suit and navy blue solid pants from another. What a baptism to the boardroom!

That night I dragged myself home and was so exhausted, I couldn't even eat dinner. I went right to bed so I could rise early on Saturday morning, go down to Wards, and wrap up some loose ends on the audit. When I got up, I felt just like I did in college after I finished my last final. My body was totally relaxed. I was enjoying a quiet breakfast and being careful not to make noise so that I didn't wake Susan. Suddenly, I heard a knock at our front door and opened it. It was our janitor. He asked me if everything was okay and I replied, "Certainly." I asked why he was asking me this and he replied, "Because your car has been running all morning in the back of our apartment complex." I said, "That is impossible, my keys are right here." But when I checked my pockets, there were no car keys. I suddenly realized that when I dragged myself home, I was so tired I just left the car without turning it off! Fortunately, I had filled the tank on the way home from work. But now, I had a quarter of a tank left and my car was so hot, I had to drive to work with the windows open on a cold wintery morning. You might say in more ways than one, I was almost out of gas!

But those were the kinds of experiences that made me grow in the firm. They were part of the initiation process into the Arthur Andersen culture in a sense. When Mobil Oil tried to acquire Marcor, they requested that Mobil's chief operating officer (COO) and the senior partner for Arthur Young meet with David Schwartz to do some due diligence before the acquisition was completed. David asked that I come along, and the two of us met them in their hotel suite. The COO introduced us to the senior partner of Arthur Young, who was their advisory audit partner, and said he needed some information from us. With that, he handed David a letter for him to sign and said, "I am sure if you want to continue servicing Marcor, you will have no trouble signing this letter." I saw David's face turn red as he read the letter to himself.

After collecting his thoughts, David turned to the Arthur Young partner and said, "If you were in my position, would you sign this?"

The partner reflected and said, "No, I wouldn't."

David then said, "Well, neither will I." In his charming way, David then asked what they were trying to accomplish and how could we satisfy their concerns some other way. We then answered their questions to the extent we could and later provided them with information that we both could live with.

To the credit of David and the firm, Arthur Andersen remained its auditor for all the remaining years that Mobil owned Marcor. As much as Arthur Young tried to get us out of there, both Mobil and Marcor felt so strongly about the way we served that account and the industry knowledge that we brought to it, that they knew they needed us. Nonetheless, this crisis and others like it were great learning experiences. Each year there were new and different challenges, but we always exceeded our client's expectations. We lived and breathed Marcor and Montgomery Ward. There were probably only a few days in any given year that we did not spend time in their offices.

Some of those sessions were especially scary. While handling the audit one year, we were all working late on a Saturday night trying to make a deadline. I was a senior then and David was the manager. We were both tired and decided to call it quits at around 10 p.m. and reconvene Sunday morning. Our batteries needed recharging. So, we left together and were crossing Chicago Avenue to the parking garage to get our cars. No sooner had we signed out of the building and got some fresh air than we saw a car speed up to the bus stop. The driver took out a gun and shot the person who was waiting for a bus. David and I looked at each other and immediately ran back into the building. We were not going to that garage until the police came and we could be escorted to our cars. It was just one of many unexpected challenges working for Arthur Andersen. Who knew when I joined the firm that I would see so much?

CHAPTER 9

Be Careful What You Wish For

When we returned from Australia, Susan and I decided it was time to start a family. After trying and failing for months, we sought counsel from Dr. Nadar Bozorgi, Susan's gynecologist. Dr. Bozorgi was very caring and showed great empathy, but he knew we needed someone else. He suggested we see a specialist, Dr. Paul Dmowski.

We naively thought it was going to be a simple process. We would see Dr. Dmowski and in a few months Susan would be pregnant. This was not the case. Each month we would be disappointed by Dr. Dmowski's prognosis and his statement in broken English that, "This is not good."

This was a difficult time for us. Our schedules were so full with both of us working. My travel schedule was hectic and unpredictable, and I was still attending monthly Army reserve meetings. I was not always available when Susan and Dr. Dmowski determined I needed to be. Such was the case when I left on a trip for one of our clients, Booth Fisheries, a division of Sara Lee. The company packaged frozen fish dishes sold in grocery stores. Van Wells was the partner on the account, replacing Al Winick, the partner who had hired me, when Al rotated off.

Van's enthusiasm quickly earned him a tremendous amount of trust from the executives of Booth Fisheries, but he had a difficult time understanding and appreciating their very complex inventory pricing procedure. Many of the activities included in the cost of processing took place at their fishing operations in Fortune, Newfoundland and Central America. Van quickly assessed that we couldn't really do our job unless we visited those places to learn exactly what fishermen do and how that is reflected in inventory costs. So, Van arranged a trip to Nicaragua. The timing interfered with Susan's ovulation calendar, but it was very difficult to arrange this trip, and as a lowly manager, I had little say in the scheduling. Not to mention the fact that I would have just felt embarrassed explaining my conflict to Van.

So, off to Nicaragua we went. We flew into Managua and I was astonished to see it. A few years prior, the city had been hit by an earthquake and the high rises were still standing, or leaning, as it were. There were no inhabitants. The city was being rebuilt farther inland, but it was still a sight to see.

During our first night in the city, we went to have drinks at the home of the partner who was servicing the account. He took us on a tour of his neighborhood. His neighbor had been assassinated a few weeks before, and he showed us the many bullet holes on the side of the house. We certainly weren't in America anymore.

The next day we were to take a long drive to their fishing operations. We were warned that the police or banditos may stop us on the way, but we shouldn't worry. The client would have things under control. Van and I looked at each other and climbed into the car. Sure enough, about halfway to our destination, we were stopped by banditos bearing rifles and donned in bulletproof vests. They yelled at our driver and client in Spanish. We were told to get out of the car and to put our hands on the roof. We were then frisked and questioned. Since they were speaking in Spanish, our client had to answer for us. Finally, the client handed money to the banditos and they allowed us to proceed. When we asked what it was all about, he replied, "They just wanted us to give them money for the policemen's ball. They are really harmless." I bit my lip. What else were we going to see?

As we drove farther down the road, the CFO told us we were going to have drinks with the minister of business. He said he would probably show up with some of his girlfriends, and we would have to entertain him so we could have a good relationship with the minister. He warned us that if the minister picked up his glass of beer, we had to pick ours up. If he drank a beer, we had to drink a beer. Those were the rules.

Sure enough, when the minister showed up at the local bar, he came accompanied. I thought Van at 250 pounds was big, but this man made Van look like a puppy. He was not only very big; he had a big beard and a big hearty laugh. Whenever he laughed, everybody around the table laughed. Whenever he picked up his beer, we all picked up our beers. But after a few hours, I'd had enough beer and shrimp. Not only was I not a big beer drinker in the first place, but I also had a tough time coping with an alcohol-filled bladder. Now I'd had more beers than I'd ever had before and I was sitting there with my legs crossed. Finally, he got up and said good-bye and we all immediately ran to the washroom. I guess the discomfort was worth it, because later that night we were told that he was going to renew the Booth Fisheries' license.

After we visited their shrimp operations near Managua, we traveled to Nicamar to see their lobster operations. These facilities were located on an island off the coast, so we had to fly via a single engine prop plane. We landed on a dirt runway and barely cleared telephone wires at the edge of the runway. From there, a small car picked us up and drove us to the boat dock. With three people crammed into the front of the stick-shift car, and Van and I both still in our suits and ties in 90-degree weather, driving along this dusty road in 90% humidity was miserable. Eventually, we were dropped off at the boat dock where a speedboat waited. One person operated the motor at the rear of the boat, and a boy with a paddle was situated at the front. The boy's job was to protect us. If a shark came too close to the boat, he was to hit it with the paddle.

Upon arrival at the island, we were greeted warmly by the plant personnel and treated to a lobster feast for dinner, complete with fried bananas and beer. The client personnel told us how their workers came from the mainland and stayed for two weeks before going home. The only thing to do at night was to feast on lobster and listen to music. Actually, we ate lobster for breakfast and lunch. I love lobster, but for a long time I couldn't look at one after returning home.

But our mission was accomplished. After spending a day at this facility and seeing what went into catching shrimp and lobster and how the manufacturing process works, we both had a much better understanding of the process and how this ends up in the inventory costs.

I was thrilled to come home and couldn't wait to tell Susan how interesting this journey was. But when I walked in the door, the last thing Susan wanted to hear about was my trip to Central America. All Susan wanted to talk about was how we were going to get pregnant. She was focused solely on starting a family.

As time went on, we were getting more and more discouraged. So Susan and I started talking about adopting a child. We were starting to get impatient. Then in September 1973, Susan finally got some good news from Dr. Bozorgi. She was pregnant! Susan couldn't wait to tell me when I came home from work that day, and the two of us were just thrilled. During the next several months, Susan grew bigger and bigger. One day, she said the doctor wanted to take an x-ray as he thought perhaps there could be twins. In those days, ultrasound technology was still new, so Susan was a little nervous. I told her I would meet her for lunch and then we could go to the doctor's office together. When the x-rays came back on a Friday afternoon, Dr. Bozorgi brought us into his office and put it upon the wall. I immediately counted two heads and screamed out, "TWINS!" I was so excited! We were hoping for twins! I turned to Susan. She was in shock.

"What is wrong? You always wanted twins," I said.

"Count again," Susan replied.

I looked up at the screen and pointed 1, 2....................3!

Susan asked, "How are we going to handle triplets?"

I looked at the doctor. He was rubbing his chin while he stared at the x-ray. Without turning his head to Susan, he said, "Don't worry, everything will be okay. Not to worry. The only thing you need to do is call Marshall Field and order two extra cribs."

Susan was doubtful. "How will we handle this?" she repeated.

We left the doctor's office with mixed feelings. On one hand, we were finally having the children we always wanted. On the other hand, we were both scared and overwhelmed. I felt bad about leaving Susan and heading back to the office while Susan had to drive home by herself. But I had to go back to work. I encouraged Susan to call her folks and best friend, Nettie Isenberg. Perhaps they could give her moral support.

That following Monday, I went back to work thinking about how Dr. Bozorgi had been staring at that x-ray. I felt he had something else on his mind and started to worry, so I called his office. When he returned the call, I asked him if he was being open and honest with us.

He said, "There are at LEAST FOUR—quadruplets."

I asked what he meant by "at least," and he said that the x-ray showed a shadow, which he could not interpret. He didn't know if it was a bad x-ray or another head. I tried to remain calm and asked him what I needed to do.

He told me, "Just call Marshall Field and tell them you need one more crib."

Dr. Bozorgi suggested we not tell Susan for a while. He had seen how she reacted to triplets and he didn't want to give her anything more to worry about. He told me to keep a close watch on her to make sure she didn't do anything too strenuous.

The following weekend, I decided to tell five people about my predicament: my folks, my mother-in-law, Susan's best friend since kindergarten, Nettie, and my best friend since the fourth grade, Carl. I figured they could give me some advice on what to do and also be able to watch out for Susan to make sure she followed the doctor's orders. The reaction from each was the same. Incredulities. After talking it through, I decided that the only thing I really needed to do was order the cribs from Marshall Field, but at least I'd gotten it off my chest and gained the support of others.

Unfortunately, this was also the start of another busy season for me. As Susan grew bigger, she became less mobile, while I continued to audit Montgomery Ward and, as always, worked longer and longer hours. I felt guilty leaving her all day. She was now getting bored, since she could no longer work as a bookkeeper at a nearby company and had to stay at home. Fortunately, she had

Nettie and her mom available to visit, along with her sister-in-law, Margie Nieder, who lived in the same apartment building. But it was still always a long day for Susan.

In March 1974, right after we completed the audit for Montgomery Ward, Susan started to get contractions. The doctors were starting to get worried and suggested that she have an alcoholic drink to help stop the contractions. Quite a different perspective than you would get today! But this was not a suggestion that Susan was eager to follow. She tried it once, but then ignored the advice.

Then, in late March, as I was getting dressed to go to work, Susan told me to call the doctor. She was not feeling right and was getting back pains and spasms. So I called Dr. Bozorgi, who immediately rambled instructions in broken English. Fortunately, Susan had picked up the other line and heard everything because I had no idea what he had said. When he asked me if I had any questions, I said I only had one. "Can you repeat what you just said?"

Susan, holding the other receiver, said, "Take me to the hospital right away and put me in the back seat with a pillow!" I did as I was instructed.

We lived in Evanston, a suburb north of Chicago, but Michael Reese Hospital was on the South Side of Chicago and it was morning rush hour. I am sure the 45-minute ride down to the hospital seemed like hours to Susan. She tried lying still in the back seat with an occasional moan here and there, but I knew she was miserable.

When we got to the hospital, I couldn't wait to hear from the doctor. We learned that Susan had been having contractions, but if the babies were born then, they probably wouldn't survive and even if they did, they would be severely handicapped. He suggested we talk to another specialist: Dr. Joseph Bieniarz. Michael Reese was one of two teaching hospitals in the country that was experimenting with a new drug called ritodrine hydrochloride that could stop the labor. Dr. Bieniarz was the only person who could administer this drug. In his strong European dialect, Dr. Bieniarz explained to us that there could be severe complications if Susan was not given this drug, and that the drug had been successfully used in Canada and Europe for years. But here in the U.S., the FDA had not yet approved it. He told us that he thought the risks were minimal—if there were any at all—and that if we agreed to the administration of the drug, we needed to sign a consent form. Susan and I signed without hesitation.

The nurses immediately began to feed her the drug intravenously. I stayed with Susan in the delivery room and slept on the chair beside her bed, hoping for a miracle. Dr. Bozorgi now suggested that I tell Susan about there being four babies, and not triplets like she thought. He figured telling her in a hospital, surrounded by doctors who could help her, was as good a time as any. So I broke the news. Her response was like everyone else's. "You've got to be kidding me!" It was probably good that I told her when we did. At this point in time, it was the least of Susan's worries.

The next day the doctor said the treatment appeared to be

working. We felt great and that night I went home to get a good night's sleep. Things were going so well that they soon put Susan in a regular room and decided to feed the medication to her orally. But, soon thereafter, the contractions resumed. Susan returned to the delivery room and went back on the IV. We prayed for things to work out for the better. Luckily, a few hours later the doctor gave us the good news. The contractions had stopped.

During Susan's stay in the hospital, I spent a lot of time in the delivery room, so much so that the doctors offered to let me stay in their lounge. This went on for days. Once Susan's IV was working well, they brought her back up to a room and administered the medication by pill. This time, it worked. I then went back to my usual schedule: get up, go to work, go to the hospital, and go home while Susan was buying valuable time.

But she couldn't plan the timing of the birth precisely. At work, we had just finished reviewing the Montgomery Ward Form 10-K due to be filed with the Securities and Exchange Commission (SEC) the next day. The attorneys for Montgomery Ward asked me to bring the 10-K with me the next morning to have it signed by the partner, David Schwartz, and then to drop it off at their offices for delivery to the SEC. So I went home feeling good. We had it all wrapped up and I quickly fell asleep.

At 3 a.m., I was awakened by a phone call. It was Dr. Bozorgi. He told me to get to the hospital right away. "We are going to let nature do its own thing."

I jumped out of bed and quickly got dressed, only to see all the signed 10-Ks sitting on the table. I thought quickly. I decided I would drop them off at the office on the way to the hospital, put them on David Schwartz's desk with an explanatory note, and hope for the best. I stopped at our offices only to find the building locked. I rang the night bell. I rang and rang that night bell, but there was no answer. I knew the watchman was there since I saw his keys and hat on the stool just inside the door, but where? I started pacing back and forth. What do I do? I had my wife going into delivery but the client's 10-Ks needed to be delivered. I noticed another person standing outside the building watching me pace back and forth. He asked me if I needed to get in. Impatiently I replied, "Why else do you think I am pacing back and forth at four in the morning?"

He answered, "I don't think you will get in because the keys on that chair are mine. I'm the guard and I locked myself out."

I couldn't believe it!!! Without hesitation, I left for the hospital with the 10-Ks. When I got to the hospital, I ran to the delivery room. The nurses asked me if I wanted to be part of the delivery or to stay in the waiting room. I chose the latter option. There was no way I would have the stomach to see four babies being delivered. I wanted to be out of the way for this miracle to make sure everything went smoothly.

I was all by myself in the waiting room, except for one other person, the worker who restocked the candy machines. At 8 a.m. on April 22, 1974, I heard a loud applause in the delivery room. Soon thereafter they strolled baby boy "A" past me, so I could get a quick look at him before they rolled him upstairs. Then, there was silence.

I started getting nervous, pacing back and forth. I wanted to hear a noise. Something, anything. Some 23 minutes later, an eternity to me, baby girl "B" was wheeled by me for a quick look. I asked if Susan was doing okay and they replied, "Yes, everyone is doing great." The candy machine man, still stocking one machine after another, congratulated me on having twins.

Eight minutes later, baby boy "C" was strolled past for a quick look. With astonishment the candy man said, "Triplets!?!" I laughed and replied, "There is more to come." With that he packed up his supplies and said, "I'm getting out of here. I don't know if this is contagious or not, but I am not taking any chances."

After another eight minutes, baby boy "D," the fourth baby, was strolled by. All seemed healthy. Good reports came from the doctors and nurses. I felt a sense of relief reminiscent of that which I felt after taking my CPA exam. The pressure was off. I'd been running on adrenaline but now I was exhausted. I was thrilled, but I had no energy. I couldn't wait until I could give Susan a great big hug and kiss.

After a period of recovery, Susan was wheeled up to a room where we were reunited. We held hands as we thought about the miracle that had just happened. The doctor said the delivery had gone as well as could be expected. However, we couldn't be certain until 48 hours passed. Susan and I are both optimistic people. We had no worries. Perhaps, we should have but we were so happy. We finally had the family we'd been yearning to love.

Dr. Bozorgi then took me aside and said I should consider having a press conference, but I couldn't understand why we needed one. Dr. Bozorgi said he told me this was a big event. The odds for having quadruplets were one in a million, and the press would naturally be interested. He advised me that if I didn't have a press conference, the press would follow us to our home until they got the story they wanted. I told him I wouldn't entertain the idea until we knew the babies were okay. I requested he keep this a secret until then. He agreed, and, with that, I said I needed to go my office to deliver some 10-Ks. Dr. Bozorgi suggested I go out a private entrance as there could be press lurking. After all, he lamented, they have a way of finding things out. I was escorted out of the hospital, relieved to be heading back to the office.

At the office, I went to see David Schwartz. He was shocked to see me. I told him what had happened. He was thrilled and said he would take care of the 10-Ks and explain to the client what had happened. He told me to go to Susan.

When I got home that night, I saw the press congregating outside my apartment building. I managed to use the back way to get in, but my phone rang continuously. It didn't take long for me to stop answering it. I called Dr. Bozorgi and he repeated the notion that the only way to stop this was to conduct a press conference. I agreed, if we kept it short.

The next day I went to the hospital and met with Dr. Bozorgi. I was escorted to a special room. As the door opened, flash bulbs erupted. At the front of the room was a table with the names of what seemed to be a half dozen doctors and one empty seat for me in the middle. I was in shock. Why all this fuss?

As I sat down and looked at the audience, I saw national and local news anchors from ABC, NBC, CBS, and WGN (In those days there were no CNN, FOX, MSNBC, etc.), as well as representatives from the various newspapers. Each started asking me questions. One that stood out was, "Why would I put my wife's life at risk by having her take this drug to prolong her labor?" I told them that we did not think this was a life-threatening risk. For us, it was the opportunity to start the family we had always desired. Then I realized what was really happening. Michael Reese Hospital was getting all this notoriety for delivering our babies, but the drug that helped prolong Susan's labor was the real news. This was an opportunity for the pharmaceutical company to share a positive story and ride the buzz it generated to get this drug approved in the United States. The story ran in papers everywhere. My friends and colleagues from around the world sent me clippings from their local papers. They came from Australia, the UK, Canada, and everywhere else I knew someone from the firm. The Arthur Andersen organization was like an extension of our family support, and they couldn't wait to share in our joy.

The next day was one of the strangest days of my life. Like every other day, I took the Evanston Express downtown and picked up a newspaper. Only this time, the front page had my picture on it. It was a picture from the press conference of me holding four baby dolls. Susan and I were the headline story on every paper. When I turned around on the train, I saw hundreds of fellow commuters holding their papers in front of their faces. I saw tons of pictures of me, yet not one person ever stopped me or noticed that I was that person! I felt like I was in the Twilight Zone as I walked to the office surrounded by images of myself.

Susan stayed in the hospital for a week or so. I'd drop by after work and visit with the neonatal unit to see our kids being fed in incubators. We could already identify a personality for each one. Baby "A" was squirmy little Jeremy. Baby "B" was the adorable Laurie. Jonathan, Baby "C," was somewhat aggressive, constantly pulling at his face. And Baby "D" seemed sensitive. We named him Brian. Each night I would have dinner with Susan in her room, and then we would go upstairs and spend our time staring at our four babies.

One day I got a call from Ed Donnell, CEO for Montgomery Ward. Ed was a graduate of Duke University. I went to Drake University, except one of the papers had a misprint, which said I went to Duke. Ed must have read one of these since he said, "We Duke people must stick together." I didn't know what he was talking about at the time, but I certainly was not going to question him. Ed continued by saying that Montgomery Ward wanted to give us a gift and asked what we needed. I told Ed that I could not accept any gifts. Our firm had strict policies about that sort of thing. All I needed was his good wishes. Furious, Ed told me those policies were ridiculous and said he was going to send a gift to my home right away. He wasn't lying. Later that day, Susan called to say Ed Donnell's driver had dropped off two twin strollers and some blankets.

I immediately went to our office managing partner, Jim Brice, and told him what had happened. Jim had served Montgomery Ward for many years and was the advisory partner on the account. Jim told me that I shouldn't accept the gift and that I should call Ed to thank him for his generosity, but tell him that I had to return the gifts. So I did, which only made Ed even more livid. He said, "You tell Jim Brice that either you accept my gifts or Montgomery Ward will look for new auditors." So there I was, caught in the middle. I went to Jim and he told me not to worry. He just had to check something with our home office. A few hours later, Jim reported that since the value of the gifts was nominal, it was not going to be an issue. But he warned me not to accept any more gifts from our client!

Despite this somewhat tense episode between us, Jim Brice was actually quite great during these times. He was sensitive, caring, and willing to stand up for his employees. Such was the case in a disagreement with our insurance company about our hospital bill. The bill was significant—compared to my annual earnings. Yet, the insurance company notified me that they were going to apply five separate deductibles, one for each of our kids and another for Susan. I was stunned that they would treat this as five separate claims. That would greatly deplete our savings at a time when our expenses were about to grow exponentially. I talked to Jim and he took matters in his own hands. Later, I was told he threatened to pull our firm's account if the insurer would not change its decision. I don't know what happened or how it was resolved, but I never had to pay for four of those deductibles. All I know is that I have Jim to thank for it.

Later that year, Jim came through for me again. Each spring, our performance reviews were followed by a pay raise. That year I had one of the highest raises for any manager. I thought it was purely for the good job that I had been doing, but not too long ago, I learned the truth. Jim overruled the committee recommendation and gave me a larger raise so I could take care of those quadruplets without too much added stress. Jim was one of the best partners the firm ever had. He was a tough cookie, but he also had a tender heart. I will always be grateful to Jim for his support in a time of need.

As this was all occurring, Susan and I were adjusting to life with children. While Jonathan and Brian only stayed in the hospital for two weeks, Laurie and Jeremy had to stay a little longer. The doctor thought this was a good idea from two perspectives. First, it would give us some adjustment time, allowing us to get used to taking care of two infants before we had to care for four. Secondly, Laurie and Jeremy needed to gain more weight before it was safe to release them. In the end, Jonathan and Brian came home on Mother's Day weekend. It was the perfect gift for Susan: a family.

Just a few days later, I had to leave. Van and I were off to visit Booth Fisheries in Fortune, Newfoundland. This was the first time I left Susan alone with the kids, but luckily my mother was visiting from Florida to help her. Fortune was a small fishing town on the North Atlantic. Fishermen would go out on their vessels for weeks at a time to catch all kinds of fish and bring them back to the manufacturing plant. We had sent our senior accountant, Don Rattner, a week before so he could go on a vessel and document the processes that took place in catching the fish and getting them ready for manufacturing. Van and I could then look at his notes and understand what took place on the boat, along with what took place in the plant.

It was bitterly cold in Fortune with snow flurries falling in the middle of May. The hotel we stayed in was very modest. There were no nice restaurants. The plant manager said he knew of a widow who loved cooking for visitors. He gave us a bucket of fish and suggested we bring it to this lady for a home-cooked meal. Our team stopped at the hotel on the way to wash up and have a drink. But there was one problem. Fortune had no bars and no liquor. It was a dry town. So we begrudgingly forfeited our drinks and went to see the lady for a home-cooked meal.

When we arrived, this sweet old lady dressed in a white apron had the Stanley Cup hockey game playing on her black and white TV. There was snow on the screen, so you couldn't see real well, even after we adjusted the rabbit ears, but it was better than nothing. Then she gave us some good news. For special guests, she kept some wine in her basement and would be glad to serve it with our fish dinner as long as we swore not to tell. Great!

We sat down around her dining room table and picked up our wine glasses to savor our first sip. One by one, our lips puckered and our eyes twitched. This was the worst tasting stuff we had ever put in our mouths and that's including whatever we drank at college parties. But we didn't want to hurt her feelings, so from then on we made sure we always had some fish in our mouths before we took our next sips. I finished my one glass and told her I'd had enough. But the halibut was fantastic. I never liked halibut, but this was the best tasting fish I ever had. Too bad it was paired with that awful wine.

But, sometimes, that's how life goes. Take the great with the bad.

CHAPTER 10

Good-Bye

Needless to say, the next few years were hectic. As we were adjusting to our new family, we quickly realized that our two-bedroom apartment would not do. The only problem was that neither Susan nor I had ever lived in a house. Not only did we not know what to look for, but we also couldn't look together. So after hiring a real estate agent, Susan would go out on her own to look for a house, while I took care of the kids. Then the next day, I would go out on my own, while Susan took combat duty. This chaotic schedule continued until we found a house that we both liked. When that happened, we put in a bid.

It was probably not as much as we should have offered. At the time, I had limited savings to invest in a house. When my folks had moved to Florida, they could not afford a condo, so I bought the condo for them, took out a mortgage, and then rented it to my folks at a nominal rate. This made my dad believe it was not a gift and that he was responsible for his own housing. I do not regret it, but because of this arrangement, we had limited funds available for a house of our own.

In the fall of 1974, we put a bid on a house in Wilmette, a suburb of Chicago. It was a four-bedroom, split-level house. The owners had just put in a nice family room addition. The location was great, right across the street from a park and a school. We felt we could put the three boys in one room and Laurie in a room by herself. The fourth bedroom would be a combination guest room and mini playroom. Unfortunately, the owner wanted more money than we could afford. After a lengthy negotiation process, she agreed to sell the house to us for $75,000. To this day, I think she felt sorry for us and our situation and accepted less than she wanted or could have gotten. I'll always be grateful to her. Life was hard enough at the time without the added stress of living outside our means.

Our social life during these next few years was very limited. The chaos of watching four kids at once meant that we could never expose our children to things that other kids their age would have been exposed to. It was 18 months before they saw a grocery store or went to a restaurant. It was too stressful. We just stuck to the basic schedule. I would come home from work and take the second shift after Susan survived another day taking care of four kids. We eventually decided we needed to get some help for Susan for one or two days a week, but we had trouble finding qualified help that we could afford. Finally, we found Gail Anderson, a recent high school graduate. She was a godsend and a tremendous help to Susan and me. The kids fell in love almost as quickly as we did.

Even with Gail's help, our life for the next two years was abnormally baby-focused. Susan would send me to the grocery store to buy baby food, and I would take a shopping cart and clear out the shelves. One time, when I was pushing around a cartful of baby food, a customer stopped me to ask where she could find an item. I replied, "I don't work here, you will have to ask someone else." The customer gave me a weird stare before glancing at my cart, clearly wondering, "Then what are you doing stocking the shelves with baby food?" Little did she know, I wasn't stocking. I was buying.

Sleep was a precious commodity in those days. I generally took the early shift. When I heard one of the babies cry, I woke up another baby so I could feed two of them at a time and then get dressed for work. That way Susan could get a little more sleep. Over time, though, the babies started getting up earlier and earlier. One day, I did my usual routine of feeding and changing the babies when they woke up. After putting them back to sleep, I walked to the train station to catch the "L" downtown to go to work. When I arrived, I was the only one there. So, I waited, and waited and waited some more. Finally, I saw a sign that said the first train didn't arrive for another 30 minutes. I was there before they even started running!

On Sundays, Susan and I were always exhausted by early afternoon. Occasionally, we took the babies to a park in Evanston, where we'd lie on the ground, each holding a baby carriage. The kids seemed to be happier outside and we were able to relax. That is, until one day when a lady saw us sleeping and started lecturing us on how dangerous this was. "Someone could steal your babies," she yelled.

When we took vacations, we stayed in town and did things that we never had the opportunity to do during the rest of the year, such as go on a picnic or visit the zoo. Susan and I had our hands full following the kids as they roamed in four different directions. Finally, we had the courage to fly to Florida over Christmas vacation to visit my folks. To handle this trip, we had Susan's folks (Gus and Marian Nieder) accompany us so each child could sit on a lap. In those days, when a plane was in the air, the flight attendants allowed our kids to crawl in the aisles. Even with this added amusement, it was still a tense trip and we were all glad when we landed.

Unfortunately, my overly excited mom had arranged for local TV crews to be at the gate to interview us when we got off the plane. Susan, exhausted from traveling, didn't appreciate all this attention. Not only did we have to survive the flight, but we now also had to cope with a surprise press interview. Although we were upset, we forgave my mom. She and her friends were so excited watching us on the news that night. At least, it was an adventurous and memorable start to our first out-of-town trip.

Life with four kids was complicated, but the firm was great to us. Occasionally, some of the partners, such as Van and Barbara Wells or David and Elaine Schwartz, came by to visit us. My career was progressing nicely and the firm wanted to make sure I could handle a more diverse group of assignments, so they shifted my client schedule. I was removed from all my retail clients and put on two very large non-retail accounts: Abbott Labs and Quaker Oats.

It was a great challenge: being brought on as manager on two large engagements with which I had no previous association. Bob Allgyer was technically the manager on Abbott Labs, but he was about to make partner. As a result, many of his duties fell to me. I had to learn quickly. Abbott Labs operated in over 60 countries and we were the auditors in most of them. Since we were required to complete the audit at the end of January, it was a very quick close for a December 31 year end. The work required extremely long hours, just like my experience at Montgomery Ward. The partners and managers worked until 7 p.m. before breaking for cocktails and dinner, and then returned to work a few more hours before getting home around 11 p.m. The next day, we would be on the road by 6:30 a.m. to do it again. The work never seemed to end. Abbott was a very active client; there was always something going on that required our services or input. I spent many hours schlepping 40 miles to North Chicago, where the Abbott campus was located. Luckily, Bob was a very patient person for a new partner, and he gave me a lot of coaching and guidance as I grew into my new role. I admired the way he developed client relations and how he could handle almost any crisis.

On a pattern of growth and acquisition, Quaker was similar except it had a June 30th year end. Abbott kept me busy in the winter; Quaker kept me busy in the summer. Both of these jobs required a lot of travel since each company had so many locations throughout the world. As a result, Susan had to rely less and less on me and more and more on Gail and her mother for help. At the same time, she started getting involved with various support groups for mothers of multiples. Out of necessity, she began to build a support system outside of me.

Despite the stress of our daily lives, Susan and I were starting to have more fun with our kids and feel more confident about our future. I was going to be considered for partner in the next year. I was receiving good feedback at work from my bosses and clients, and I was enjoying working in a window office overlooking the city center. All was well. We were settled. Then, complications arose.

Susan was turning 30 on March 20, 1977, and I thought I would surprise her by buying six tickets to the circus for March 19. We planned to spend the day taking our kids on a real adventure going to the circus and then dinner. However, no sooner had I made those plans than Bob Grottke, the audit division head, called me into his office. Bob was a great guy, but very energetic and somewhat aggressive. Bob greeted me with a smile and asked me to sit down. Something was going on; this rarely happened. At first, I thought he was going to fire me, but I couldn't have been more wrong. Bob told me that the firm thought highly of me and was going to put me up for partner next year. I smiled. He continued. However, the firm wanted to transfer me to Dallas, Texas. My smile faded.

The reason was Zale Corporation, the largest jewelry store

chain in the world with almost $1 billion in sales. They had fired their existing auditors, Touche Ross (now called Deloitte & Touche) and wanted the remaining Big 8 to propose. Our Dallas office was primarily an oil and gas practice at that time so the firm wanted to transfer in a retail person to handle the work. My transfer was conditional upon Zale selecting Arthur Andersen as its auditor. Bob said they wanted Susan and me to visit Dallas the weekend of March 18 so we could visit the city and meet the Zale client service team.

I was shocked. All I could think was, "But I have six tickets for the circus!" My second thought was, "What am I going to say to Susan?" This was quickly followed by my third thought. "How can I say no, when I'm up for partner?" I was totally confused.

On the train ride home, I thought about how I was going to break the news to Susan. I knew how she would feel, but no matter what I did I was going to break somebody's heart. After we put the babies to sleep, I told Susan that I was going to ask my brother and his wife to take the kids to the circus. Susan asked why, so I told her my story. At first, she thought I was joking. Part of me wished I had been.

I told her that there was a one in seven chance that this transfer would happen, since all the other firms were proposing as well. We had no choice but to take the first step and visit Dallas. There was no point in jeopardizing my standing at the firm by turning down an opportunity that might never even happen. Susan questioned me thoroughly about it, but she was an extraordinary soldier. She agreed that we needed to make the visit. So, on Friday, March 18, 1977, we flew to Dallas and stayed at the downtown Fairmont Hotel while my brother, Bob, and his wife, Burdette, had the joy of taking our kids to the circus. I still wish I could have been there.

Dallas was a much different city than it is today. It seemed small compared to Chicago. Most of the area north was either new housing developments or cotton farms. I settled into my hotel, and then met with the Dallas team. Frank Rossi, office managing partner, was in charge of orchestrating the proposal. Bill Meenan, head of the tax division, was going to be the lead tax partner. Rich Howell, who had transferred from Milwaukee, was going to be audit partner. David Ewing, the consulting division head, would serve as consulting partner. They were assembling a large support team below that group.

We sat down to discuss the proposal, and they told me the story of why Zale was changing auditors. They gave me a copy of D Magazine, which had a feature article titled, "Who's telling the truth at Zale's?" Apparently, Zale was mired in a series of accounting irregularities that involved the brother-in-law of one of the Zale executive officers. This brother-in-law was embezzling money and having an affair with another Zale officer's secretary. If that was not lurid enough, that officer was also having an affair with this same secretary. When the company was under investigation by the criminal division of the IRS and the Securities and Exchange Commission for filing erroneous financial statements sometime later, the brother-in-law and the secretary unsuccessfully tried to commit suicide. Although these investigations went on for years, the brother-in-law was acquitted on fraud charges when he somehow convinced the jury that the Zale family had authorized his appropriation of these funds as a way for him to pay himself a bonus. Although the brother-in-law was found innocent of embezzlement, his innocence did not last long. Soon thereafter, he threatened the company, claiming that he would go to the IRS and divulge other improper transactions, unless he was handed a suitcase full of money. The brother-in-law met with a Zale executive at the Fairmont Hotel, where they had adjoining rooms. The suitcase of cash was handed to the brother-in-law. As he left his room, he was greeted by the FBI. Ultimately, he was convicted on extortion.

This was a story of intrigue. There was embezzlement by a relative of the owners, sex between executives and employees, attempted suicide, extortion, accounting errors, SEC investigations, IRS investigations, criminal investigations, and the possibility of restating the financial statements for the current and preceding two years. Under this scenario, the company had to select new auditors and complete the audit by Memorial Day when they had a March 31 year end. In short, this was a real mess, and Zale's was marred by the controversy. They needed a fresh start and new auditors.

That's where I came in. Arthur Andersen, with my advice and expertise, could help them, but I didn't know where to start. I was out of the loop. I had never set foot in Texas. Susan and I knew no one. I had never heard of the Zale family. Should I believe all these stories? Plus, I was hesitant to do my best. If we were selected, I would have to start right away. That meant commuting every week to and from Chicago and leaving Susan at home with our two-year-old quadruplets. Susan would have to take charge of the move while I'd be working my tail off in Dallas. That Sunday morning, I quieted my doubts when the firm took us out to breakfast at a nice restaurant before Susan and I were to head back to Chicago. Since we hadn't had any time during the weekend to talk, Susan and I couldn't wait to be dropped off at the airport. We needed to discuss this.

As we flew back, I realized I had screwed up Susan's 30th birthday. I just took her through a birthday weekend that was the last thing she would have wanted to do. We were now travelling home, sitting in first class, when I turned around and asked her one of the most overused of all questions, "So, what do you think?" Susan broke down and cried. She was dead set against moving to Dallas. I told her that if she felt this strongly that I would decline the transfer. Bob Grottke would have to empathize with our situation. It was just too difficult with four two-year-olds.

I was actually not against moving out of Chicago. I never liked the winters and always wanted to work in a warm climate, but what came to my mind was California, not Texas.

Despite how great the opportunity was, I felt I could not betray my wife's wishes. On the train ride to the office that Monday morning, I kept rehearsing how I would tell Bob that I couldn't accept the offer. I knew he would either refuse me or try to override me, so I was thinking about how I was going to respond. When I got to the office, my phone rang. It was Susan.

Now, Susan and I always had an agreement. She would only call me at work if it was an emergency. If it wasn't an emergency, we could talk about it that night. I waited to hear what she had to say. Susan told me she had given this more thought. Since there were seven firms proposing, why not go through the proposal stage? Odds were we would lose out to another firm. The firm would then see my commitment to them and my chances for making partner would not be hurt, but we wouldn't necessarily have to move to Dallas. It was a great idea!

So I took it to the next step. Along with four partners, I made a presentation to the Zale family and their board. Our presentation seemed to go well, but we had no idea how it compared to the other six. The Zale family said they were going to cut it down to four firms who would then have another round. As David Schwartz, an advisory partner on the proposal, flew back to Chicago with me, he kept telling me what a great opportunity this was for me and for the company. I kept thinking that I hoped we would get the good news that we didn't make the cut. Unfortunately, that was not the case. By the time I got home, there was a message on the phone from Frank Rossi. We would have another round next week.

The team worked even harder in preparation for this next go-around. We already had enough information to determine how we would proceed should we get the work. We even had the troops all lined up and ready to go. Frank Rossi was drooling. He saw Dallas as a cosmopolitan community, not an oil and gas community, and he was transferring in managers and partners from everywhere to develop practices in manufacturing, banking, utilities, etc. Now he had a potential client with a March 31 year end. That meant work in April and May, the two slowest months for an accounting firm. This could enhance office profitability considerably.

In round two, Zale's Bruce Lipshy, the son of Ben Lipshy, a senior officer who was the brother-in-law of the founder, M.B. Zale, took a more active role. With ambitions to be CEO one day, he wanted to work with younger, more aggressive people. He seemed to feel comfortable with me since we were around the same age. Donald Zale, the son of M.B. Zale, on the other hand, hit it off real well with Frank Rossi. Rossi had the rare ability to blend into almost any setting. He was Italian; Zale was Jewish. But watching him interact with Zale at those meetings, you might have guessed Frank was Jewish as well. That is, if you didn't know his last name.

When we finished our presentation, Zale said they were going to narrow the search to two firms. I knew we were going to be one of the two firms, and I was right. It was now down to Price Water-house and Arthur Andersen. Both firms were willing to transfer a retail industry partner to handle the work. Both were committed to having the resources necessary to get the audit done on time.

We were asked to make one final appearance. David and I flew to Dallas to help with the presentation. When we finished, all I wanted to do was fly home. I didn't want to hear the result. I had my fingers crossed they would pick our competitor. I didn't have the stomach to tell Susan if we won the work. I said my good-byes and was about to head to the airport when Frank stopped me. "What's wrong with you? You can't leave. Don't you want to stay and hear the result? They are going to call us within the hour," he said. I blushed. Frank could tell I was uncomfortable, but sure enough within the hour, Frank got the word that Don Zale was on the line. He ran into his office to take the call.

A few minutes later, Frank came out with a box of cigars. Arthur Andersen had been selected! Everybody was excited. That is, everybody except for me. I couldn't even stand. My knees started shaking and I sat down. How would I break the news to Susan?

On the flight home, I couldn't think. I caught a limo at the airport and on the ride home, I still couldn't think. When I got home and opened the door, Susan greeted me with a big hug and kiss, and I still couldn't think. Then she said, "Congratulations!" I was shocked. "How did you know?" I asked. Susan showed me the bouquet of flowers that Frank sent her and told me about the nice follow-up call she'd received from him assuring her that we would love Dallas and that he would do everything in his power to make us feel at home. Susan was committed. She said it would all work out. At that moment, I loved her more than ever. She was always there for me no matter what.

After that, I began commuting to Dallas, leaving every Monday on an early morning flight and returning on Friday evening. I rented an apartment in Dallas but didn't spend much time there since I worked from morning until late at night every day supervising a large staff on the audit. Charles Napier was my lead staff person. He was very talented, but lacked retail experience and always wanted me to work the staff harder. For the first time in my life, I was accused of being soft. Unfortunately, I followed his advice, and quickly got a reputation that stayed with me the rest of my time in Dallas. I became known as the insensitive one.

As we were working on the audit, some problems arose. One of the high-risk areas was federal income taxes. In those days, retailers were allowed to defer the gross profit on installment sales until the customer paid for the goods. The calculation was quite complex and Zale recorded a deferral for such taxes. However, as I got into it, my calculations showed that the deferred liability should be significantly higher. Obviously, I had to be wrong since these numbers were previously audited by Touche Ross, one of the premier accounting firms.

So, I asked my dear friend and Chicago retail tax manager, David Carlson, to come down to review my work. At first, David resisted coming to Dallas since he had a phobia about flying. His only coping solution was to stand up during the flight and smoke cigarettes. Luckily, good-natured David survived the flight. David was a stickler for details. Each morning he hand-pressed his shirts to make sure there was not a wrinkle in them. Bringing this attention to detail to his work, David pored through the calculations, made some calls back to Chicago, and quickly came to the conclusion that my findings were correct.

This was one of many adjustments that we found while auditing Zale's financial statements. Since this was considered an error, we had to restate the prior years' financial statements, and Touche Ross had to review our work and subsequently reissue its opinion for those years. Touche Ross didn't cooperate. They took the position that their prior numbers were correct. As a result, if you look at the Zale March 31, 1977, shareholders report, you will see a full page of two auditors' reports. One report was from Arthur Andersen and contained our four-paragraph opinion on the matter. The other was from Touche Ross and contained a five-paragraph opinion, disclaiming our adjustments. A typical audit report in those days was only three paragraphs. Because Touche Ross refused to cooperate, we had to go back to the earlier years and review enough of their work to feel comfortable. It all resulted in more work for us. Everything changed except our deadlines.

Pretty soon, my commuting started to take its toll. After getting back late on Friday, I'd spend Saturday and Sunday with the kids and doing household chores before leaving Monday morning on an American Airlines flight. One day, I got a call from David Schwartz saying he was going to come down next Monday. He wanted to know my flight number. I gave it to Dave and he called back saying he could not get on that flight, but there was a Braniff flight leaving around the same time. He asked if I would change my flight to accommodate him, which I was glad to do. I grabbed four more suits after deciding I needed more on hand in my apartment. Carrying these four suits in hand, I told Susan good-bye, kissed her, and said I'd see her later. Susan was coming down later that day on another flight to start looking for houses.

Our plane left on time. The unfriendly stewardess did not like me from the start because I dared to hang my suits in a closet she said was reserved for her. She took them out, rolled them in a ball and put them in the overhead. Annoyed by how she treated a first-class passenger like me, I took them out of the overhead, put them back in the closet, and took her stuff out and put it in the overhead. Needless to say, I didn't make a friend.

She started serving breakfast. All of a sudden we heard a loud noise. I looked over to David. What was that? The plane started descending. It felt like we were gliding, just drifting down slowly. David, ever the jokester, was not laughing anymore. Remembering that a Delta Airlines Flight had recently attempted an unsuccessful landing on a highway in Georgia, I asked David if he could see a freeway. David shook his head. "No."

Now this lovely stewardess went into the cockpit, came out, slammed the door, closed her eyes, and whispered to herself, "Oh my God!" She then took out a megaphone and said, "Now hear this. Now hear this. We are landing in mid-America, USA." With that, she started clearing our trays, throwing them in the lavatory, and giving us instructions on how to prepare for an emergency landing. At this time, all I could think about was the family I was leaving behind and wondering why I ever took this assignment in the first place. Realizing that this was not doing me any good, I started thinking what I should do if we crashed. I concluded it would be best to grab some blankets and head out the exit as quickly as possible. I'm not sure what good that would do, but I couldn't think of anything else.

As I looked around the plane, there were all sorts of reactions. Some older men behind us continued to play cards. A lady across the aisle was screaming and pulling at her hair. David was stone silent, staring out the window, hopelessly looking for a highway or someplace for us to land. All we could do was wait.

Miraculously, we eventually landed safely on a short runway in a small town in Missouri. Everybody applauded when the plane finally rolled to a stop in the middle of a field. As soon as the steps of the plane hit the ground, I grabbed my suits and got off the plane. My knees were still shaking when the pilot came out and inspected the engines, which were all carved up. He thought we must have hit a flock of birds, but he didn't know how since birds could not fly at 30,000 feet. He had no idea what could have caused the damage. Fortunately, we had one working engine that helped us land safely.

From there, we were bused to Kansas City and put on another plane. We arrived in Dallas later that same day. David decided to turn around and fly back to Chicago, since he had meetings the next day. I figured I'd wait at the airport for another hour or so to meet Susan, who was flying in to look for a house. David called his wife, Elaine, to tell her his change in plans, but before Dave could say a word, Elaine asked, "David, are you okay?" David asked why she was concerned. She replied that early that morning she'd had a mysterious feeling that David was in some kind of trouble. David, who couldn't believe what he had just heard, told Elaine the story.

After saying good-bye to David, I went to the gate to meet Susan. When she got off the plane, I told her I beat her by an hour and then explained what had happened. She couldn't believe it. How close she'd come to losing me. She hugged me, and we left the airport.

Otherwise, Susan's visit was successful. She managed to find a house she liked and was starting to get excited about moving to our new home. I went to see it and immediately supported her decision, since it cost less than what we were getting for the sale of our Wilmette house. I thought we would live in Dallas for a few years and then return to Chicago. I figured the house would serve us well for the moment. I left the details to her as I focused on my work.

What complicated work it was. In addition to working with the auditors, we also had to work with the attorneys. The criminal division of the IRS was investigating the Zale family. They were represented by Fay Vincent, future CEO of Paramount Pictures and Commissioner of Major League Baseball, currently of the prestigious Caplin and Drysdale law firm in Washington, D.C. Fay had a razor-sharp mind and defended Zale and the family quite well, but his mobility was curtailed as a result of his falling off a fraternity house roof in college. Like me, Fay commuted to and from Dallas weekly, so I occasionally left with him on Friday afternoons and drove him to the airport. In those days, you could park right in front of the Dallas/Fort Worth terminal and go directly to the gate. There was no security or long lines, but Fay still needed some assistance to make it to the gate, so I'd help him. These adventures went on until the end of May, when we completed our arduous audit. It was such a relief to get the audit done successfully and on time, but a lot of people had to make a lot of personal sacrifices to do it. Finally, we could breathe, but only for a day or two.

Now, it was time for Susan and I to pack things up and bring our kids to Dallas. We spent our last night in Chicago at the Hilton Hotel by O'Hare Field. Susan's folks, Gus and Marian Nieder, drove us to the airport. I watched Susan's father hug and kiss his daughter good-bye, knowing she might never live near him again. A man who rarely showed any emotions, Susan's father closed his eyes as tears started rolling down his cheeks. I felt like such a schmuck, stealing his little girl and grandkids.

The next day, on June 9, 1977, our ninth anniversary, we flew to Dallas. It was another special day that went by without much celebration. Instead, we were starting a whole new life.

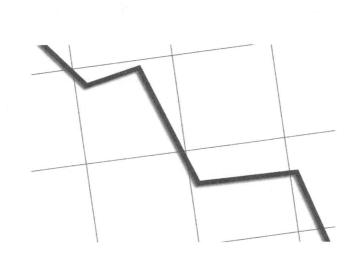

CHAPTER 11

Partnership

Our helper-cum-lifesaver, Gail Anderson, moved to Texas with us to help in our transition. She stayed for the summer and then went home to Chicago. Thank God we had Gail. Without her, the transition would have been all but impossible. She was a godsend that summer and somehow conquered the task of teaching all of our three-year-olds how to swim. By the end of the summer, they were jumping off the high dive and paddling to the side of the pool. Comforted by my family's easy adjustment to life in Dallas, I could focus solely on work.

With the completion of the Zale audit, I was able to shift my focus to other clients. The office assigned me to General Portland Cement and Pearle Vision Centers. Taking on General Portland Cement was relatively easy even though I knew nothing about the industry. The CFO was from Chicago and worked with a number of our Chicago Andersen people, whom I knew quite well. Because of this, the relationship was relatively easy to develop. The amicable nature of the relationship empowered me to step outside of my comfort zone, working proactively to learn new things like depletion allowance. Through the General Portland Cement, I greatly expanded my knowledge.

However, its effects were not limited to my professional life. They reverberated through my life outside of work. My work at General Portland Cement inspired me to quit smoking. I had started smoking Old Gold cigarettes when I went to Drake. Susan also had started smoking at Drake but had successfully quit when she was pregnant and never resumed. I was still addicted. That is, until I saw what it can do.

General Portland was located on the top floor of a building just off the LBJ Freeway near Central Expressway. It had a great view of the city and with it, the city's pollution. As we were completing the audit in January 1978, I looked out the window and saw this brown haze. It got worse as the day went along. I finally asked one of the Texans, "What is that in the air?" The reply came back quickly, "New Mexico." I didn't know what they were talking about until I went outside. We were in the middle of a dust storm that was blowing in from the west.

When I got home, Susan's brown 1974 Ford station wagon was covered with it. I started coughing terribly as dust got trapped in my throat. There was dust everywhere in our house: on the drapes, the furniture, and the floors. It looked like the house hadn't been cleaned in months. When I made it upstairs to change clothes, I opened my closet door and noticed my carton of Old Golds. I realized smoking was just like breathing in the brown dust around me, only every day. I didn't want either of them to enter my lungs ever again. I decided right then and there to quit, and I haven't smoked since. That carton stayed in my closet until we moved to another house in 1985.

Even though it was in my specialty—retailing—auditing Pearle Vision Center was a much more difficult assignment. A relatively small company, with only $54 million in sales when I took over the account, Pearle was a begrudging client of Arthur Andersen. Stanley Pearle was the founder and chairman emeritus, and Don Phillips, a Harvard graduate and very astute business leader, was the CEO. His CFO was a true blood Texan who did not appreciate Yankees from the North. Neither officer had a very strong relationship with the firm. The only reason they were using Arthur Andersen was because they were now owned by GD Searle, a Chicago pharmaceutical company and an Andersen client.

After spending some time at the company, I began to realize why they didn't like working with Andersen, and I couldn't blame them. Our Dallas office had no retail expertise, and none of our people visited their operations. We handled it as a "referral" audit, doing whatever the Chicago office asked us to do, no more and no less. So, I asked Don if I could visit his best locations and worst locations on Andersen's dime to get to know the company. He complied by lining up some visits for me to their stores in Minnesota. When I came back to Dallas, I met with Don to discuss what I observed. He was very grateful for my objective insights, and my

AND YOU THOUGHT ACCOUNTANTS WERE BORING

investment in his success opened the door to a close relationship.

Little did I know this relationship would lead to one of the most important decisions of my life; 1978 was a big year for me. I was being nominated for partner, but it was not without its trials and tribulations. Most of my time was spent with clients, and the second year auditing Zale was not much easier than the first. The ongoing investigations and the significant changes in management and the accounting department made things difficult. I spent most of my time at Zale working with Frank Rossi, the managing partner, and Rich Howell, the Zale audit partner. Because I was so insulated from my other coworkers, I started to hear things like, "We need to get to know him better. He needs to spend more time with people other than those who work on Zale. Perhaps we should wait a year before we nominate him, since he has been with the firm only 10 years. Most people make partner after 12." I felt dejected. As far as I was concerned, I had done everything the firm asked me to do and more, but most of my support was in Chicago. If the Dallas partners did not nominate me, that support meant very little.

One day, in the midst of this turmoil, Don Phillips, the CEO of Pearle, called me and asked me to go to lunch. While we were eating lunch in his office, he asked me about my career plans and if I would be interested in coming on as the executive vice president of finance of Pearle Vision Center. He wanted me to work directly with him to build Pearle into an international retailer. It was an amazing opportunity rendered all the more appealing by the tension surrounding my proposed partnership in the Dallas office of Arthur Andersen.

Susan and I talked it over and she said it was my call. I went back to Don seeking more details, including salary. At this time, Frank Rossi also called me into his office to tell me the good news: I had been nominated for partner. I should have been crying with joy, but I had no reaction. It was news I didn't want to hear. My mind was already dreaming about Don's vision for Pearle. Frank wanted to know why I was so subdued, so I told him. I was not sure I wanted to be a partner. Frank was livid. His face turned red, his eyes widened, and his eyebrows rose. He told me I had to be pulled off the Pearle account immediately, since I now had a conflict of interest. He told me that this partnership was just the beginning of my career with the firm. He and his colleagues had high hopes for me in the Dallas office. Frank said the firm wanted me to talk at the worldwide partners meeting on how we got Zale as an account, an opportunity that would greatly increase my firm visibility. I was now totally confused. Frank said I needed to make up my mind sooner rather than later.

I needed advice, so Susan and I discussed these two totally different opportunities. Eventually, I decided to take the partnership and my reasons were probably entirely ego-driven. I liked working in a professional office environment. Pearle's corporate office was located in the same building as their factory. The people I worked with in the firm were all smart and professional; that was not the case at Pearle. Pearle was a subsidiary of GD Searle and did not always have the same flexibility as Arthur Andersen. The CEO of GD Searle was Donald Rumsfeld. Yes, that same Donald Rumsfeld who later became Secretary of Defense for the United States. I had made a presentation to Donald in his office in Chicago and seen his dictatorial style in action. Would he let Don carry out his vision? What would happen if he didn't? What if Don left? I knew Arthur Andersen would be around forever. Would Pearle have the same security?

So, I decided to go for the partnership. Looking back, I don't know if it was the right decision or not. Going to Pearle Vision Center certainly would have been another life-changing event for the Katzen family. As it turned out, Don later hired Cece Smith for this position. When Pearle was spun off by Searle into a separate public entity, its management team was suddenly inundated with golden parachutes. When they subsequently sold the company again, they had even bigger parachutes. With their newfound economic clout, Phillips and Smith started their own retail buy-out firm and excelled. They thrived and, ultimately, Pearle outlived Andersen. On the surface, it may appear to have been the wrong decision for me, but I gained many irreplaceable and spectacular memories and experiences through my work with Arthur Andersen. I don't regret the decision I made. But, perhaps, that is just my prideful self-preservation talking.

After all, my first year as partner was far from a perfect one. It was one marred by conflict. My first partners' meeting was held at the new Marriott Hotel on Michigan Avenue in downtown

Chicago. Our CEO, Harvey Kapnick, gave a brilliant opening speech highlighting his certainty that the SEC would soon require consulting firms to be separate from auditing firms. The implications were shocking; it would mean two separate organizations at Arthur Andersen.

The consulting partners were up in arms. They were a small group in the firm and didn't want to be off by themselves. They didn't like that our "One Firm" philosophy was being questioned. We all wanted to stay as one firm. Harvey didn't like what he was hearing and ordered all the partners to stay another day to discuss the issue further. He arranged for the hotel to accommodate all 1,000 plus partners for an extra night. It was a waste of his effort. At the end of the next day, the partners adamantly advised Harvey to abandon his idea of splitting the firm and strongly urged him not to communicate with the SEC on the topic. A few weeks later, Harvey ignored the suggestion and was asked to leave the firm. We appointed a new CEO.

At the end of the year, our earnings were off, and the firm made a capital call to all the partners; each partner had to contribute a significant amount of money to the firm to bolster our cash assets. To pay my capital call, I had to sell my 1974 Buick and begin leasing a car. I earned more as a manager than I did as a first-year partner. I prayed that this chaos and discontent did not foreshadow things to come.

CHAPTER 12

Putting Things in Perspective

Life in Texas was great. We were making a lot of new friends and always had visitors, whether they popped in from Chicago or Dallas. Many of my clients would even come by to visit our kids. M.B. Zale, the founder of Zale Corporation, and his wife, Edna, would drop by with ice cream cones, while Richard Marcus, the CEO of Neiman Marcus, and his wife once came over and played with our kids on the floor. It was a blessed life, and I cherished it.

In 1979, Dallas finally landed an NBA Basketball team thanks to Don Carter, who started one with a $12 million expansion franchise. Like the Bulls, Dallas selected players from other teams before supplementing them with top draft choices. Their new coach was none other than Dick Motta, the same coach who had made the Chicago Bulls so competitive. Knowing how much enjoyment we got from watching the Bulls, I couldn't wait to see them play, so I went down to their new offices to inquire about season tickets. Since Reunion Arena was still under construction, it was hard to visualize what was being offered to us, but I managed to convince three Andersen employees—Jordan Roseman, Bruce Bernstien, and Craig Hamilton—to trust me enough to pick out the four seats we would share each season.

Our seats cost more than I paid for the Chicago Bulls tickets, but we couldn't complain too much. For $15 a ticket, we were located in the second row right behind the Maverick bench. Like he had done in Chicago, Dick Motta created an entertaining team. Future drafts enabled him to assemble an impressive team comprised of the likes of Rolando Blackman, Sam Perkins, Mark Aguirre, Brad Davis, and Derek Harper. Sadly, the team was plagued by some of the same issues as the Bulls. Like Chicago, their weakest position was at center. The best they could muster was James Donaldson, and like Chicago, they would frequently lose heartbreaking battles against the Lakers in the Western Conference championship. Despite these sad moments, we still had some great times. I enjoyed taking my kids to the game, my eyes crinkling as they complained about the players being too tall and blocking their views. Eventually, I convinced my fellow partners to move our seats behind the basket. My kids saw the game better, and I didn't have to deal with as much pain in my herniated neck. These were the great years in Dallas, the years when Susan and I really settled into life there.

In 1979, Susan and I joined the Columbian Country Club. When I'd signed the Andersen partnership agreement, I'd agreed to join a club. The firm did not reimburse us for the cost, but it was our obligation to join the club to increase our visibility in the community. So, starting on my 33rd birthday—February 19, 1979—I took golf lessons every week from a pro, John Darling, and spent several hours each week practicing. This went on from February to May. I never played, just practiced. I had this idea that all members who joined a country club were great golfers and I didn't want to go out there and embarrass myself. After all, this was the club where the famed golfer Lee Trevino started as a groundskeeper.

That all started to change in May of 1979, when we proposed for a new client. The owners had several businesses, one of which was the Coca-Cola bottling distributorship for the Monterey Peninsula. In the course of doing business together, Ed Hoffman, the owner, asked if I played golf. When I told him I had just joined a club, he excitedly suggested, "Let's meet out there at the end of the month. We can see my business and play some golf." It just so happened that I had a retail industry meeting in San Francisco around that time and Susan was going to be joining me, so I agreed to play with him and then meet Susan in San Francisco.

Ed hosted me at The Lodge at Pebble Beach. The last time I had been at Pebble Beach was on a weekend pass in 1968, when I was stationed at nearby Ft. Ord. Not only did I not play golf in those days, but I was not even interested in the sport. I went to Pebble Beach in my Army fatigues to read a book behind the 18th hole, facing the Pacific Ocean to get my mind off the Infantry. Now, eleven years later, I was staying at this prestigious resort. My life had changed so much.

The next morning Ed drove us to the plant, where we spent all of five minutes before going to Cypress Point Golf Club, one of the most exclusive and prettiest golf clubs in the world. Here I was, a newbie playing this course on my very first round since taking lessons! I was shaking from the very first tee. I had to hit my tee shot over 17-Mile Drive. I paused as I thought about which club to use. I was not about to use my driver, which could go in any direction. I picked up the club that John Darling had been working on with me for all those months—my trusty 5 iron! I don't know what I shot on my first round of golf that day, but it turned me onto the game forever. The course was breathtaking. It was a beautiful sunny day. There was wildlife all over the course, and several holes majestically bordered the bright blue Pacific Ocean. From then on, I was hooked.

On day two, we played Pebble Beach. Feeling more courageous, I used my driver on the first hole. Perhaps I was a little too confident. My errant tee shot hit golf carts parked to the left of the tee box. My cheeks tinged red, but my love of the game refused to fade. If I could play these two courses, I could certainly could go home and play the Columbian Club.

Upon returning from the West Coast, it wasn't long before I had to go to Chicago. Arthur Andersen had bought St. Dominic College in St. Charles and converted it to a training facility. At first, this university slept just a few hundred people. Later, it was expanded to accommodate more than 1,000. The initial training session I had taken at the Marriott Hotel was now conducted in St. Charles, and as part of my initiation dues for becoming a partner, I had to spend two weeks as an instructor.

One of my dear friends, Alan Gilman, a partner from the Detroit office, was also an instructor. His class was in the room next to mine, a coincidence that incited many a hijinks. Whenever Alan and I were together, our senses of humor seemed to control the conversation. Some may say we were funny. Others might say we were immature. I like to think it was a mix of both. It was not long before I walked into my class to see all kinds of nasty words printed on my blackboard, courtesy of Alan Gilman. A series of escalating pranks ensued.

This competition eventually culminated in a 16-inch softball match between our classes. Alan and I agreed that the losing team would buy the other team beer. The game took place on the next to last day of the two-week session. Both Alan and I were great motivators. We both riled up our classes to make sure each person performed at his or her best for the team. Alan and I pitched for our respective teams, a feat that was hilarious on its own at times. The game had a lot of spirit and soon got carried away, especially at the end when Alan started throwing bean balls at our team. That was it. Fortunately, someone suggested that we should end the game in a tie. The students were stymied when they saw Alan and I give each other a big hug and then laugh hysterically. It was fun for us and certainly memorable for the new employees of Arthur Andersen.

Things were going great. My kids were starting to become more independent. My career was progressing well, and Susan and I were starting to get some financial breathing room. But I knew it wouldn't last. I have a philosophy in life that the "good evens out with the bad." My philosophy, inspired by retailers' paranoia of bad days ahead, soon proved true.

Soon after Susan and I married, my mom, Marion Katzen, had been diagnosed with breast cancer at age 46. She made it through the surgery and treatment successfully. The doctors thought if she survived the next five years, she would live a long life. The five years came and went, our fears leaving with it. But then, more than five years later, her cancer came back. Only this time, it was terminal. When they operated on her at Sloan-Kettering Hospital in New York, they closed her up and said there was nothing they could do. Undiscouraged, my mother vowed to keep fighting.

In February 1980, I had to deliver a speech in Florida, so I stayed at my parents' condo. It was a long night. I couldn't sleep. My mother was in so much pain. I was sleeping in my parents' bedroom with my dad, but I could still hear my mom's moaning from the guest room. I knew she wanted to die. The next day I said my good-byes after listening to her lecture me about my career and how I needed to make sure our family was taken care of. I walked out the door, knowing I'd probably never see her again. I don't know how I delivered my speech that day, but I did. When I got back to Dallas, I called my brother, Bob, and encouraged him to visit our parents as soon as he could. He immediately went to Florida. It was the last time he saw our mom.

On March 17, 1980, I got a call from my dad. He said, "Larry, it's over." My heart tightened. He could hardly talk.

I immediately called Susan to tell her. I left the office early and came home to my supportive Susan. Wrapped in her arms, I started to cry. I couldn't remember the last time I cried, but this time I couldn't stop.

We asked Gail Anderson to come stay with our kids while Susan and I flew to Florida for the funeral. In accordance with her wishes, my mother was cremated and her ashes dropped by helicopter over the Atlantic Ocean. My father and my brother flew up in the helicopter to do the nasty deed, while I stayed on the ground and waited for them to return. As I watched them fly away, I thought back on my mom's final years. How she and my dad had opened a children's clothing stand at a flea market. How she would constantly give my kids clothes from their inventory. How happy my mom was to be a grandmother, spoiling her grandkids whenever they came to visit. She was so happy. Now, she would never see them grow up.

My mom was only 61 when she died. Now, I had to worry about my father. I knew he would not see a doctor on his own, so I concocted a plan. First, I called his doctor to make an appointment for him. Then, one day after our visitors left, I asked my dad to go with me for a drive. Trapped in the car, he could only watch as we got closer and closer to the doctor's office. I'd already paid for it. We were already on our way. He couldn't get out of it.

After the physical, his doctor gave him a clean bill of health. Still concerned, I asked him, "What if something happens when we are gone?" Unfazed by such a common question, he suggested that we leave nitroglycerin by each phone along with the doctor's business card. If something happened, my dad could pop a nitro and call him. I felt uncomfortable with that solution and begged my dad to return to Dallas with us, but he refused. So, a few days later we said good-bye. It was our last.

En route to Dallas, Susan and I stopped in New Orleans. It was Easter weekend so we'd had a tough time getting a nonstop flight to Dallas. We were going to stay in New Orleans for the night before continuing our journey. We had a nice quiet dinner and returned to the hotel. When we got into the room, our message light was on. The message was from my sister: my father had died of a heart attack in his condo. They'd found an open bottle of nitroglycerin on the floor next to him.

Susan and I immediately tried to change our air reservations to go back to Florida and called Gail to tell her we would not be home for a while. When we got back to Florida, we started making the necessary arrangements and phone calls. This on its own was hard enough to bear, but the next evening we got a call from Gail. She had taken our kids out for dinner with our family friends, Mona and Joe Robinson, when our house was robbed. The thieves had taken all our valuables and sentimental possessions. The house was a mess and the kids were too scared to sleep there. Mona and Joe, who had two kids around the same age as ours, had offered to take our kids to their house to sleep, but Susan and I knew our kids needed us, or at the very least, one of us. So, Susan flew back to Dallas while I stayed for my dad's funeral. Alone.

In just ten days, I'd lost everything—my mother, my father, and many of my possessions. I lost it all.

CHAPTER 13

Building a Retail Practice

The first half of the 1980s was a time of much growth and prosperity in my career at Andersen. Frank Rossi had been right. Dallas was a very cosmopolitan town, and it provided an excellent opportunity to serve the retail industry. Our only limitation was finding good people. So, we started pulling them from other offices, transferring in several employees to help alleviate my workload. Each one helped me leverage my time so that I could more effectively lead Arthur Andersen's retail organization.

I could focus on taking advantage of the Texas retail market, where we had very little competition. There were no other firms with our retail experience. To increase our visibility, I decided to work with other retail executives to start a local chapter of the National Retail Financial Executives Association. Many company executives soon agreed, including those at Pier I Imports, JC Penney, Pearle Vision Centers, and Neiman Marcus. It was networking at its finest. As I was inviting these companies to join, I always met at their offices and got a tour of their facilities. I left with a personal connection and a professional understanding of their business and their needs, both of which ultimately led to a discussion of how Arthur Andersen could help them out.

For them, we were a delight. They had finally met professional accountants who understood their business, a rare thing in the Texas market where our retail expertise really set us apart. The National Retail Financial Executives Association gave us the opportunity to show them. For example, Horchow Catalogue had long been audited by KPMG. In the course of garnering support for the association, I got to meet with Roger Horchow, the CEO, and learned that he had just built a home in Nantucket and was facing a significant tax bill. He asked us and several other firms to come in and propose solutions to help reduce his tax bill. I brought in Jordy Roseman, tax partner, and Craig Hamilton, tax manager. At first, Jordy did not want to propose. He thought Horchow would take our ideas and do it without our help, but I convinced Jordy to at least go through the process. After all, we had nothing to lose, and no one else had our expertise in the local market. At the very least, we could begin building a strong working relationship with Horchow. Sure enough, we had the best idea and later, based on our retail expertise, we got all of Horchow's work.

We began working with Roger and his president Clay Johnson, George Bush's roommate at Yale, Governor George W. Bush's chief of staff, and ultimately Assistant to the President for Presidential Personnel under President George W. Bush, before being appointed Deputy Director at the Office of Management and Budget.

Forging great relationships came easily for us because our knowledge of the business produced great results. In this case, I had significant mail order experience from serving clients like Montgomery Ward, experience that enabled me to produce ideas to improve Horchow's business. For example, Horchow had some outlet stores that they were going to close because they were believed to be losing money. But on further investigation, we found that this was not the case. The merchandise was bought for the catalogue and, when it didn't sell, was transferred to the outlet store at full price. The outlet store then took the markdown before selling it to the consumer. We convinced Horchow that if the merchandise were transferred at the marked-down price, since it was the catalogue's problem and not the outlet stores', the outlet stores would be profitable. We were right, and they didn't have to close.

Sometimes, our advice was ignored. I would sometimes travel the state to study the various retail markets. I was fascinated by how each of these smaller towns had family-owned stores that dominated their individual markets. However, they all operated on a regional basis and were limited to expansion opportunities in those markets. There was The Popular in El Paso, Strike it Rich in San Angelo, The Fair in Beaumont, Gibsons in Odessa, and Cox Department Stores in Ft. Worth. Each had its own warehouse, credit operation, merchandising organization, and financial organization. I met with them to show them that if they could combine and operate as one, they would all be so much more profitable. Perhaps, they should form some kind of joint venture. Many were fascinated by the idea, but each one believed it had the best warehouse, best credit operation, best merchandising organization, and best financial organization. Thus, although we did work for each of these retailers, we could not get them to make the big decision. Today, most of them are gone or operate modestly.

As my knowledge of the state grew, I began to look towards expanding into the Houston market. We already had an office in Houston, run by Randy McDonald, but its focus was on oil and gas. The Dallas office, run by Frank Rossi, was growing in banking, manufacturing, and retail. Our two offices were rivals, but Houston had no interest in developing a retail practice, so I started spending more time in that market. I spoke at its National Retail Financial Executives Association meeting, which enabled me to meet and schmooze with many retailers.

Quickly, we picked up Sakowitz Department Stores as a client. Bobby Sakowitz was like a rock star in Houston. I remember taking him and his girlfriend to dinner while attending the National Retail Merchants Association convention in New York. Upon entering the restaurant, Bobby helped his attractive girlfriend out of her magnificent white mink coat that he had just gotten her for Christmas. We were sitting at a table at this quaint Italian restaurant, enjoying some idle chitchat, when Bobby noticed a familiar face at the adjoining table. It was Rex Harrison, the star of My Fair Lady.

According to Bobby, a number of years ago they were both in England at a wine auction. Soon, Bobby realized that the two of them were bidding up the price of each case, so he called a time out and met with Rex in the lobby. The two of them worked out a deal; one would bid on the even-numbered lots and the other would bid on the odd-numbered lots. This way both of them would save money. Upon my insistence that there was no way Rex would forget a story like that, Bobby decided to write a note to Rex and asked the waiter to give it to him.

Rex glanced at the note, looked up at Bobby, and then gave him a big smile. He came over to our table, and we asked him to join us for dessert. What a great evening! Not only did it help Bobby get more comfortable with me and Arthur Andersen, but I also got to meet one of my favorite celebrities. It was a night to remember.

Despite all this activity, I still spent a lot of time serving Zale. Only now, I had some experienced people around me. In 1981, Zale bought a chain of jewelry stores based in Frankfurt, Germany called Keller Christ. It was the largest chain of jewelry stores in Germany, and Zale purchased the bankrupt retailer with relatively little due diligence. They had trust in the CEO and were going to keep him on to operate those stores. But soon after the acquisition, Zale believed there were accounting issues and that the CEO had been aware of them. In November, the company asked me to visit Keller Christ to coordinate with our Frankfurt office to dissect this problem. Willie Jung was the partner on the account in the Frankfurt office. He was approaching 60 years of age and handpicked a bright young manager, Christoph Gross, to work with me on his behalf. Gross spoke excellent English, and we soon developed a nice relationship.

Being Jewish, the last place I ever wanted to go was Frankfurt. The memories of the war were still fresh. My own dad had fought in World War II and had been stationed in Europe. Although he was proud to serve, he rarely talked about his heroics, and the little info I gathered came in tidbits. Sometimes, drunken tidbits. Like that time we went on a vacation in Michigan and he met up with an old Army buddy for drinks. That was one of the few nights he talked.

I knew he served in France and I knew he came home after being injured, and he told me once or twice that he'd driven General Eisenhower around in a Jeep. His silence haunted me. Now I had to fly to Germany.

I flew out with Bill Pavony, CFO and executive VP of Zale. Bill had an unusual personality, which at times could rub a person the wrong way. However, Bill had a lot of experience in Frankfurt. He'd been stationed nearby when he was in the Army and had spent a lot of time there with his previous employer. But all of this would have done nothing to placate me were it not for the fact that he was also Jewish. If he could handle it, so could I. He assured me that times had changed. He was partially right.

The day Bill and I were to leave, I had to help out at my kids' sixth birthday party. It was held at a roller skating rink, and the sheer chaos of it all acted like a tranquilizer. I spent the entire afternoon helping kids put on their roller skates and listening to their yelling and screaming. By the time I tied up the last laces, the party was practically over. I was totally exhausted and ready to get away.

We boarded a nonstop Lufthansa flight to Frankfurt from Dallas. In those days, there was a smoking section on the plane and despite my traveling first class—the only seat available was in that section. The last thing I wanted after a day of chasing kids was a plane ride choking on smoke. Fortunately, I was able to trade seats and quickly fell asleep thanks to the barbiturate-like effects of the day's activities combined with a smooth cocktail. Hours later, I was awakened by a message from the pilot. "I have some good news and some bad news. The good news is that we will be landing ahead of schedule. The bad news is that the airport is being sabotaged and you will not be able to leave." I was concerned, but I looked around. The other passengers didn't seem too alarmed. I guess I'd just have to wait and see what this was all about.

When we got off the plane, we couldn't leave the airport. Police were patrolling the building with Doberman Pinschers. The riotous raucous of hundreds of shouting demonstrators could be heard just outside the doors. But Bill told me not to worry. He knew how to get to the train station and we could take the train into the city. When we got there, though, the escalator to the train was blocked by demonstrators. They would not let us pass, chastising us with slurs and insults in a tongue unbeknownst to us. Again, Bill said not to worry. We could take the train outbound from the city and then catch a cab back in. I followed him blindly to the subway. There, we waited for a train. And waited. And waited. Then there was an announcement.

People started scurrying in all directions. Parents were passing their children to their spouses as they climbed over live train tracks. People were leaping up the steps two at a time, pushing people out of their way as they went. People were running everywhere while Bill and I just stood there confused. I stopped someone—hoping she would understand me—and asked her what was happening. She curtly replied, "Train sabotaged. No train." With that message, I told Bill I was done listening to him. He had to follow me now. We saw a stairwell and opened the door. It was dark, but we could tell it led upstairs. Carrying our luggage, we ascended the steps until it led us back to one of the airport doors. The only problem? It was guarded by police.

We tried to explain what happened to us through stilted German and English and showed them our tickets. Eventually, they let us in, and Bill and I spent the night in the airport. There was no way we were going back out there until we were told it was safe, although we had no idea when that would be. As we looked out the window, all we could see was fire and protests.

By morning, it had miraculously calmed down. We were told that these demonstrations were in protest of the airport's plans to build a new runway that would require the removal of the surrounding trees. On the way to the city, we saw all the damage from the night before. Flame-licked buildings. Trash-filled streets. It seemed like a lot of violence for so small an issue, but at least we were finally on our way to work.

When we arrived at Keller Christ, it was the beginning of a long process. Despite most Germans being able to speak and understand English, here, they only spoke German. Whenever we asked a question in English, they would reply in German and then we would have one of the Arthur Andersen people tell us what they had said. This made for a very long and difficult inquiry. I quickly convinced Bill that we needed to rely on our Frankfurt office to handle this work. We would simply be getting in the way. I laid out the program of what needed to be done and they performed the work, apprising me of their progress regularly.

By the time the investigation was wrapping up in May, we were convinced that we needed to make some adjustments to the financial statements, in order for them to comply with generally accepted accounting principles. The question was, to what degree? Jerry Grubstein, the Zale Controller, and I returned to Frankfurt to meet with the team. I spent a week with our people understanding what they'd done, what they'd found, and the extent to which the financial statements had been misstated. Then, I needed to figure out how to communicate that to the Zale family in a way that they would understand when we returned to Dallas. It required me to do a lot of independent analysis, which in turn raised all sorts of additional questions and issues. After identifying all of these, I put a presentation together in English. It took us all week to finish the presentation and have all the parties involved agree to it.

Not all of my trips to Frankfurt were so uneventful. Some were quite memorable. During one of my visits, my Frankfurt audit partner, Willie Jung, invited me to his apartment for a drink. I climbed up to his third floor apartment, where he served me a beer and turned on the Masters Golf Tournament. As his wife served us appetizers, Willie noticed the apprehension on my face. Here I was: a Jewish man in a German apartment. It was surreal. Willie started talking about how some of his clients were Israeli and how he spent a lot of time in Tel Aviv. While it made me feel a little more comfortable, I kept wondering where he was and what he had been doing from 1941 to 1945. My doubts materialized when we passed a kosher butcher shop on the way to a nearby restaurant. It was boarded up and covered with anti-Semitic expressions and sayings. Willie saw my face and explained that this was done a long time ago. It was all in the past. I just kept walking until we came to a park with a giant chess set on the ground. Each chess piece was over five feet high. I was admiring the sheer ludicrousness of the set when I noticed several swastikas sprayed on the wall behind it. I stiffened. Willie told me that these were the work of "crazies" and apologized, but my discomfort lingered. I walked to dinner with a mind mired in a somber reflection.

Over dinner, my discomfort slowly dissipated. Willie started talking about his time in the German navy and how some of his best friends had been thrown overboard for not following orders. His honesty and open critiques of his country helped me relax, as did the fact that some of his closest friends were Jewish. We had a long discussion that night and, afterwards, I felt much more comfortable around Willie. We eventually became friends, and years later, we played golf at my Jewish country club when he visited Dallas.

On my last trip to Germany, I went with Lou Grabowsky, an audit manager I'd had transferred from the Cleveland office. Lou was anxious to take on more responsibility, so I thought this would be the perfect opportunity for him to do so. We decided to take our golf clubs with us, since we planned on stopping in Scotland afterwards to play at Gleneagles and Troon, two of the most famous golf courses. When we arrived in Germany, however, it was a holiday. There was nothing to do. Since we needed to stay up late in order to adjust to the time change, we asked the concierge at the Grand Kempenski Hotel if he could get us on a golf course. He graciously accommodated our request.

We took a cab to the course, passing through the main entrance to find ourselves surrounded by woods. My mind wandered. I started imagining how Jews were probably running through these forests some 40 years ago, trying to escape from the Nazis. I felt my sweat trickle down my forehead. I breathed. It wasn't the '40s anymore.

When we arrived, there was a beautiful old clubhouse that looked like an English Tudor mansion. Just past the clubhouse sat the golf starter, a heavyset German lady. We walked over and told her that the hotel had made a tee time for us. She asked us for our names. Lou Grabowsky gave his first, and she replied, "Oh, a nice Polish name." Lou smiled politely. Then I gave mine, and she asked, "Cotzin? What kind of name is Cotzin?" My knees started to shake. I said, "What do you mean?" She repeated, "Cotzin, what kind of name is Cotzin?" "Italian," I mumbled before quickly moving on.

Despite this ominous start, it was a beautiful day. In fact, it was one of the few days I ever saw the sun shine in Germany. The temperature was very mild when Lou and I teed off. Our golf was terrible. The long flight and jet lag had caught up with us, and the round was very slow on this holiday, but we still had a lot of fun. When we finished, we headed to a restaurant on the roof of the clubhouse overlooking the golf course.

We sat at some large picnic tables and started perusing our menus until we realized they were entirely in German. Lou and I were trying to make out some words when a couple at the next table over started laughing and asked if they could help us. The lady spoke perfect English, so we immediately took her up on her invitation to join them at their table. Otherwise, who knows what we would have been eating? With her help, we had a wonderful dinner of wiener schnitzel and beer.

We talked about a variety of things. She told us that she was a stewardess for Braniff Airlines. He told us he was an executive at Deutsche Bank, and so on. But the most memorable discussion was about the club's history. The boyfriend was a member of the club and said the clubhouse used to be the home of a prominent

Jewish citizen. Some 40 years ago, he donated the property to the city of Frankfurt, and they later turned it into a golf club. I quickly did the math. Forty years ago was 1942. I'm sure he "donated" it. No problem. Did he really expect me to believe that for one second? I stiffened at the thought, but soon reminded myself: the past is the past. These people cannot be held accountable for what their country did before them. Plus, they were also kind enough to drive us back to our hotel in their Mercedes convertible. I couldn't stay mad for too long.

This international experience expanded my global perspective of and reputation within the firm. I had now worked in Australia, Germany, England, and countless other offices in various countries. Having spoken at our worldwide partners' meeting and getting more involved in our firm-wide retail industry program, I was beginning to get calls from around the world asking for my assistance. One of those calls came from South Africa.

A few years before, our firm had bought a local company in South Africa called Schwartz Fein. It was a predominantly Jewish firm with a large retail practice, so they asked me to come down to lead some retail industry training and do a couple of presentations for clients. Since I had just led an initiative to develop our basic and intermediate retail schools for our U.S. employees, they wanted me to bring the same thing to them.

It was January 1982, and since that is summer in South Africa, I thought it would be a nice relaxing break before I headed back to Dallas for the busy season. I fondly remembered my experiences in

Australia, where it had always been pleasure first, work second. But this was not Australia. This was South Africa. It was work first, work second—at least during my trip.

My schedule was completely booked. So, I decided I really needed to sleep on the flight from London to Johannesburg. I was on South African Airways Boeing 747. The seats reclined almost into a bed, and I was the only one in first class. It was perfect. When I boarded, I was exhausted from a hard few days of work in London. Sleep should have come easy, but there was one problem; I was freezing. Before we'd taken off, the stewardess had come by with a glass of orange juice and laid it on the armrest. The glass was not very stable and when I got up to get something, the glass wobbled and fell onto my lap. The stewardess came over to wipe it up and handed me some blankets. She suggested I take off my trousers to let them dry, but I was too embarrassed. So there I was, sitting there with the air-conditioning blowing on my wet trousers. I eventually relented. I called her over to take her up on her offer. I went into the bathroom, removed my pants and underwear, and gave them to her to hang and dry. I fell asleep in the buff wrapped in blankets, until we stopped in Nairobi to refuel. By then, my pants were dry and I could sit in the clothed comfort for the last leg to Johannesburg.

From the moment our plane hit the tarmac in Johannesburg, I was busy. There, someone handed me a ticket to Cape Town. When I arrived in Cape Town, I was met by Gerald Diamond, our retail partner. Gerald took me to my hotel, where I made a quick change of clothes and went to a nearby club to make a dinner presentation to a group of retailers. The next day, I met with three other retailers before heading to Durban for meetings with the employees in the office there and more clients. Then, I flew to Johannesburg, did some retail industry training, and met with prospective clients. Every minute of my time was booked. The South African offices were going to take full advantage of my presence.

It was a great success. It ended with a beautiful Sabbath dinner with Gerald and his family at their home. I was taking a late night flight to London before changing planes to fly to Dallas. I was waiting in the terminal, when I saw a rack of postcards and decided to buy some for my kids. They were calling passengers to board, but I decided to wait a few minutes to take some time to write some nice notes to my kids. There was enough time. I'd just quickly drop them off in a mailbox before boarding.

As I was writing the cards, I heard a familiar voice ask me what I was doing. As I looked up, I saw it was the comedian Jackie Mason, who had just finished a performance in South Africa. After I replied, he asked how many kids I had and how old they were. When I told him, he asked what I did for a living. I told him I was an accountant. He quickly quipped, "I never met a Jewish accountant before who had quadruplets!" No. I don't suppose many people have. It wasn't always easy, but I wouldn't change a thing.

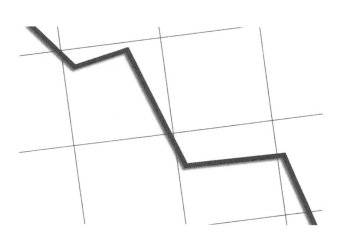

CHAPTER 14

Time with the Quads

The summer of 1980 was one of the hottest summers in Dallas history, breaking the record for most consecutive days over 100 degrees. As I sat by the pool on one of those hot steamy days, I overheard people talk about skiing during the upcoming winter. I had never skied before in my life. After hearing about their plans, I turned to Susan and suggested we take our whole family to learn how to ski together. Sadly though, when I tried to book reservations in Colorado, the places I called were already booked for the Christmas holidays. Susan and I figured we'd have to abandon the idea for this year.

As fate would have it, in the fall of 1980, I got a call from our Salt Lake City office asking if I could help them on a proposal to become the auditors for a jewelry manufacturing/retail company. The Zale Corporation was the premier recognized name in the industry, and our Salt Lake City office thought it would be helpful if I were on the team. We delivered the proposal in an outstanding fashion. When we finished, one of the owners of the company asked if I would participate on the audit. I jokingly replied, "Yes, if you ask me to come during the ski season."

He took the comment seriously. No sooner had I returned to Dallas than I received a call from him saying they booked us a Christmas vacation in Sun Valley, Idaho. They had a three-bedroom condo reserved in our name at Sunburst in the Elkhorn Resort adjacent to Sun Valley. I thanked him and immediately made reservations to fly us all out to Salt Lake City. We would spend the night there in a motel before driving to our destination the next day.

The trip wasn't easy. It was snowing when we landed in Salt Lake City. The sidewalks were slippery, the roads icy and wet, and we had to deal with the lovely task of picking up a rental car and getting our four rambunctious six-year-olds settled into an unfamiliar motel. Susan and I took two adjacent rooms, where we each had two of the kids who eventually decided to sleep. It was a long, long night.

But the next day made it all worth it. We loaded up the car and made the long drive to Sun Valley, where the kids got to see snow for the first time since Chicago. They loved it. They wouldn't come inside no matter what we did. They were having so much fun. Right then, I knew my client's suggestion to visit Sun Valley had been right. It was going to be a great trip.

The next morning we took our skis and went to Dollar Mountain, a small beginners' mountain near our three-bedroom condo.

This was no easy task, as we had to carry our skis and climb through the thick snow to get to the ski area. Susan and I then tried to put the skis on each of our kids, but it was all but impossible. By the time we started putting skis on the second child, the first one would already be falling over or sliding down the hill. Finally, the ski instructor came over to help us. We told her that none of us had ever skied before, so she immediately took us aside and begged us not to be in the same class as our kids. She said if we wanted our kids to learn and have a good time, we needed to let them be on their own.

I told her that we came up here to learn together and that we didn't want to split up! But she persisted, so we eventually relented and said good-bye to our kids. They cried and cried as we were leaving. They wanted to be with us and were afraid. Susan and I almost couldn't bear it, but we kept going at the ski instructor's insistence. She assured us that we would see smiling faces upon our return.

She was right. At the end of the day, not only were our kids smiling, but they were skiing better than we were. We couldn't get them off the mountain. That night, we all went out to dinner at the Western Café, and they were talking so much they barely had time to eat their food. We had a great time hearing about all the fun they had learning to ski.

Even though we had only stayed in Sun Valley for less than a week, we loved the area so much that we looked into what condos cost. Surprisingly, they were much cheaper than we expected. Each day, Susan and I spent our lunch breaks looking at condos. By the end of the week, this conservative accountant became the owner of a furnished Sunburst three-bedroom condo for $90,000! For the next 13 years, we enjoyed our summers and winters in Sun Valley. It was our vacation spot, and we no longer had to cope with the stress of having our quadruplets staying in multiple hotel rooms while on vacation. Sun Valley became our home away from home.

This time was a time of family memories, but it was also a time of great professional growth. I was introduced to a privately held company called Glazers. It was one of the largest liquor distributors in the U.S. and was controlled by the Glazer family. Robert Glazer was a principal owner, and he loved to talk.

Sometimes, it was hard getting one short word in as he chatted away. I met him at a Christmas party and we hit it off from the beginning. For the next several years, Robert frequently told me that he wanted the firm to take over his auditing work, but he never made a decision to do so. Finally, he invited me to his annual sales party. I was coming in from out of town and I knew I would be tired, but I told him I'd try to be there.

It was pouring rain when I got off the plane. The last place I wanted to go on a Friday night was to the Marriott to listen to Robert. But I forced myself to go. It was hard to hear Robert over the loud music and commotion, so he asked me to go to his suite. Already exhausted, I listened to him talk until 11 p.m. I hardly said a word and he poured his frustrations on me. Finally, I told him I had to go home. Realizing I was about to leave, Robert suddenly said that I was more helpful than anyone else he had ever met, and that my support that night had convinced him to give Arthur Andersen all his work. I stood there in shock. I got the account because I said absolutely nothing!

Robert was a very insightful person who gave me countless life-changing tips. One of the most important ones was a suggestion on how to tie business with spending more time with my kids. He suggested I take one of my kids with me on a business trip. It made a lot of sense to me. Since I spent less time with Laurie than the boys, I decided to take her with me to New York when she was nine years old.

While I was there to give a presentation at the National Retail Merchants Association's annual convention, the more memorable moments were the ones with Laurie. She flew out with me on Friday and we spent the weekend together. We visited the FAO Schwartz toy store, went to a play, shopped, and dined at some wonderful restaurants. It was just Laurie and I without any disruptions for the first time ever. On our last night, I decided to take Laurie to an upscale Italian restaurant. When the waiter came over, he asked Laurie what she wanted for dinner. Decked out in a new dress we'd bought for the trip, my little girl looked up at the waiter and said, "Pizza." Her face fell when I told her this type of Italian restaurant did not have pizza. She wasn't disappointed for long though. Laurie soon tried her first Fettuccine Alfredo and loved it. It was magnificent!

Robert had been right. It was a weekend neither of us would

ever forget. On Sunday, I put Laurie on a plane and she flew back to Dallas alone, while I stayed and attended the convention. This trip was such a success that I thought I would do it with Laurie again. However, my three sons would not allow that to happen. They said it wasn't fair and they were right. So from that point on, they took turns.

The next year, I had two free American Airlines tickets to fly anywhere in the world. So, I asked Jonathan where he wanted to go. An avid basketball fan, Jonathan replied that he wanted to go to Houston to see the season opener between the Los Angeles Lakers and the world champion Houston Rockets. Since my passes had to be used by October 31, I used those free tickets to save $58 on round trip tickets from Dallas to Houston. A few days later, American Airlines called me to say I must have made a mistake. My tickets could be used to fly anywhere in the world. Surely I didn't want to use them to go from Dallas to Houston? I replied that it was no mistake and explained that this was where my son wanted to go.

The agent repeated, "But these tickets could be used to go anywhere in the world."

I repeated, "But this is where my son wants to go."

So that is where we went. We had a great weekend seeing the Rockets' opener and visiting the National Aeronautics and Space Administration (NASA). We saw the space shuttles, learned about the training astronauts went through, and even how computers had been used to manage the moon missions. Watching Jonathan's expression as he learned about the wonders of space travel was priceless. It was an amazing trip, more than worth my using those two vouchers for so short a trip.

The next year, I took Jeremy to Atlanta to see his favorite player, Spud Webb, and the Atlanta Hawks. For Jeremy, the shortest of the boys, Spud Webb was somewhat of an idol. He loved watching him play, dominating the court despite his shorter stature at 5'7". We also visited the Cable News Network (CNN) studios while we were there, but Jeremy found them rather boring. Like many kids his age, he was much more interested in a basketball game, and I can't say I blame him. All in all though, it was a wonderful weekend where I finally had the chance to talk to Jeremy, and Jeremy alone, without interruptions.

The last child to go on a trip with me was Brian, an avid Los Angeles Lakers fan. His room was decorated in purple and gold, and pictures of Magic Johnson and Kareem Abdul-Jabbar covered the walls. He wanted to go to Los Angeles for a Lakers game, so we did. We also planned to take in an Oakland Raiders/Chicago Bears football game. I rented a convertible, thinking it would be warm in sunny California, despite it being December.

We got off the plane, put the top down on the convertible I'd rented, and headed to the Los Angeles Coliseum to see a football game. It was December in California so I figured it would be sunny and warm enough, but we were chilled so I put on the heat. There was no way we were going to put the top up on our convertible. As we were driving, people kept staring at us. We didn't know why until we turned on the radio. Apparently, this was a record cold day for Los Angeles!

The next day, we decided to drive to Tijuana, Mexico, and do some shopping. On the way to Mexico, I couldn't understand why I saw signs promoting Mexican car insurance. We just kept going until we crossed the border. It was warmer in Mexico, so we could legitimately enjoy driving with the top down. Soon, we came across some familiar store names. I was looking for a parking spot when we were stopped by a police officer. He walked up to the car and said, "Señor, can you show me evidence of your insurance?" So, I showed him my insurance card. He replied, "Señor, I need to see your Mexican insurance card." I replied that I had no Mexican insurance.

With that he said, "Then I must impound your car and jail you for driving illegally in Mexico." Brian started to cry. I then used an old trick that my father-in-law had taught me back in my Chicago days. I said, "Perhaps if you told me what the fine would be, I can give you the money and you can pay the fine for me." With that, the officer replied, "How much money do you have?" I took out my billfold and said I had $125. He replied, "That is exactly the amount of the fine." So he took my $125 and said I needed to follow him to the border and leave the country immediately.

When we got to the border, the line out of the country was long and my gas tank was nearly empty. There was no way I could stay in the line, so we jumped to the front. Fortunately, the border officials understood, and we made it to a gas station near San

Diego. I filled up with gas and used my last 25 cents to call our San Diego Office for a cash advance. But no one was answering. I called and called. Finally someone answered and I told her who I was and what I needed. She promptly directed me to the office.

Brian and I drove to the building. I showed my Andersen ID and received a $200 advance, and Brian and I drove back to Los Angeles, stopping at a Tony Roma's for ribs and to watch Monday Night Football. Thank God for the firm. I don't know what I would have done without their help.

The next day, we went to the Lakers stadium, bought souvenirs, watched the Lakers practice, took pictures with the players, and saw the big game with the 76ers. It was another trip to remember. Brian loved it and the two of us definitely had some stories worth telling afterwards.

But, as I said, the good always evens out with the bad. For the last several years, I'd had a lot of good.

CHAPTER 15

When It Rains, It Pours

One of my areas of expertise in the firm was my knowledge of the retail LIFO (Last In, First Out) method of accounting. I would never have guessed that this would be the case, since I flunked only one test in my time at Drake, and that was on the retail LIFO method! It was a very difficult concept to grasp, but now, years later, I was one of the experts in this field for one of the largest accounting firms in the world.

The retail method of accounting is an averaging approach to price inventories. Since department store retailers carry thousands of Stock Keeping Units (SKUs), before computers, it was virtually impossible for them to price out each individual item at cost, so the IRS allowed retailers to use this convention. It involved grouping like departments of inventory and then coming up with an average markup to reduce the inventory from retail to cost. In effect, retailers would accumulate their inventory in retail dollars and then convert it to cost using an average markup.

The IRS allowed retailers to use a retail LIFO (Last In, Last Out) approach for income tax purposes, whereby they would price their inventories at the earliest cost versus the latest cost, thereby removing any inflation from the ending inventory. This would allow a retailer to have a lower ending inventory and lower profits, permitting the retailer to pay less income tax. The IRS required one to use the same method for both financial statement purposes and income tax purposes. A retailer could not use FIFO (First In, First Out) for financial statements and LIFO for tax purposes. Therefore, unlike almost any other area, tax law dictated how a company would apply the retail LIFO method for financial statement purposes.

In the late 1970s and early 1980s, there was tremendous inflation in jewelry. It was not uncommon to have gold, silver, and diamond prices go up by as much as 25-50% in one year. Yet, Zale was pricing its inventory using the retail FIFO method. Thus, they were paying taxes on inflated prices. I approached Zale with the idea of converting to the retail LIFO method, which could save them tens of millions of dollars each year. At first, Zale objected since it could not use the department store Bureau of Labor Statistics inflation indices. The IRS published these indices for department stores and had this rule that, in order to use these published indices, a store had to use at least three different merchandise categories. Since Zale was a jewelry specialty store, they were not able to use three different categories. Further, at this point in time, few, if any, specialty retailers had ever calculated their own inflation index.

I suggested that they hire us to see if we could construct their own inflation index for them. Since all their jewelry was centrally purchased and distributed from one warehouse, perhaps they could construct an inflation index from the prices and mix of inventory at that central warehouse. Seeing the potential for significant tax savings, Zale agreed.

I led a group that visited the Zale warehouse in New York so we could all understand exactly how diamonds were procured, made, and distributed to the stores. I learned the four Cs (carat, clarity, cut, and color), all of which determined the value of a diamond. We spent weeks learning the diamond business. Then, we visited the stores to make sure that the mix of inventory at the stores replicated the mix of diamonds at the warehouse. After all this work, we were convinced it was legitimate to calculate an inflation index and use it to convert Zale to the retail LIFO method of accounting. Needless to say, it would be a complex process and require significant documentation to support an IRS examination.

Zale successfully converted to the LIFO method and did, in fact, save tens of millions of dollars in taxes, a multiple of what it cost to convert to this method. However, inflation continued to accelerate to even greater rates in the years that followed, and I knew that one day the IRS would want to investigate. To prepare, I saved every article that described diamond price increases that appeared in the Wall Street Journal or Jewelers Circular magazine, as evidence that our calculated inflation index was realistic and reasonable. We knew the government would question our findings, so we waited for them to call.

Sure enough, the day of reckoning came. We got a call from Zale that an IRS agent named Rob was at its door and wanted to examine their retail LIFO calculation. So, Zale requested that the firm make a presentation to the agent that would explain our approach in a way that Rob could easily understand. Our tax team suggested that I make the presentation to Rob. This was most unusual. Generally, an audit partner would not be asked to present, but our tax people felt that since I had spearheaded the project, I should make the presentation.

On October 25, 1983, I made a presentation to the IRS on our method. There were very few questions. One was when Rob asked me how he could learn the retail LIFO method. I told him that I learned it in college and could give him my intermediate accounting book. I also suggested he visit the Zale warehouse to understand how diamonds are procured, manufactured, and distributed to the stores. He took me up on both offers.

For the next several months, I spent a lot of time being as open and honest as humanly possible to try to get Rob to understand what we did, why we did it, and why the answer made sense based on outside independent evidence. Rob seemed grateful for our assistance, but we both knew he was out of his element.

In the midst of this chaos, one of our clients in St. Louis, May Department Stores, needed to rotate audit partners as required by the SEC. This was one of our firm's largest retail clients. May operated multiple divisions throughout the country. Jerry Loeb was the new CFO, and he requested that the firm nominate three candidates to take over his work. None of the candidates were to come from St. Louis, since they wanted the most experienced retail partners as candidates, and there was not much retail in St. Louis, other than May.

The firm recommended Bob Grottke as the partner. Bob, the man who'd transferred me to Dallas, was the partner in charge of our retail division in Chicago, but his primary expertise was food retailing. Despite the client's request, the St. Louis office insisted they put up one of their partners as a candidate. Both individuals met with Jerry and the feedback was that Bob Grottke would be the new partner. However, Jerry still wanted a third candidate.

So, the firm decided to put my name in the hat. Frank Rossi, the Dallas office managing partner, presented the scenario to me. May would select Bob Grottke. They just needed me to meet with Jerry Loeb. It was a formality. I told Frank that I had no time for this. I was involved with many retail clients in Dallas, and if I had to serve the May company from Dallas, it would adversely impact what we were doing here. But Frank insisted that I go through the motions.

So, on June 28, 1983, I flew to St. Louis to meet with Jerry Loeb. As I left the meeting, I felt that there was no way he was going to pick anybody other than Larry Katzen. I may have been the third option, but I was their first choice. I knew it. I told Frank he was assessing the situation incorrectly and that I would be selected to handle the work. Frank just laughed.

A few months later, Jerry Loeb called to request a second visit and meet with him and David Farrell, the CEO of May Company. I returned on December 15 for another visit. Within a year, I was meeting with the May audit committee. The decision was made. I would be replacing David Schwartz as the next audit partner for May Company. Jerry made it clear, they loved David Schwartz and he would continue as advisory partner. The advisory partner was someone who would be available to the client, should they have an issue with the firm that could not be handled by the lead audit partner.

I knew very little about May Company. It was now time to learn. I had the audit manager, Mark Wuller, feed me information on its merchandising strategy and merchandising performance by category, so I could begin to learn more about the company. The big question: how would I handle Zale and their ongoing IRS investigation, May Company, my other Dallas retail clients, and grow our Dallas retail practice, all at the same time? When it rains it pours.

At this time, my career in the firm was all-consuming, but my reputation within it was being established. I was asked to go to Chicago and be tested by David Morrison, a psychologist, who tested partners on the leadership track. So on December 20, 1983, I flew up to Chicago to be tested. I was tested all day. I even took tests at a nearby restaurant while having lunch, before returning for more testing. At the end of the day, I met David in his office and asked for his feedback. He said nothing. Not a word. Instead, he piled books on a table until they were up to my eyeballs. David told me to read the books and come back when finished.

I felt the guy was a quack. With everything I had going on, there was no way I had time to read these books. I was glad to get out of there and head back to warm, sunny Dallas. Unfortunately, or perhaps fortunately, my flight was canceled because of a snowstorm and I was stranded at O'Hare with nothing to pass the time but these books. I began to read them. The more I read, the more interested I got. The books were about my type A personality. I could relate with everything I was reading. As it ended up, this day changed my life; I ultimately developed a wonderful working relationship with David.

When I got back to Dallas, the IRS wanted more of my time. On January 5, 1984, we began to meet with them. They turned into group meetings with Rob bringing reinforcements. He did not understand retail LIFO and he was in over his head. These people did not like Zale. They remembered Zale from the previous scandals and were determined not to trust the company and to challenge everything. The more answers we gave them, the more questions they asked. They suspected that this was another way Zale was trying to scam the government. Yet, it was the furthest thing from the truth. I never saw any company that tried to accommodate the IRS the way Zale did.

While this was going on, I was getting involved with my new client, May Company. After completing my research, what became evident was that May Company was vulnerable to being acquired. I was in process of completing a presentation for the

National Retail Federation on why retailing would be the next industry to consolidate. Many of the reasons supporting this thesis were evident when I looked at May. Their balance sheet was cash heavy and their operations continued to generate more cash. The company owned much of its real estate, most of which had a much higher market value than what was recorded on their books. There were far too many department stores in the market, and shopping center developers were continuing to build new locations. Many of the organizations were thin on top management talent. They also consolidated their back offices and with new technology had the capacity to manage a larger number of locations. Many of these chains, such as May, operated too many divisions, with each division having its own management team.

With this as background, I had my first meeting with Jerry Loeb and David Farrell. I shared my thesis on retail consolidation and asked what end of the consolidation continuum they wanted to be in. If they wanted to be acquired, I had not much to add. But if they didn't want to be gobbled up, then I thought they needed to monetize their real estate and make a major acquisition.

I thought my comments would be appreciated, but Jerry Loeb responded in a shocking way. He snapped back that I was brought in to be their auditor and not their advisor. He said I needed to stick to my knitting. I had the utmost respect for Jerry. He was probably one of the smartest individuals I had ever worked with, but he was also one of the toughest. I liked his being direct and honest, even though I disagreed with him. In this instance, I felt I knew more than he did, but I left in silence. In my heart, I thought May would not be around more than a few years.

Meanwhile, back in Dallas, the Zale Corporation had a March 31 year end, and we finished our audit around Memorial Day. It was always a tough audit. The conversion to LIFO made it that much more difficult and complex. But having finished the sign-off by Memorial Day, I had the benefit of having a three-day weekend to relax with my kids around the swimming pool of the Columbian Country Club. It helped recharge my batteries after weeks of working long hours.

I came to work on the following Tuesday all relaxed. It was a long time since I had been in the office, and I was eager to catch up on some of my negligent office duties. Without my noticing, a stranger came into my office and asked if I was Larry Katzen. After confirming that I was, he then gave me papers to sign, at which I asked him who he was and how he got in here. He said he was with the IRS criminal investigative division (CID) and "that they have their ways." I asked him to show identification. He pulled out a badge in a leather case and threw it on my desk. It went flying across onto my lap. I said there must be some mistake because I had the firm prepare and file my income tax returns. He said this was not about me, but about Zale. He accused me of conspiring with Zale to avoid federal income taxes and informed me that I and others were under special investigation. I told him I was not going to sign anything without talking to my attorney.

At the same time, other IRS agents were doing the same thing to the others who were involved. The Zale CFO and other officers were approached, as were an Andersen tax partner and tax manager. This had a significant impact on me for the next two years. A lot of my time was devoted to fighting these allegations. The firm had to get its attorneys, and Jordan Roseman, Craig Hamilton, and I had to get ours. The firm took the position that it is possible that our interests might be different from its interests and, hence, we needed separate attorneys. Zale did the same with its executives. For me, it was painful. I always thought I was part of the firm. But now the firm and I were on different pages.

I was represented by Chuck Meadows and Bob Davis. Bob had been the head of the IRS criminal investigative division just a few years before, so I felt comfortable. However, for the next few years we were not to be seen with any of the Zale executives. This was tough, since I considered them friends, as well as clients. But my attorneys made it clear that we needed to be separated. The firm also made it clear that my career was on hold until the issue was resolved. For the next few years, I would be rehashing the whole Zale LIFO incident with my attorneys. We would be discussing every meeting and every detail to prove our innocence on something we felt we had done nothing wrong. The firm would be spending millions of dollars on our defense.

In the meanwhile, my other responsibilities continued. Later that year, May Company received notice that the Haft Brothers, a wealthy family from Washington, D.C. who owned a specialty book store chain, made a major purchase of May stock. Rumors quickly spread that this was the first step in a hostile takeover attempt. Immediately, I got a call from Jerry Loeb and David Farrell asking me to come back and talk to them about my theory on retail consolidation. Suddenly there was a change in their level of interest. I encouraged them to consider making a major acquisition and to reduce their real estate holdings.

Jerry indicated that, for years, they were exploring possibilities to dispose of their real estate, but nothing seemed to work because of the high income taxes that would result. Any idea that we would offer was rejected. So on January 21, 1986, I had Howard Wood and Les Small, two St. Louis tax partners, find the smartest real estate tax partners in the firm and invite them to our Dallas office for two days of brainstorming. During those two days, we sketched every idea possible. I then laid out Jerry's goals and objectives. We matched every idea to that list. One by one, we discarded each idea until there was one left. It was a perfect match.

The following Saturday, I invited Barry Wallach, a Chicago tax partner, to St. Louis to present the idea to Jerry. It was a cold beginning until Barry recognized a famous mathematician's paintings on Jerry's wall. It seemed like that got Jerry's attention and established Barry's credibility. The ice melted. Jerry said he liked our idea, but needed to think about it. Finally we made some progress!

That winter I also learned more about Jerry Loeb and the May culture. At the end of the audit, we prepared a closing presentation for management and the audit committee that summarized the results of our audit and included any observations we had that could improve their operations. Since I was new on the account, I thought I would give them my fresh perspective and make the presentation different from prior years.

Although May was considered a very cost-efficient department store operator, like most department stores, May operated on a decentralized basis. Each division had its own administrative function, credit department, warehouses, etc. I thought there was an opportunity to consolidate those operations so they would operate on a larger scale.

In the closing presentation, I showed a picture of the United States with all the May warehouses plotted on the map. Then, I contrasted that with the Limited Stores, which had billions in sales and operated with one large warehouse in Columbus, Ohio.

On the Friday before our audit-closing meeting, I met with Jerry Loeb to review the presentation with him. Jerry was so displeased with the presentation that his face turned bright red. He stood up pacing back and forth and started screaming at me. He tried to call David Schwartz to tell him he would not tolerate such a presentation. Fortunately, David was in a closing meeting in Chicago with the Montgomery Ward management, and the secretary would not get him out of the meeting.

Jerry, then, emphatically told me to revise the presentation and meet him on Saturday morning at 7 a.m. I cancelled my flight to Dallas and was prepared to honor his request. I asked our team to show me some of the board presentations of the past. It became obvious to me that it was a relatively simple issue. Their presentation style was different than mine. There were no pictures, only words and numbers. I simply had to adapt, or perhaps in this case devolve to suit Jerry's preferred style. So we worked late into the night and redid the presentation into words. I took out all the pictures, but left my message the same.

On Saturday morning, I showed Jerry the revised presentation. He reacted positively. I passed his test. The following week we gave the presentation to the audit committee. They were very pleased with our insights and said this was one of the best presentations they had ever seen. Jerry turned to me and smiled. I had finally earned his respect.

Later, I was called to New York to meet with May management and their outside legal counsel to discuss possible accounting ramifications related to proposed real estate transactions. There was strong disagreement among May management as to which direction to go. Jerry Loeb and Henry Lay, VP of Real Estate, got into it pretty good. We left the meeting with them asking me to come back the next morning with the accounting ramifications for each of the scenarios.

That night I went back to the hotel with Mark Wuller, the audit manager. As we checked into the hotel, we were told there was no heat in the hotel. It was extremely cold outside, but it was not much warmer in the lobby. The hotel we stayed at was a favorite of Lou Garr, the vice president of legal for May, who encouraged us to stay at this hotel. We went out to dinner and hoped the heat would be on by the time we got back.

This was wishful thinking. I went to my room and started doing research on the appropriate accounting for the real estate transaction. While I was doing this research, I was delivered a fax from my attorneys in Dallas. It said there was a meeting with Zale and the IRS the next day. They wanted me to read the document and get back to them first thing in the morning. The document was more than 20 pages long.

I didn't know what to do. Do I spend time on the IRS document or do the May research? I just couldn't decide, so I got up and took a walk around the block to collect my thoughts. It was bitter cold and the wind was blowing hard, but it seemed to clean out some of the cobwebs in my brain. I decided to focus on May Company first and prepare for my meeting the next day.

I got back to the room and took out the Arthur Andersen books to research the accounting issue. The light in the room was dim, so I went to my bed, turned on the light and started reading. I lay there in my suit and overcoat as the room was just too cold. Slowly, the darkness and exhaustion got to me. I eventually fell asleep. When I awoke in the wee hours of the next morning, I noticed my books were on the floor and my glasses were off my face. I reached over to grab my glasses and saw my research books on the floor. Miraculously, the page was open to the exact issue that addressed the May situation. I grabbed the book and started pulling my notes together for the morning meeting.

Then, I read the Zale IRS paper and collected my thoughts. In those days there was no email, so the only way to communicate quickly was by fax. I faxed my attorneys that I would call them during my break from our May Company meeting.

The next morning, I met with Mark Wuller and we discussed our research. Mark was going to contact our Chicago office to verify what we had found. It was now time to discuss the results of our research with May management. The company was pleased with our quick response. Now it was time to call my attorneys in Dallas.

The key issue I had with the IRS paper was that it asserted I said certain things in a meeting held several years ago. I didn't remember that meeting or any of the subject matter. I told them I would check my calendar when I returned to Dallas. As a result, they had sought to delay their meeting with the IRS.

Back in Dallas, I researched my old desk files to see where I was on August 30, 1984. To my surprise, my calendar confirmed I was meeting at Zale with the IRS. How could I not remember such a meeting? I researched my pocket calendars and found August 1984. A big smile came to my face. On August 30, I was sick and never went to work. My best friend, Carl La Mell, was marrying his third wife, Maita, in New Jersey that weekend. I was standing up for the wedding and didn't think I would be able to make it. I rested at home and felt well enough to fly to New Jersey the next day. Now I knew why I didn't remember that meeting!

I immediately called my attorneys, who drilled me over and over to make sure I had the right facts. I assured him that this was the case and if he wanted, I could show them my trusty pocket calendar as evidence. We were all extremely relieved to know that the government's accusations were in error.

Later that summer, I was at the Columbian Club, playing golf on the day before Father's Day. I was looking forward to the next day, as the club was having its 9-hole father-son golf tournament. My boys were now 12 years old, and I was going to play three 9-hole matches, one with each son. The club was curious as to how I would handle the logistics.

When I got home that Saturday afternoon, I got a call from Jerry Loeb. Jerry said they wanted me at the Sullivan & Crowell's office in New York on Father's Day, Sunday at 10 a.m. He asked that I bring a tax partner. I asked him if he wanted me to bring anything else and Jerry replied, "Yes. Bring your brain and all your knowledge of pooling accounting."

Pooling was a method used for accounting for acquisitions. Under this method, we prepared the consolidated financial statements as if the combined companies were always owned versus showing their results from the date of acquisition ("purchase accounting"). So that afternoon, I went to the office and pulled some material on pooling so I could read it on the plane the next morning. Then I gave the disappointing news to my kids—no father/son golf tournament.

At Sullivan and Cromwell's office were the four top May executives, the two Arthur Andersen representatives and two representatives from Sullivan and Cromwell. The topic was a hostile takeover by May Company of one of its chief competitors,

Associated Dry Goods (ADG), a company that at the time was a little larger than May. It owned a number of prominent retail chains, such as Lord & Taylor, Robinson's, Goldwater's, Caldor, Loehman's, and other regional department store chains. During that day, the strategy was laid out, assignments made, and the process began. David Farrell commenced the activity the following Friday by delivering a letter (known as a "bear hug" letter) to his peer at ADG with an offer to buy the company.

For the rest of that summer, I led a team working on the acquisition. For most of it, we were stationed at Sullivan and Cromwell's office. Bob Karn, a St. Louis partner, and Mark Wuller, a St. Louis audit manager, were the key players on our team. Bob worked behind the scenes in St. Louis, while Mark and I were in New York. Mark also brought in Mike Crooch, a technical guru from our Chicago office. Our job was to keep working the numbers as changes in negotiation took place, make sure that pooling accounting could be preserved and be ready to do due diligence and to start auditing the target company when needed.

That summer, my kids went away for their first overnight camp. I spent my time in St. Louis or New York while Susan was home by herself. We were going to enjoy our first summer without kids, just as we were going to enjoy taking the kids for the first time to the circus. But like the circus, my commitment to the firm took precedence.

The ADG deal closed later that summer. In looking at flights that were returning to Dallas, I saw that I could catch a flight and make it back in time to meet the kids, who were coming back from overnight camp. I decided to stop at a hotel, shower and shave, and then go to the airport. The first hotel I saw was the Intercontinental. I went in the lobby at around 4 a.m. to ask for a room. They were sold out. I said, "You must have one room." I was not even going to sleep there, just shower and shave. The attendant said the only thing they had was a suite. They quoted the price and were not going to budge from it. As much as I wanted to tell them to take that suite and stick it, I had no choice. I took the room and freshened up. As I was leaving, I looked around the room, went back and messed up the bed. At least they now had to clean the room.

On the plane I thought about the last two years of my life. A period of great stress, but also one of great learning. I hoped life would finally start calming down.

It was not long after, when I was giving a presentation to our business leaders at our St. Charles training facility, that I was handed a note saying my wife was on the phone. Since I never wanted my wife to call at work unless it was important, I was startled. I finished the presentation and returned Susan's call. Susan said she had put a $10,000 deposit on a house at 6402 Riverview. If we wanted it, we needed to sign a contract within 24 hours; otherwise, they were going to sell it to another couple. You have to understand my wife to know this had to be something special. She frequently took hours to pick out a dress before deciding whether or not to buy it. This house had to be impressive. I immediately took a plane home and went to see the house. I fell in love with it as well, and we moved in the summer of 1985.

Susan and the kids spent much of that summer at our home in Sun Valley, Idaho. I commuted and took my vacation there. But now, we had to move to our new house, so Susan went back to Dallas for a few days and she and I moved to our new house, while our kids stayed with friends in Sun Valley.

As we were moving into our new house, I got a call from our Sun Valley neighbor, who said our son Brian had been shot in the neck while on the rifle range at camp. Although Brian was okay, she said he and his siblings were upset. I immediately left Susan with the movers and took a plane to Sun Valley. It was normally a long flight anyway, but this one seemed particularly long. We were lucky. The doctors said a bullet fragment from another rifle just missed Brian's artery.

I hoped the chaos of the past few years was finally over. I didn't know how many more crises I could take.

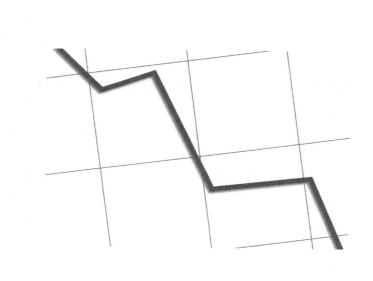

CHAPTER 16

I'm So Excited

The more I worked with my attorneys, Chuck Meadows and Bob Davis, the more confident I became that we would win our case in the Zale matter. However, Jordy Roseman and Craig Hamilton were Mr. Doom and Gloom. They had much more experience with the IRS and knew how difficult the agency could be. They kept reminding us of the dire consequences to our careers if we lost. But, in my heart, I knew we had done nothing wrong and would be vindicated. It was just terrible going through this process and not being able to communicate with my close friends at Zale.

Bob Davis was speaking at a conference in Los Angeles regarding IRS criminal investigations. He thought it would be helpful to us to attend. I accepted, but Jordy and Craig wanted no part of it. Their nerves were already frayed. I was glad I took Bob up on his invitation. It certainly helped alleviate my fears. I learned that the vast majority of IRS criminal cases involved capturing drug and other narcotic dealers. Professionals who acted in good faith were rarely convicted. I left the conference feeling more confident than ever. I felt the injustice of going through this terrible process and what it was doing to my career. I could no longer service Zale, and as a result, Lou Grabowsky had taken over my partner responsibilities. Fortunately, I had the May Company account to keep me distracted and challenged. I also was able to spend more time growing our retail practice and working on such recent client additions as Maison Blanche in Baton Rouge, Accessory Lady in Dallas, Gibson Discount Stores in Odessa, and others. The best therapy for going through IRS scrutiny was to keep busy on other more productive assignments.

In October 1986, I was asked to present at the Arthur Andersen worldwide partners' meeting in Atlanta, Georgia in front of 2,000 of my peers. I was ready to deliver my talk after the next break, when I saw a message for me on the message board. It was from Bob Davis. It read, "Call me ASAP—important." I didn't know what to make of it.

I looked at my watch. I could run upstairs to my room and make a quick call before I made my presentation. Then I thought again. If this was bad news, how would I be able to deliver a speech to my partners? On the other hand, if I didn't check with Bob, I would be nervous and distracted, trying to guess what the call was about. I decided to go for it. I ran upstairs to my room and made the call.

Bob answered right away and said he had good news. The Justice Department thought the IRS criminal investigative division did not have a strong enough case. As a result, the IRS had dropped the case against all parties involved. I was thrilled. I told Bob that I needed to leave to give the presentation. Perhaps he could send the IRS notice to me? Bob said there was no written notice. "Then, what evidence is there?" I asked. "None," Bob replied. I couldn't believe it. Two years ago, an agent invaded my office demanding that I sign papers. Now, I am cleared and I get nothing? Bob said that is how the IRS works. "Don't worry. The case is done." I couldn't believe how our government worked, but was thrilled with the outcome.

Relieved and relaxed, I calmly gave my presentation. It went well. I received countless compliments from my partners.

That night, after the partner dinner, the firm offered entertainment at an old Atlanta theater. I will never forget how the Pointer Sisters put on a fabulous performance and sang "I'm So Excited." Boy, was I excited! What a great day! I could now return to Dallas and lead a more normal life and without having to deal with attorneys. Not that I didn't appreciate Chuck Meadows and Bob Davis, but I no longer had to invest time to defend myself on an alleged crime that was never committed. It had been a wasted time and effort, merely to return to the same starting point.

Even though the criminal cases were dropped, the IRS pursued a civil case to challenge the LIFO method and threatened not to approve its adoption, which would have required Zale to remit millions of dollars in tax savings from adopting LIFO. This case dragged on for years. In the end I was told that Zale won their case and was awarded an additional refund for minor misapplications that went in the company's favor.

Although this ended happily for all concerned, it was a lesson to all and a harbinger of things to come. You can't trust the government. In good faith, we tried to do the right thing and to be open and honest, only to go through years of aggravation and major expense to defend what was always right. Prior to this episode, I always thought that something like this could not happen in a democracy. But it did. It also made me more aware and sensitive to what could happen in the future. It would not be the last time that the firm and I had to defend ourselves to the government for some false accusations.

With this mess cleared up, it was now time to return to a more normal life. My kids were about to celebrate their 13th birthdays on April 22, 1987, and would be having a B'nai Mitzvah—more than one Bar Mitzvah at a time. The kids' B'nai Mitzvah was held on May 9, 1987. Friends, family, and clients came in from all over the country for this joyous occasion. For some, it was their first Bar Mitzvah. In his sermon, our Rabbi, Ken Roseman, said he had searched all Jewish records and talked to colleagues, and no one could identify a Bar Mitzvah ceremony for quadruplets. The Jewish religion is over 5,000 years old, yet nobody had ever experienced what our family was experiencing! I was so proud of our kids for the way they handled the occasion. I took such joy in buying them their first suits, navy blue with pink ties. Susan bought a beautiful pink dress for Laurie to match our boy's ties. They looked great and performed even better.

After the ceremony, we were greeted by our friends and relatives. It was difficult to hold back the tears of joy. I then tried to corral our kids for a picture and realized I could not find my son Brian. I looked everywhere except the sanctuary. It was the last place I had to look.

When I opened the door to the sanctuary, there was Brian staring up at the pulpit and ark. I asked him what he was doing.

Brian turned to me with tears running down his face and asked, "Dad, this is the happiest moment of my life. Why am I crying, if I am so happy?"

I grabbed Brian and gave him a big hug. I then looked in his eyes, as tears started rolling down my face and said, "Brian, it is natural. I am just as happy."

It was a beautiful moment amidst years of tension. The party that night was held at the Columbian Country Club. Susan planned the whole event and, true to form, did a magnificent job. I made sure the band played my new favorite song, "I'm So Excited."

Later that summer, our family continued to celebrate by taking a special vacation. We went to Hawaii and stayed in a beautiful condo that had everything, except air conditioning. However, we managed to cope without it. The kids loved playing at the beach and building sandcastles. They enjoyed each other's company, and Susan and I reveled in their happiness. But we also had something to tell them, which we knew would break their heart.

Now that the Zale case was done, my career was no longer on hold. Dick Measelle, the firm's audit division leader, asked me to consider a transfer to Columbus. I was asked to be the managing partner of the office and take over partner responsibilities for Les Wexner and The Limited Stores. David Schwartz was rolling off as partner because the SEC required the engagement audit partner to rotate off that role every seven years.

Earlier, The Limited had purchased Lane Bryant stores. Deloitte & Touche (D&T) were the auditors of Lane Bryant. When we took over the work, we found accounting adjustments that had to be made. Had the adjustments been known, The Limited would not have paid as much for Lane Bryant. So, The Limited sued D&T and asked us to testify against them. However, our CEO, Duane Kullberg, had a policy that we would not testify against another accounting firm. Les Wexner was livid and threatened to dismiss us from the account. I couldn't believe this was happening. We had been their auditors since they started with one store. It was also an inopportune time for David Schwartz to be rotating off the engagement. Like all his clients, The Limited loved him. The firm knew I replaced David on May, and now they wanted me to replace David on The Limited.

So while we were in Hawaii, we had to break the news to our kids that we might be leaving Dallas. We knew they would not like it, so we decided to wait until the end of our vacation to tell them. We didn't want to cast a dismal glow over the whole trip. My boys' reactions were essentially restricted to lamentations that Columbus didn't have a baseball team. When I told them that Columbus was between Cleveland and Cincinnati and that they could see both the American League and National League teams, they were happy. My daughter was another case.

Laurie first turned her chair so her back was facing me. She then started to cry and tell her mother that she was not moving. She would stay with her friends in Dallas.

When we got back to Dallas, Susan and I visited Columbus and started looking at houses and schools in Bexley, a suburb of Columbus. Susan was a real trouper. She knew the move would be difficult but was already looking at the positives. I was meeting with The Limited people and their attorney, when I got a call from Jerry Loeb at the May Company. He asked where I was and I told him. Jerry was furious.

I told Jerry that I would still represent the May Company and give them the great service that I had given them while I was living in Dallas. He said there was no way he would allow me to service The Limited. If I chose to do that, they would retain another accounting firm. Jerry was particularly sensitive because, several years before, The Limited had tried unsuccessfully to buy Carter Hawley Hale, May's competitor.

Jerry informed me that May was going to do the real estate deal that we had presented to them. He wanted me in New York that night. He also wanted David Schwartz to be there. I told Jerry there was no way I would get to New York that night. I could get there tomorrow. He replied, "Then rent a plane," and hung up the phone.

Fortunately, David was with me in Columbus. I told David what had happened and he just laughed. We were both accustomed to Jerry's outbursts. However, anyone who dealt with Jerry knew he was not kidding. Jerry demanded plenty, and this was typical Jerry, so David and I rented a plane and flew to New York. The next day, Susan returned to Dallas. In a way, she was relieved. She knew there was no way the firm would risk the May engagement. She was right. Columbus was done. It was off to New York to do another deal. Laurie would be thrilled. Although to be honest, so was I a little bit.

Back in Dallas, it was good to renew my estranged relationship with Don Zale. Don graduated from Texas A & M, and Zale was helping support the university's retail industry program. However, they were reducing support and asked our firm to help. We met with Len Berry, retailing professor, and agreed to sponsor their monthly newsletter and support an annual retail symposium, by bringing in outside speakers.

Our first event was held October 1, 1987. CEOs from some of the most successful retailers in the U.S. spoke. I, also, gave a presentation on the consolidation of the retail industry. This program grew to be nationally prominent. It was a great way to educate our own people and meet with prospective clients. It was a great marriage that lasted many years.

Although Columbus was off the radar screen, the firm was ready to apply my talents elsewhere. I was eager to oblige. I started spending more time on firm-wide retail industry matters and at May Company. I had less and less contact with our Dallas partners. It was not long thereafter that I was asked to transfer to the Chicago office and split my time between the home office and Chicago. The managing partner for Chicago was Jim Kackley, the same Jim Kackley who was my instructor at my first training program in the firm (where I bombed the inventory case).

So, I went to Chicago and started looking at houses. The more I looked, the more depressed I got. Prices there were much higher than Dallas, and we would get a lot less for our money. How could I look Susan and the kids in the eye and say that this move would improve our standard of living when, in fact, it would be quite the contrary. Further, when I talked to Jim, my role in Chicago was somewhat undefined. I liked my role with the home office, where I would be helping on strategy, but that was somewhat ill defined as well. In any event, I could do the strategy part from Dallas. There was no need for me to move and uproot my family. I decided to turn the offer down no matter the consequences. Fortunately, the firm supported my decision. I agreed to do the firm-wide work, but without a move to Chicago.

During this time, May Company continued to keep us busy. The ADG acquisition went well and the May management did its usual outstanding job in integrating the new operations. They left no detail unturned. The acquisition strengthened May considerably. They were now ready for the next move.

Federated Department stores was their chief competitor, and after Robert Campeau did an unsuccessful leveraged buyout (LBO), it was not long thereafter that the company was considering filing for bankruptcy. As part of the reorganization, they were going to sell certain divisions. May was eager to gobble up two of them: Foleys, in Houston, Texas and Filenes in Boston,

Massachusetts. Once again, May asked us to help them on the due diligence. Mark Wuller and I started making weekly trips to Boston and Houston to help our local office teams. The final purchase price was based on the closing balance sheets, which we were to audit. It was a similar story, with long hours and hectic travel to help May fill big market voids. Dan Archibald, a partner in our Boston office, led the effort at Filenes. Butch Eller of our Houston office led our effort on Foleys, supported by our Dallas office.

Upon completion of our work, the purchase price was reduced based on the final audited balance sheet, but Federated later objected to some of our proposed audit adjustments. The acquisition went through, but the terms of the deal called for third-party arbitration to resolve the remaining differences. Each organization selected a partner from an accounting firm to serve as the arbitrator. If there were different names, the process continued until there was agreement on the individual and firm selected. We knew what firm we wanted. We also knew that whatever person we would name, Federated would disagree. So, we held off on our preferred choice until the second round. Sure enough, we objected to Federated's first choice and they objected to ours. But on the second round, we found a match, and we got the person and firm that we had wanted.

We were later asked by May to help prepare for the arbitration. The arbitration went on for months, and I quickly learned that, in any arbitration, neither party will end up completely happy. The arbitrator looks through both eyes and tries to find a happy medium. We won a lot of issues, but not all of them. Arbitration never goes exactly how you want it to. Nevertheless, it did result in a lower purchase price, and May appreciated our effort.

In the spring of 1988, our audit division managing partner, Dick Measelle, assembled a few leadership partners to develop a new vision for the audit practice. Dick wanted to hear the voices of our younger partners and added two names: Barry Wallach (the same Barry Wallach who helped come up with the real estate tax idea for May) and me. Dick got Michael Doyle, an outside facilitator from San Francisco, involved to help guide the process. Our first meeting was in Williamsburg, Virginia, where we stayed in an old bed and breakfast.

At first, it seemed ironic for us to be staying in this antiquated building with a dimly lit conference room while we were talking about our Vision 2000, but this was just the first of several meetings that would change the future direction of the firm. We still had more time to solidify our ideas. The consensus of our group was that our industry might consolidate, and by the turn of the century, the Big 8 could become the Big 4. (Little did we know that, years later, we would be right on the number, but unfortunately wrong on the composition.) We went through an exercise to determine if we should initiate a merger and, if so, with whom? We decided that, given our strong position, we should not be the one initiating a merger. But, if one of our competitors merged, we should identify with whom we should merge.

After much discussion, we identified Ernst and Whinney as the best match. Their industry strength complemented ours, and we were the only two firms who were not based in New York. If

Ernst and Whinney was first to merge, our Plan B would be Price Waterhouse (PW).

Price Waterhouse served the largest clients in the world, but mostly on the traditional audit and tax side. They provided fewer services to their clients. If we could bring our skills to their clients, this would represent a wonderful synergy between the two organizations. Our concern was one of culture. Most of our partners came from modest backgrounds and worked hard to achieve their position. Price Waterhouse had a large, well-known client list; many of their partners came from wealth. In addition, we had an open system, whereby each partner knew what the others earned. They had a closed system. Finally, they had a very lucrative unfunded retirement plan that was much more generous than ours. While we were concerned whether we could mesh, there was a strong business case to merge.

It was not too long before the first merger was announced. Ernst and Whinney would merge with Arthur Young to form Ernst & Young. There went our first choice. We implemented Plan B and approached Price Waterhouse (PW). PW reacted positively and the two firms began due diligence on one another. Although our logic was confirmed, our concerns were also confirmed. Our two cultures would not mesh for a variety of reasons. Both firms called off merger discussions. Arthur Andersen was going to operate alone.

These visioning sessions were not a complete waste, though. Other ideas came out of them. We challenged ourselves to identify other services we could provide to our clients. We became the first firm to develop a contract internal audit practice, in which we performed internal audits for companies. Since we could train our people to perform this work, we could do it better than many of our clients. In addition, many companies did not have an internal audit department. We could fill that void. We ultimately grew this to a multimillion-dollar practice before any other firm even considered developing such a practice. We were ahead of the game.

The audit division also launched the "Expanded Services Task Force," led by Dale Kessler, who left Dallas to work in our home office audit division. I continued as a member of the task force, in which representatives from a number of offices worked with Bain Consulting to identify new services offerings. One of these offerings was expanding our Mergers and Acquisitions program.

There are a number of private equity firms in Dallas, and I assisted one in performing due diligence. Hicks and Haas, a Dallas buyout firm, gained its initial fame buying Dr. Pepper. Tom Hicks later broke up with Bobby Haas and formed Hicks and Muse with John Muse. Now, they were buying a wholesale dental supply company in Boston. Since the owners were Orthodox Jews, Tom Hicks thought it would be good to get a Jewish partner involved. I led a team that investigated certain acquisition issues, many of which were considered deal breakers.

For one, the inventory valuation seemed very questionable, so I asked to meet with the Coopers and Lybrand partner who handled the work. He was vacationing at the time and reluctant to visit with me. So, I used a David Schwartz technique and told him that we were now aware of some questionable items in inventory and it would be to his advantage to meet with us to give his side of the story. With his curiosity perked, he drove in to meet me. It didn't take long before he gave us the details to complete our investigation.

We also learned that the key to the business was a family member who was in charge of marketing and sales. Everybody told us that this person was the key to the business; yet, we learned he had no intention of staying after the sale. This would adversely impact the future of the business, so we questioned the viability of the acquisition, particularly at the proposed price. Unfortunately for Hicks and Muse, that deal went through. It ended up as one of the few unsuccessful deals they made.

I, then, worked on the Sound Warehouse deal. Sound Warehouse was our client and was being acquired by Shamrock Holdings, a private buyout firm owned by Roy Disney. Dave Scullin, the audit partner, and I helped our client understand the process and prepare for the sale. The Shamrock people liked us so much, they hired us to help them with their due diligence and to close the deal. We received written approval from the Sound Warehouse CEO to participate on both ends. From his perspective, he knew of our competence and knowledge of the company and that it would make it easier for both sides to complete the transaction. We worked with Stanley Gold, Roy Disney's partner and a very sharp individual. Stanley was a delight. The deal closed right before the Jewish holidays. I caught a plane from Burbank to Dallas to make it back in time for services.

During this time, I also developed a close relationship with Ted Strauss and Shelly Stein at Bear Stearns. On January 28, 1988, Shelly asked that I participate in a Bear Stearns dinner at the Mansion Hotel, featuring one of their partners, Larry Kudlow (who now has his own national television show). I can remember them introducing a "surprise guest." It was Jerry Jones, the new owner of the Dallas Cowboys, who had just fired the famed coach, Tom Landry. I never witnessed such a cool reception for a new owner. It was almost embarrassing.

I worked closely with Shelly Stein on a number of projects. Soon, I was faced with another decision. I had to pick between two job offers. Shelly thought I might fit in well at Bear Stearns. They wanted to boost their retail industry practice, and Shelly felt I could lead that practice. Shelly arranged for me to meet with several of his partners in New York, who offered me the position. They even accommodated my request to live in Dallas, rather than move to New York. Susan and I talked it over. It certainly would enable me to earn more money, but the more time I spent with the Bear Stearns people, the more I realized that it would be a tremendous cultural adjustment for me. Yes, I would get great financial reward, but would I realize the psychological reward? The people at Bear Stearns never could appreciate that thought, but I was convinced I made the right decision to stay with Andersen. Ironically, 20 years later, neither firm would be in existence. I would go through tragedy no matter whom I selected.

In 1989, I was also asked by my partner, Tom Kelly, to work with David Morrison, who had tested me in Chicago, and Marvin Zonis, economics professor at the University of Chicago, on a unique project to help our partners deal more effectively with CEOs. We called this the "Trusted Business Advisor" program. Tom was once part of our Andersen Consulting practice, and he and I had worked together on Zale. We also worked on Pier I imports, where Tom led an effort to design and implement their merchandise systems.

At that time, Pier I was led by its founder Luther Henderson. Luther was a very private person and somewhat odd in stature. He was 6'4" or taller with a crew cut and skinny as a stick. Rarely could you get him to smile, let alone talk. I will never forget the time we did our initial preliminary design and had to propose its final design and implementation. Luther asked Tom, "How much will this cost?" Tom, with a cigarette shaking in his hand, nervously whispered, "$1 million." Luther shouted back, "How much?" Tom reiterated the $1 million with a little more confidence. In the end, Luther accepted our offer, which became one of the first $1 million assignments ever for Andersen Consulting. Later, Andersen Consulting would turn down projects that small.

In any event, Tom was now part of our home office, leading our strategic planning efforts, and we were working together to help our partners become "Trusted Business Advisors" for their clients.

We hired David Morrison and Marvin Zonis to meet with 25 CEOs from all areas of business—large companies, small companies, and not-for-profits—to study whom they used as their trusted business advisors and why. The study was fascinating and led to the development of a three-day training session for our partners. We piloted it for the audit and tax division heads and office managing partners for some of our larger offices.

Although it was a lot of work, I learned much from working with these people and helping put this seminar together. It was also very emotional for many who attended, as it required considerable self-reflection. Many in the room could not control their emotions, and for the first time in front of partners, tears were rolling down their faces as they related many of the topics to their own lonely lives. Worried that leaders of our practice should never cry, Jim Hooten, audit division head, killed the training session, which was never held again. When we finished the session, I was ready to unwind. No problem. I left with my family on a one-week vacation to our home in Sun Valley. That was the place where I could always escape and clear my mind.

There was a lot going on in the firm in the 1980s, and I had a lot of pleasure helping shape its direction. The firm was always looking forward and anticipating and preparing for what might happen. It was no accident that they were always one step ahead of the competition. I was now looking forward to the future and the start of the 1990s.

CHAPTER 17

The Best of Retailing

Dallas was booming in the late 1980s after the city attracted two giant companies from New York: JC Penney and Exxon.

Hearing about the JC Penney move, I contacted our retail team in New York about its relationships with these executives. They replied that they had none and encouraged me not to waste time trying to develop one. KPMG had been their auditors since day one. Regardless, I gave Bob Amick, the JC Penney corporate controller, a call and asked to visit with him. Bob, a pleasant, down-to-earth guy from North Carolina, welcomed the idea.

I remember my first visit as if it were yesterday. Bob had a great sense of humor and was most interested in hearing about our retail expertise in Dallas; JC Penney was taking a fresh look at its service providers. I came over expecting a 15 or 30 minute meeting and was there for hours. Bob Amick called Bob Northam, the CFO, who came down and introduced himself. Northam was a former partner at Peat Marwick Mitchell (now known as KPMG) but did not seem to be emotionally attached to them. Soon, my visit paid off. I reached out. They reached back.

We started doing some work for the company. Our first big project was a review of its credit department, where we provided ideas to improve their efficiency. Brad Forsberg, one of our top retail managers, assisted me on leading the project. Pleased with our work, shortly thereafter, JC Penney asked us to help them centralize their store accounting functions. JC Penney had hundreds of stores; yet, each one was operated independently. Each store had its own buying function and its own accounting function. Management wanted each store to be run as if it were their only one. They wanted to encourage this entrepreneurial spirit, despite being a multibillion retailer. The concept was great, but it was also very costly. Eventually, management agreed that they should centralize their back offices and asked us to help them.

I enjoyed working at Penney's as much as I enjoyed working with any other client. They treated everyone with respect and dignity. Unlike some of their competitors, they valued their vendors as much as their own employees. They believed in strong relationships.

To foster ours, I met with some of the company's top executives from the treasurer to the CFO to the CEO. Most of the executives at JC Penney loved to play golf, so we played together, an informal setting compared to a boardroom. It enabled me to get to know them, not just as clients, but also as people. Because of our shared interests, JC Penney asked us to co-chair an LPGA Skins

Tournament at Stonebrier Country Club in Dallas. Wanting to bolster our relationship with the company, I was eager to help, but the problem was getting my office managing partner, Dale Kessler, to approve. Dale had recently returned to Dallas to replace Frank Rossi after he was appointed COO. Unlike Frank, Dale was not a golfer and he had trouble seeing the value of his partners being involved in golf. It was not easy to convince Dale to be involved in the LPGA.

In fact, the only thing more difficult for me that year was teaching each of my 16-year-old quadruplets how to drive a car. I quickly gave up on the idea and ended up hiring a Sears' driving instructor to teach them. The most frightening part of that experience was the day they all went for their driving test. I took the day off work, and Susan and I drove all four kids to the department of motor vehicles. Our biggest concern was what would happen if some of them failed? Fortunately for the peace of the household, they all passed. Hesitant to buy each kid his or her own car, Susan and I decided to buy two used cars and pair up the kids so that two would share one car. One would have it from Sunday through Saturday and then hand it over to the other child. We also gave each one a gas credit card, so if the other child did not leave gas in the car, he or she could fill it up without any fighting. The technique seemed to work well, but it didn't take long for these cars to look like they'd been in demolition derbies. Within a month, all four kids had gotten into accidents, usually within a one-mile radius of our house. One kid side-swiped a parked car. Another backed out of a parking spot and into another car. Another kid hydroplaned into another car. Fortunately, no one ever got injured, but unfortunately, all of these accidents were their faults. It didn't take long before one of the cars was totaled and we had to replace it.

Compared to that stress, convincing Dale to co-chair the JC Penney Skins Tournament seemed easy. I told Dale that I would do all the legwork for him. All he needed to do was say yes and help fund it. I would do the work and he would earn co-chairman credit. After deliberation, Dale eventually agreed.

The first Skins Tournament was a complete success. We all got to know executives and clients on a more personal level. But more important, Dale Kessler enjoyed the weekend and quickly saw the value of his involvement and participation.

During that weekend, I got to know W.R. Howell, CEO of JC Penney. He was and still is a real gentleman. I admired him for his openness and honesty and how he lived and breathed the JC Penney culture. Later that year, I invited him to the three-day Columbian Club member-guest golf tournament. The event really brought us closer. W.R. and I played as a great team in a best ball format. We ham and egged it to finish in the money, but W.R. had a conflict and couldn't stay for the closing ceremony. He left, not knowing how we finished for the three days. The following Monday, I called W.R. to see if he wanted to get together for lunch, but he said he was too busy. I then told him I had some cash for him from our winnings at the tournament. He quickly replied, "Why don't you come over today?" I laughed and our friendship was born.

W.R. and I continued to play in this event for a few more years.

A month after the first Skins event, I visited the JC Penney accounting center in Salt Lake City, Utah, with Bob Amick and Leo Gispanski, and invited them to join me at our home in Sun Valley to play golf over the weekend. With my partner Lou Grabowsky in tow, we all had a great time. Amick and Gispanski felt so comfortable with me and the firm as a whole that they decided it was in the best interest of JC Penney to switch auditors. They wanted to get rid of KPMG and hire Arthur Andersen. However, we would need to get W.R. Howell's support and approval.

My time was now being dominated by May Company and JC Penney, but I had to act differently with each. May was all business. There were no personal relationships. JC Penney would not do business with you unless there was a trusting relationship.

May Company did have a special celebration one time on February 12, 1992. It sponsored a dinner in St. Louis with David Farrell, CEO, and Jerry Loeb, CFO. We had five partners attend, including our CEO, Larry Weinbach. We celebrated the 25th anniversary of the May/Andersen relationship. It was one of the few times I saw May ever celebrate anything. Farrell gave each of us a little memento commemorating our years of service. We all felt good that night, particularly after working together on so many difficult assignments.

In the spring of 1992, I was invited to the JC Penney shareholder meeting in Kemmerer, Wyoming, the town where James Cash Penney opened his first store. The store is now a museum in this tiny town. We flew to Salt Lake City and then boarded busses to Kemmerer. The shareholders' meeting was held in the high school auditorium, and each attendee received a fossil stone unearthed from the surrounding area. W.R. gave a wonderful speech on the history of the company as it celebrated its 90th anniversary.

My kids were now graduating high school and about to leave for college. Knowing I would not be able to handle this on my own, I hired a college counselor from the neighborhood. She helped each kid decide where he or she wanted to go and figure out how to get there. She helped them through the whole process. At first, each wanted to go to a separate college, but it didn't end up that way. Brian selected the University of Texas (UT), Jonathan went to the University of Missouri (Mizzou), and Laurie and Jeremy opted for the University of Arizona (U of A).

By August, it was time to send the kids to college. Jeremy and Laurie were the first to depart. Susan and I hugged and kissed them before they boarded a plane to Tucson, Arizona. We both cried as we drove our empty car back home without any kids in the back seat. Jonathan and Brian were next, and we decided to split the parenting duties.

Susan helped Jonathan get settled in Columbia, Missouri. Meanwhile, my brother, Bob, who loved to fly and had his own plane, agreed to fly Brian and me to Austin. After we flew to Austin and drove to the dorm, Bob and I began to help Brian unpack his bags, but we could see that Brian didn't want our help. He wanted his independence. I asked Brian if he wanted us to leave. That brought a smile to his face. So we kissed good-bye and left. This time, there were no tears.

Susan and I were now alone for the first time. Our sadness lasted about one day. It didn't take long to appreciate being able to live a life that we had not experienced for 18 years. It was like a second honeymoon.

The fall of 1992 was our first brush with a long series of parents' weekends. We had U of A October 3—4, Mizzou November 6–8, and UT November 13–14. Susan and I made our plans early and were looking forward to seeing our kids in their new environments. Then I got a call from W.R. Howell.

"Larry," he said. "What are you doing November 13–14?"

I replied, "I have parents' weekend in Austin."

"How about November 6–8?" he countered.

"I have a parents' weekend in Columbia," I answered.

He sighed. "Oh well, I'll get you another time."

I asked him what he had in mind. He said he was getting a group together to go to Augusta to play golf at the world-famous course where the Masters Tournament is held. I would have done almost anything to play there and asked W.R. to give me a day or two to sort things out. That night I came up with a solution. I would fly Laurie in from Tucson to take my spot for the Mizzou Parents' Weekend. Laurie wanted to come home anyway, and this would be a good bonding experience for her and her mother. I approached Susan with my grand idea, without telling her why. She thought I was crazy.

"Why wouldn't you want to go to Jonathan's parents' weekend?" she implored.

She had a right to be annoyed. After all, I had left her alone with the kids for so many weeks and weekends throughout my career while I traveled the world. Now, I was asking her to let me do it again. I told her about Augusta. To my surprise, Susan said that I had to say yes to W.R. It was a once-in-a-life time experience, she said. I happily called W.R. the next day.

The trip to Augusta was everything I thought it would be and more. I flew out on the JC Penney plane with two of W.R.'s friends: Don Finn and Joe Haggar III. Tom Hutchins and Chris Sears of JC Penney also flew with us. W.R. later joined us in Augusta with Larry Rawls—CEO of Exxon—and Joe Williams—CEO of Warner Lambert. Half of the group stayed in the Bobby Jones cabin and a few of us had rooms in the main lodge of the club. We played 36 holes in each of the two days. I will never forget dinner that first night and seeing a green jacket at every table. I appreciated the history and tradition of the club almost as much as the golf. When I left, I could describe every hole and how I played each shot.

On the second day, we were to tee off ahead of the Warren Buffett group. W.R. introduced each of us to him and his group. I remember Warren dressed in his Cornhusker red and bringing a radio so he could listen to the University of Nebraska football game. I couldn't understand why he was feeling troubled being in beautiful Augusta, Georgia, instead of attending the game in Lincoln, Nebraska.

On Saturday afternoon, the Dallas contingent flew back on the JC Penney plane, listening to country western music. It was a clear night and you could see all of Dallas as we landed. Susan was still in Columbia, so I decided to go to the office to collect my mail.

I got to my office to find this high pile of paper on top of my desk. I sat in my chair and turned around, viewing the magnificent Dallas skyline. I started thinking about the weekend and what I had just experienced. I didn't feel guilty about not going to parents' weekend. I knew Susan and Laurie would have a great time, and that Jonathan would be more interested in being with his friends than being with me. I just sat, stared out the window and reflected. I was in total heaven.

I then turned to my desk to face reality. I started going through my mail. I stopped. I threw it in my briefcase and brought it home. It would still be there tomorrow.

When Susan returned the next day, she talked about the great time she had in Columbia. I told her how I wished I could have been there with fingers crossed behind my back. I wouldn't have traded my weekend with W.R. for anything.

The following summer, I reciprocated by taking W.R. and a couple others to Barton Creek in Austin, Texas. Prior to playing, Bob Northam, CFO, and Bob Amick, Controller, told me they were going to recommend to W.R. that Penney change auditors. They asked me to try to get W.R.'s reaction before they presented the idea.

After our round of golf, I asked W.R. if we could meet in private. I then posed the question: would he be supportive of changing auditing firms? W.R. reacted negatively. He said KPMG had been their auditor since day one. He felt Amick and Northam needed to first express their displeasure to KPMG and give them a chance to correct their service issues before seeking out another firm's services. It was only right. Although I was disappointed, I admired W.R. for his loyalty. It was only fair that KPMG be given a second chance. Soon thereafter, KPMG transferred a partner from another office to take over the account, and Arthur Andersen never did become the auditors for JC Penney.

In 1992, the firm embarked on an ambitious program, in which each of our industry teams studied major companies within its specialty area and published its "Best Practices." In this way, we were able to factually compare our clients' methods to these "Best Practices." I led the retail industry initiative. Dave Phillips, who oversaw the entire project, was a demanding guy who set a tough deadline. Group leaders expressed their concerns about meeting these deadlines, but David ignored them. He responded by saying that he gets two hours of sleep a night himself and he wished he didn't have to have any! There was no way Dave was going to budge from the timetable.

The retail industry team decided to study two areas:

merchandising and customer service. We identified the top retailers around the world and which partner had the best relationship with each. He or she would then be responsible for completing the study of that retailer.

I quickly realized that in certain geographic areas we had no relationships with any major retailers. I decided to approach the famous Stanley Marcus, the former CEO and chairman emeritus of Neiman Marcus, to ask him for his help. Stanley was a heavyset guy with a full beard and a low voice. In the backyard of his Dallas home, he had a herd of cattle. Only they weren't real cattle. They were painted sculptures. He didn't have enough space for a real herd, but every time you went over to his house, he'd point to those sculptures and say, "That's my cattle." Basically, he was unlike anybody else. He was a real genius. His job would be to introduce us to various retailers. In return, he could participate in the study with us. Being "Mr. Customer Service," Stanley said yes.

Stanley quickly identified retailers in Japan and arranged visits to their facilities. The flight to Japan was fascinating. Stanley told me one story after another from his erroneous store placements to his successful sales ventures. It was like getting an MBA in retailing. I learned much from this retailing genius, such as, "You point to bears, not to people." That was his reaction when a customer wanted to find something and the sales associate pointed and said, "It's over there." Stanley believed it was important for the sales associate to escort the customer to the area.

After arriving in Tokyo, we had to change planes to Osaka. I could see that Stanley was tiring. He was getting up in years, and the trip was grueling. I insisted that he rest on a bench. When we arrived in Osaka, I made sure he and his wife were settled in the room and told him he could stay there and rest the next day. I would visit the retailer with my Japanese partner, Hyo Kambayashi, and tell the company representative that he was not feeling well. Stanley agreed.

The next morning, I was surprised to see Stanley waiting for me in the lobby. He was ready to go. He was fully committed to his job. There was no way he was going to miss those sessions.

During the first interview, I could see that management felt honored that Stanley was there. Communicating through interpreters, we had a cordial discussion before we got underway. We inquired about their merchandising organization and were surprised to hear they didn't have one. Japanese department stores were gorgeous. How could there be no merchandising organization? We must be losing something in translation. So, we rephrased the question, but we received the same answer. Finally, we began to understand. These stores were really real estate companies that leased space to various vendors, each of which was responsible for merchandising and selling its product. Vendors were paid a percentage of profits (not sales) to the store. Sales people were dressed uniformly, but were actually employees of the vendor. Stanley and I were fascinated. It was so different from what we were used to in the U.S.

This visit, however, was just one of many. Throughout 1992, I travelled the globe meeting retailers in order to understand their best practices. Then, I helped our local offices. I visited Nordstrom in July, Costco in August, and other well-known retailers. We finished each visit by meeting with local management to confirm our findings. On October 3, 1992, every partner involved with the assignment met at our training facility in St. Charles, Illinois. Each person shared the results of their findings. We were determined to let each office's findings be used for the betterment of all. The retail initiative culminated with Stanley and me making a presentation at the National Retail Merchants Association annual convention in New York in January 1993.

Soon after, I traveled the world to share our Retail Best Practices presentation with the companies that helped make it possible. In February 1993, I went to Australia; in March, it was Europe and South Africa; and in June, it was Canada. In May, Stanley and I were invited to the Dayton Hudson management retreat in Santa Fe, New Mexico, where Ken Macke, CEO, asked us to present to his management team. We stayed for the entire session.

Being in charge of the firm's retail practice increased my travel schedule considerably. After getting a broader view of the world, our team realized how provincial retailing was. For the most part, U.S. retailers excelled in what they were doing yet did not operate outside our borders. We thought that the industry was ready to go global. So, we assembled our teams around the globe to help retailers think and act globally. We wanted to make sure that if a retailer wanted to open in a certain country, we would have a team available to help.

Life was going so well, Susan and I were prepared to spend the rest of my career in Dallas. She hired a decorator to remodel our house. I settled into my new jet-setter lifestyle. We were ready to stay there.

CHAPTER 18

Meet Me in St. Louis

Both Susan and I were excited and content with our new life. Susan was redecorating our new family room, and I started thinking about what to do for our 25th wedding anniversary. I decided on a trip to Italy and got in contact with some of our partners there. I wanted the trip to be special and asked for their help coming up with an itinerary. After that, I contacted a travel agency to book the trip.

It was not long thereafter that I got a call from Terry Lengfelder, the regional managing partner for the Midwest. Terry had an offer for me. He said they would like me to move to St. Louis to become office managing partner. I was in complete shock. After all, only a few months earlier, the firm said I would be spending the rest of my career in Dallas. Our firm-wide retailing program was humming. We had a new strategy and the team was on board and excited. We started to make some big things happen. Why did they want me to move now?

Terry was honest with me. He said the St. Louis office was a turnaround situation through no fault of its own. The office had lost some large clients due to circumstances outside of its control, including General Dynamics when it relocated to Washington, D.C. On top of that, the tax division was losing money, primarily due to one large client that outsourced its trust tax return work to us. The work was priced so aggressively that it resulted in a built-in loss for us. The office needed new leadership, and the firm wanted me to do it.

In keeping with his honest nature, Terry added that I was not his first choice. He had initially identified a tax partner in our Milwaukee office, but the partners in St. Louis felt strongly that he was not the right fit. In frustration, Terry asked the partners to come up with some names of their own, and my name surfaced. He said not to let this deter me. This was a great opportunity for me, and since May Company was based in St. Louis, they would be thrilled as well.

I didn't know how to respond. I thought about Susan. She was already redecorating our house and was totally set on staying in Dallas. After some silence, I responded to Terry with that most classic of lines, "Thanks, let me think it over."

The next day, I went for a long run to focus my thoughts. But it was hard to think. I was still in shock. The only things I could think about were the personal negatives. We had a lot of friends in Dallas. I had a lot of business contacts that took me years to develop in Dallas. I had a 25th anniversary trip to Italy planned.

There was no way I could move to St. Louis and then leave for a two-week vacation. The more I thought about it, the longer my list of obstacles became. I decided I needed more time to think.

So, that afternoon, I cancelled my lunch date and went over to Turtle Creek, a beautiful park just outside of downtown Dallas. I bought some lunch and sat on a bench, staring at the ducks floating in the pond. It was a beautiful spring day and I was in the perfect place to really think.

I forced myself to start thinking of reasons why I should accept this opportunity. Although I was based in the Dallas office, most of my time was spent working with other offices or helping out on home office assignments. I really didn't feel a part of the Dallas office anymore and was actually extremely frustrated with its leadership. Inspired by the books that David Morrison had given me, I had always wanted to be in charge of an office so I could apply some of the motivating principles that I had learned. I observed so many flaws in the way things were run in Dallas. It was different after Frank Rossi left, and the Dallas and Houston offices were now part of one region. Relatively cosmopolitan Dallas now reported to the primarily oil and gas-focused Houston. The two offices frequently disagreed.

I thought back on one of these disagreements. Years earlier, the two offices recruited at the University of Texas on a joint basis. The firm spent a week there. We were the dominant recruiter, hiring more recruits than any other firm and attracting the best students, yet I noticed we never hired any Jewish students. I asked myself, where else could these Jewish students be? TCU—no; Texas A & M—afraid not; Texas Tech—no way. They must be at the University of Texas! So I went there and reviewed the entire recruiting list. I saw only one Jewish-sounding name and volunteered to meet with him. After learning that he was a member of a Jewish fraternity, I listened to his story.

He told me Arthur Andersen had the reputation of being anti-Semitic and that the Houston office was viewed as being an especially "redneck" office. There was no way Jewish students would sign up to interview with Arthur Andersen. I told him this was obviously not true. I was living proof. I then told him that I would stay an extra day and interview any Jewish student who wanted to meet with me. The next day, I interviewed three more Jewish students, none of whom had previously signed up to interview with Andersen. The result: the Dallas office hired its first two Jewish students.

I was thrilled and, the next year, volunteered to recruit again but was told I couldn't return. Ron Ebest, our HR partner in Dallas, said that the Houston office recruiter had accused me of favoring Jews. They did not want me to be part of their recruiting team. I was livid and flew there to meet with this person. He said that one of the students told him I was favoring Jewish students, and this recruiter believed him without even asking me to share my side of the story. It was an ideological difference between the two offices.

I defended myself. Between our Houston and Dallas offices alone, we had thousands of accountants, and virtually none of them were Jewish. How could I be accused of discrimination? I was merely trying to right a long-standing wrong, to erase our anti-Semitic image. I demanded an apology from him, threatening to take the matter to Larry Weinbach if he did not apologize. Larry was the New York office managing partner and a member of our board of partners. He was also Jewish. He would undoubtedly see my side of the argument. This recruiter refused to apologize, so I stormed out of his office telling him that the firm would not tolerate this bigotry. He called me the next day to half-heartedly apologize, and I moved on.

But the episode made me realize, not everything in Dallas was so great. As I started to think about what I was leaving behind, not all the memories were good. In Dallas, we had just appointed new audit leadership. Since not all of the partners supported this change, I could see how the morale and performance of the office might continue to erode and how the pressures from the Houston leadership would only exacerbate the issue. Perhaps it was time to transfer to a new location.

I now had to discuss this with Susan. Surprisingly, she was receptive to the idea. She commented on how Dallas had changed since we moved there. It was no longer the quiet little city that we once knew and loved. She felt Dallas was becoming very materialistic. Going back to the Midwest would be a welcome change. The kids were now all in college, so it wouldn't matter to them where we lived. She encouraged me to go for it on one condition—that we throw out our old furniture and start from scratch. I said that would be okay on three conditions: First, she needed to hire a decorator that she really liked. Second, she needed to give me a "not to exceed budget." Third, she must not ask my opinion on any of the furnishing decisions. I had complete confidence in her taste and did not want to be bothered picking out furniture while taking on new responsibilities. Susan agreed, and we had a deal!

On July 20, 1993, I called Terry Lengfelder and told him that I was interested, subject to my learning more about his expectations for the office and me. I flew to Chicago and had dinner with him. He told me St. Louis was his worst performing office and in desperate need of bold, fresh thinking. He also said that there were not many instances of partners asking for new leadership by name. The St. Louis partners had nominated me themselves. This was an excellent opportunity for me to make an impact. He was absolutely right. I couldn't wait to take on the role.

Before I left for St. Louis, Susan and I decided to celebrate our 25th anniversary by going to Bermuda for one week. It was far from the two-week Italian adventure I'd planned, but it was an opportunity to recharge our batteries. We learned that August was not a good time to go to Bermuda. It was exceedingly hot and humid. But it was good for us to get away and talk about not only the past 25 years, but also our new future.

I began commuting to and from St. Louis in the fall of 1993. St. Louis was so different from Dallas. First, there were trees—lots of trees. Second, the people were down to earth and unpretentious—a far cry from dramatic Dallas. Third, the houses came with lots of land and the roads with much less traffic. I started to fall in love with the city fairly quickly.

On one of my first visits to the office, I got a call from Jerry Ritter, CFO of Anheuser-Busch (AB), one of the largest companies in town. Jerry greeted me warmly and welcomed me to St. Louis. But before I could say thanks, he informed me that in a few minutes I would be receiving some papers on a lawsuit that they were filing against the firm. I didn't even know that we did work for AB, let alone what we allegedly did wrong.

Before I could even breathe, I was embroiled in a crisis. As the story was told, years ago, we had been hired to verify the "winning numbers" on a Budweiser beer promotion. Customers who peeled the label back and had the right number won a speedboat. The promotion was so successful that they called again saying they were going to run the same promotion. However, despite our preferring to do otherwise, this time, they did not want us to go to the printer to verify the winning numbers. They wanted us to confirm the winning numbers over the phone. We obliged.

Naturally, the printer printed the wrong winning numbers, and AB ended up giving away more boats than they wanted to. Jerry said his boss, August Busch III, felt that all three parties involved should split the damages; one-third for AB; one-third for the PR firm; and one-third for Andersen. Our share came to $3 million, when our fees on the assignment were less than $25,000! It was just one more lengthy controversy to add to my to-do list—one that the firm would fight to the bitter end. But that end would not come until a few years later.

In the interim, Susan came down to look for houses. Our choices turned out to be somewhat limited. Earlier in the year, the May Company had closed its New York buying office and transferred a number of executives to St. Louis. As a result, there were fewer houses available in our desired neighborhoods and in our preferred price range. At first, we thought we would buy an old house on a tree-lined street and renovate it. But for one reason or another, each opportunity fell through and I ended up renting an apartment across from Shaw Park for the first six months. In the end, we bought a Dallas style house with few trees on a small lot! In Dallas, they would call it a zero lot line house. In St. Louis they called it a condo, even though it was not a condo.

Susan was not to be discouraged. She immediately set to work with her decorator, and soon fell in love with St. Louis. The people made her feel more comfortable than Dallas, and the city itself was beautiful.

That fall, after our worldwide partners' meeting in London, Susan and I went to Israel with two of my partners and their wives. We had an interesting time visiting Palestine and getting exposed to its rich history and modern conflicts. However, Susan and I had to cut our visit short in order to return to St. Louis for a May Company audit committee meeting. Our friends helped us get a taxi at the Golan Heights and negotiate a fee to Tel Aviv. After saying good-bye to our friends, we got in the cab and drove a mile or two to an apartment building where the driver left us in the cab, saying he would be right back. A few minutes later, another man got in the cab and started driving. We were scared. We did not know where this guy was taking us. Luckily, we made it to Tel Aviv in one piece. We later learned that the second driver was the brother of the original cab driver. He was taking his spot because his brother had to play in a band that night.

The next day, we flew to London, where we were to connect on a flight to St. Louis. Unfortunately, American Airlines went on strike, and we missed our connection. I called May Company and told them I could not make the meeting, and arranged for others to take my place.

When our friends returned to the States, they called us to see if we had made it back okay. Susan and I said there was no problem. We were fine. They said they had been concerned because after going out to dinner the night we left, they went dancing and could have sworn that the bandleader looked just like our cab driver. We told them it probably was!

When I returned to St. Louis, I felt I needed to meet with every person in the office so I could get a clear understanding of our issues in the St. Louis market. I knew there were major problems just by the way the partners walked to the water fountain. Their heads were slumped over, their gait slow. Just like a quarterback who lost a big game. I started to look at market analysis and meet with our major clients. To learn more about the community, I got involved with civic boards and started meeting other CEOs. Each was very gracious and shared with me their perception of the firm and the market.

After a few months, I started to see immense opportunities. Most of our competition provided basic audit and tax compliance services and not much else. We were very proud of the high quality audit and tax services we provided, but I also saw how we could expand our level of service by deploying other skill sets. This of course would cost money—lots of it. Contrary to what the firm thought, instead of shrinking the office, I saw a need to expand it. I felt we needed to develop a comprehensive written vision and strategy and get buy-in from the firm and the other partners.

On December 22, 1993, I went back to Dallas for sinus surgery. I would not be able to fly for two weeks, so I brought home all my notes and materials to use this time to develop our new strategy. When I came back a few weeks later, I met with our partners and senior managers to review my creation. I knew they would probably be resistant to my ideas because they involved significant change, change in the office direction and change in our attitude.

There were three sections to our new strategy. I asked that each partner sign up for one of those sections. I named a captain for each team. I gave them two weeks to analyze and recommend changes to their respective section. When each team came back with their changes, I approved them all. I knew not all of their ideas were perfect, but I figured it was more important to have their commitment than to have a flawless strategy. I now had their commitment. What we needed were some wins.

Terry Lengfelder came to St. Louis for his monthly meeting.

I shared our new strategy with him and what it would cost. It showed him our commitment to growth and profitability. His first reaction: there was no way we could grow that fast and be that profitable. Nonetheless, Terry approved my recommended investments which were in excess of $1 million. He showed 100% support for the office's moving forward.

Our first major audit proposal that spring involved Gardner Denver. It was being spun off by its parent company as a separate public entity. Gardner Denver was located in Quincy, Illinois, a two-hour drive from St. Louis. Its auditor was Ernst & Young. All the other large firms were proposing as well. Since this was a manufacturing company, we had our new manufacturing leader, Rick Siebert, lead the effort with Phil Smith, a new manager who'd transferred back from Washington, D.C. Our team spent hours and hours on that proposal. I got along well with the new CEO, Ross Centani, and our team understood the company and what they wanted. Our proposal was well received. The management team was complimentary and gave us encouragement. I thought there was no way we would lose. Believing that success breeds success, I made sure we did everything possible to win.

It was Friday afternoon. I was in a conference room with Rick Siebert and others when my secretary came in and said Mr. Centani was on the phone. I rushed to my office, where Ross and I chatted for several minutes. He then informed me that they were sticking with E&Y. I was in shock. Ross said it was a tough call, but the board recommended they stay with E&Y. I wished him well and hung up the phone. This was the first competitive proposal in which I was involved that the firm did not come out the winner. I returned to the conference room and relayed the message to Rick and the team. They were devastated.

I caught a plane back to Dallas and all weekend thought about our loss. The more I thought about it, the more convinced I was that I had not misread the situation. There must be some other reason why we lost. When I returned to St. Louis on Monday, I called Ross and told him how I felt about serving them and how I could not believe that I read him and his management team wrong. Ross said he had wanted Arthur Andersen, but the board went with the firm with the lowest cost. I asked him about E&Y's fee.

He replied, "It's a few thousand dollars lower."

I asked Ross, "If we match their fee, will you support us?"

Without hesitation, he said, "Absolutely!" He knew we were the better firm.

So, in March 1994, we got our first major victory under our new strategy, when Ross reversed the board's earlier decision and convinced them that Arthur Andersen was the right firm.

In April, we got another big win when we were selected as the auditors for the Mexican operations of Edison Brothers, a specialty store retailer based in St. Louis. It wasn't easy to get it. I got to know the co-chairs, Andy Newman and Martin Sneider. They were having problems with E&Y in Mexico, and I asked for the opportunity to show how our "One Firm" concept would work for them. I flew to Mexico City and handpicked our audit and tax team, which was led by Walter Fraschetto. We visited stores, met the people, and had them visit St. Louis to spend time with Edison tax management. Edison St. Louis actually prepared the tax return for the Mexican operations. Our team reviewed the return, found errors, and discussed how best to correct them. We then delivered the audit and tax proposal in person to St. Louis financial management. They felt comfortable with our team and with me supervising it. That night, Susan and I had the team over to our house for dinner to celebrate our victory.

Then, in May 1994, the City of St. Louis audit went out for bid. Under Greg Kleffner, the head of our governmental practice, we began another disciplined approach to the proposal, with rehearsals, visits, and needs identification sessions. This was an important proposal as the work was done off peak and would fill a void in our staffing. Greg and his team produced another victory for the good guys.

All of these successes confirmed my belief that we didn't need to shrink the office. If anything, we needed more people. I started bringing them in. Mark Wuller, who had worked with me for so many years on the May Company audit and had been transferred to Omaha a few years back, let me know that he would love to return to St. Louis. I now had the ammunition to make this happen. It was great to bring Mark back, both for him and his wife, Mary Kay.

Later that summer, Terry Lengfelder came for his monthly visit and was pleased to see our progress and the number of opportunities we were chasing. I asked Terry if he would like to spend some time in the marketplace with me instead of just spending his time in the office. Terry began his career in St. Louis and felt he knew the office and the high quality work we performed. He said he would love to take me up on my offer.

In August, I called Walt Galvin, the CFO of Emerson Electric, one of the largest companies in St. Louis, and asked him if he would meet with Terry and me. Walt encouraged the visit. During our meeting, Walt said he had heard from all the other firms in town, but never from Andersen. He assumed we weren't interested in doing business with them. Terry assured him this was not the case. We left the meeting feeling excited about our opportunity to serve Emerson in some capacity in the future.

I took it upon myself to spend time at Emerson to get to know them and what they were about. The people there were friendly and open. KPMG was their auditor, but Emerson had many other needs. In the beginning, we performed a review of their internal audit department and later helped their internal auditors on various projects. As we got to know them, they shared with us their dissatisfaction with KPMG's audit services in Asia/Pacific and asked us to submit a proposal on their statutory audit work for the Asian countries in which they were active.

On December 4–5, I flew to Hong Kong to meet with John Burrows, our managing partner for Asia Pacific. I had worked with John when I lived in Melbourne, so I already knew him quite well. I explained the opportunity to him, and John quickly handpicked partners to work with me on the proposal. They, in turn, put together teams of people in each country who then visited their respective locations to learn more about what was expected and needed. We assembled a proposal to present to Emerson management in Hong Kong.

It was Susan's 48th birthday, but once again I would not be there to celebrate it with her. Duty called. On March 20, 1995, I flew to Hong Kong with Bob Cox, executive vice president of Emerson. That night, I met with our Asian team and rehearsed the proposal. It was a difficult night as I had to make a number of changes. I reinforced what was communicated to me by Emerson management in St. Louis. I had to make sure that the team understood who was buying our services and what we needed to address. Yes, we needed to work in harmony with local management, but the decision-maker is corporate and its needs must be met. They expected high quality audit services and wanted to be informed of all issues.

The next day, we delivered our audit proposal and showed how we worked as "One Firm" throughout the world. It appeared that our approach was clearly different than our competitors.

A few weeks later, we learned that the Emerson Electric Audit Committee, headed by August Busch III, approved us as the auditors for most of the audit work in Asia Pacific. I led the coordination effort from St. Louis. Emerson Corporate dealt with just one person—me. I coordinated and communicated with all our offices to make sure we were meeting the company's needs.

Fortunately, we had Mark Wuller returning to St. Louis to help me service them.

The wins now started to roll in. To meet this growing demand for employees, I began hiring and transferring in new people in order to grow our skills and deliver multiple services to the marketplace. We brought back Rick Mayhall, a former Andersen employee, to help develop and expand our middle market business consulting services. We hired Steve Beluk, the former director of internal audit at Anheuser-Busch, to lead our contract internal audit practice. We added Steve Stoffel to lead our international tax practice and Joan Malloy to lead our family wealth practice. Our strategy was being implemented.

During these first six months, I also had to address our tax division and work out the famous "Boatman's Bank Contract." We had agreed to do the tax returns and perform other services for its wealth management group at a set fee per customer. We assumed that, between the efficiencies to be gained and the timing of this work, it would be profitable. Instead, we were losing significant sums of money. Bob Merenda, who had taken over the tax department, inherited the problem. He said our tax department would not be profitable as long as we had to service this multi-year contract.

I met with the management of the bank and was open and honest with them. I explained how we had to make this win-lose arrangement into a win-win one and proposed several options, some of which would save them money and improve the overall level of service. However, each idea was rejected. They kept relying on the contract we originally signed. I kept trying to be nice and they kept trying to play hardball. Finally, I met force with force.

I told them that if they did not want to modify the contract, we would not help in the transition from one firm to another when the contract ended. They would be on their own. Eventually, after months of negotiation, we reached a compromise. There was a light at the end of the tunnel and we would eventually get rid of the draining business. The tax department could now return to profitability and Boatman's could perform their work in a more efficient manner. It was a win-win.

Susan moved to St. Louis in April 1994, and arrived to an empty house with no furniture. She immediately began decorating and thankfully honored my request not to bother me about it. One day, I left an empty house in the morning and came back to a furnished house that night. Every wall had artwork and every room was full of furniture. Susan and the decorator stood at the doorway anxiously awaiting my response. I only had one comment, "Perfect." It was amazing. Susan and the decorator had done a magnificent job, so we celebrated by dining at Café Napoli.

It was undeniable. Susan and I were off to a great start in St. Louis, both professionally and personally. Jerry Loeb, executive VP for May Company, sponsored us so we could join the Westwood Country Club, where we later met a lot of our friends, and I continued to revitalize the St. Louis office by boosting morale through bonding experiences. Things were looking up in St. Louis.

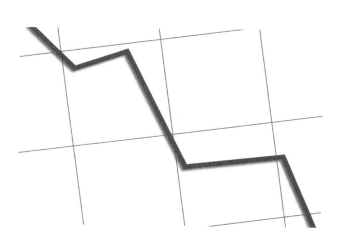

CHAPTER 19

A Global Education

In March 1994, I got a call from Dick Measelle, who was in charge of our firm-wide audit and tax practice. Dick was going to meet with Tom Kelly, partner in charge of strategic planning, and asked if I could join them in San Francisco. The purpose of the meeting was to lay out a framework and method for assembling 100 partners from around the world to develop a vision and strategy for our audit and tax practice. Dick felt the developing nations were growing rapidly and that this could have a significant impact on our business. We needed to address it.

The three of us met in San Francisco on March 31 and April 1. We developed a process to identify the partners we wanted to participate and the places we wanted to study. We kicked off the session at our St. Charles training facility, and then met in East Berlin and subsequently Singapore. We used Michael Doyle, the outside facilitator we used several years earlier, to help us develop a vision for our U.S. audit and tax practice.

Our first session was on June 1–3 at our St. Charles training facility. We brought several outside speakers, who were visionaries in and of themselves. The purpose of this first meeting was to have everyone get to know each other and focus on the future so that we were prepared to operate in the 21st century. The meeting served its purpose. We scheduled our next session for the week of July 11th in East Berlin. After Berlin, we then met, the week of August 12th, in Singapore, one of the fastest growing countries in the world. By meeting in such disparate places, we got a sense of Eastern Europe and Asia, and obtained enough data and perspective to start identifying our new future strategy. We planned to share our findings and thoughts at the worldwide partners' meeting the following October.

We had our meeting in East Berlin at the new Hilton Hotel. We spent the week studying the changes taking place in Eastern Europe and how this part of the world was developing its economic presence. We were starting to see a whole new picture of the world. Outside our hotel you could see unprecedented development. One crane after another was being used to erect new buildings and infrastructure. Berlin was being integrated into one city, free from Communist rule.

Despite all my past trips to Germany, this was my first visit to Berlin. I got there a day early with several other partners and we hired a driver to show us the city. We saw Checkpoint Charlie, fragments of the old wall, the location of Hitler's bunker, and the synagogue that was burnt during Kristallnacht. When the rest of the partners joined us, we visited buildings once used by the Nazis. Government officials shared how the buildings were used during World War II, and how they are used now. We learned about their future plans for the city, how this part of the world was changing, and what it would mean to our practice.

At night, we went out in groups to various restaurants and saw old Berlin versus new Berlin. It was an amazing metamorphosis. By the end of the week, we all had different perspectives and started thinking of how this rapid growth and development of the city might change our business. We were then assigned to different groups to study various areas and prepare to share this at our Singapore meeting.

I made plans with two other tax partners, Barry Wallach from Chicago and Alan Cohen from Boston, to go to Poland after the meeting. We were to fly to Warsaw and then visit Cracow, where we had tours arranged to two concentration camps, Auschwitz and Birkenau. We were also going to visit the famous factory from the movie Schindler's List. However, after the meeting, Dick Measelle wanted to go out to dinner with Tom Kelly and me to rehash the week's activity. So, I told Barry and Alan to go ahead and I would meet them in Cracow.

The next day, I flew to Cracow. I told Barry and Alan to leave a note in my hotel as to where I should meet them for dinner. Our hotel was a small establishment off the town center. Cracow was one of the few Polish cities that had not been destroyed in World War II. The Germans had occupied the city and made one of the old castles their home base. That night, we ate outside at a nice little restaurant.

The next day, we visited Schindler's factory. This was now considered a "high tech" factory, but to us, there was nothing high tech about it. We visited all the familiar spots where the movie was made and were running a little late for our visit to Auschwitz. Barry had previously arranged a private tour, so he asked to borrow a phone. We were escorted into the hallway and saw something we had not seen in many years—a rotary phone. So here at this high tech factory, we used a rotary phone to call in late.

Finally, we arrived in Auschwitz.

We passed through the gates and saw the glass containers filled with old shoes, luggage, and toiletries—all stolen from the prisoners.

We saw the cement cell where men scrambled over one another, fighting for a gulp of fresh air through a tiny pinhole in one wall.

We saw the gas chambers and the furnaces. We saw where millions of bodies were burned.

I tried to picture it. I tried to imagine it.

I could see Auschwitz, but I was seeing nothing at all.

Auschwitz stood next to another concentration camp, Birkenau. Here, Jews were transported in cattle cars and dropped off at their barracks. On one side of the tracks, as far as you could see, were the female barracks. On the other side were the male barracks. At the end of the track was a memorial. The Germans had tried to blow up the furnaces, and their remains were left intact with a sign explaining what had happened. The sight of all the barracks surrounded by guard towers and barbed wire was terrifying. It was 80 degrees that day, but I felt a shiver down my spine.

It was a silent four-hour train ride back to Warsaw. Each of us spent the time silently flipping through our souvenir books. That night, we went to the old city of Warsaw, the part of the city not destroyed by the war. There was a giant courtyard with outside dining. Finally, we talked about what we'd seen.

This was the shortest vacation I had ever taken, but it was among the most impactful.

In August, our strategy group met in Singapore. I had been to Singapore before, since Emerson Electric had operations there. On one visit, I had toured the entire island in a cab. It was a small country, but economically powerful with a number of large financial institutions. I loved Singapore, with its modern look and orchid-laden highway overpasses. The subways were particularly magnificent, true feats of modern technology.

When I thought of subways, I thought of Chicago where I grew up hearing loud rattling and squeaky rides. But trains in Singapore made no noise. You could ride with the windows open and talk to the person next to you without raising your voice. Unlike in Chicago, the stations were safe. Even at night, kids were playing in them.

Our Singapore meetings awakened us to business trends in Asia Pacific. Various outside speakers talked to us about their respective parts of the world and shared their tremendous projected growth rates. Representatives from China talked about how their country was going to grow like never before. By the time our visits ended, we all recognized that our firm needed to make massive investments outside the U.S. to take advantage of this growth. We were committed to transferring people from the U.S. and other countries to other parts of the world, to consider acquisitions and to consider expanding the types of services that would be in demand.

Each of us was assigned to talk to a client with significant operations in Asia to validate our assumptions. I met with Bob Staley, Executive Vice President for Emerson Electric. We talked for hours sharing each other's experiences and views. I was convinced more than ever that our strategy to invest in Asia was right for the firm. I later enrolled at the Aspen Institute for a one-week dialogue on China. Also attended by people from China, U.S. government officials, and CEOs of companies that were doing business in Asia, this institute helped me hone my perspective on the region.

From this meeting, all 100 partners participated in a presentation at our worldwide partners' meeting in Chicago to share what we learned and our vision of the future. Everyone was excited about the new possibilities.

Arthur Andersen always believed in training. We believed that a business professional needed to continually learn to stay relevant. In June 1995, I enrolled with other partners at INSEAD University in Paris, France. INSEAD is an international university on par with our leading institutions in the U.S. A course taught there was "Technology from the CEO's Perspective." The one-week course was very interesting and involved a lot of homework, yet we still found time to indulge in some late night dinners at a few fine French restaurants.

After attending the session, I realized how little I knew about technology and how rapidly it was changing, so I enrolled in another course in San Jose, California. In Silicon Valley, the world's most respected leaders talked about what was coming down the pike and how it was going to change business. After attending the seminar, I was convinced that I needed to start using some of this technology to become more productive. But I knew there was still more to learn. There always is.

My training and development continued the following year. In January 1996, I invited Roger Merrill, co-author of The 7 Habits for Highly Effective People, to come to St. Louis and spend a few days with our senior team. Although our office was improving and was now profitable, I felt we could work better as a team. I suspected that we were not always open and honest with each other. There was fear among the partners, and understandably so. After all, for the previous three years, the firm was dissatisfied with the financial performance of the St. Louis office, so there was concern on the part of many that their careers were at risk. I felt that structures needed to be loosened if we were to achieve our full potential. Those were a great few days and the outcome was tremendous. Not only were our people more confident, but several of the attendees even went on to become certified teachers of the "7 Habits." This training was so successful, we eventually required our entire management team to take this training.

One of the trainers was our HR executive, Jan Torrisi-Mokwa. When I first got to St. Louis, our HR activities were handled by various partners. One might be in charge of recruiting; another in charge of training, etc. I wanted our partners out servicing clients, not hanging out in the office. It was also my feeling that we needed to get a full-time HR executive and ask for referrals. There must have been 10 interviews conducted before I knew what I actually wanted. Many HR executives are only focused on things like compensation, which were directed by our home office. What I needed in St. Louis was someone who could interface with our people and be a resource for them when they had issues with me or any of our partners; someone who could sense the pulse of our office, a real people person. Unlike in the past when we mostly transferred in talent from other offices, our strategy to grow the office might require us to hire people who came from other organizations with different requisite skill sets. I needed an HR strategic partner at my side to help them transition.

Jan Torrisi-Mokwa was that person. She had worked at McDonnell Douglas and, from the moment I talked to her, I knew she was the person I was looking for. A real innovator, Jan was strategic, creative, and personable. She was exactly what I needed. Jan eventually accepted my offer, and I think that was the best decision for both of us. She helped build trust internally and made sure our people got "7 Habits" training once they reached a certain level.

Like my employees, I continued to learn. In the fall of 1996, I completed another leadership program at the Center of Creative

Leadership in Colorado Springs, Colorado. A number of us from different offices attended the session, and it reinforced the principles that we were exposing in St. Louis. It convinced me that I was on the right path.

Our growth strategy was in execution mode, and we divided the office by industry and functionality (i.e., service line). Everyone was part of a team. Each team developed a plan that was integrated into our overall plan. Each team had goals and responsibilities on how to deliver quality services and grow the practice. We met regularly to talk about these goals and how they were progressing. When they needed help, I was there to make sure they got the help.

Now, there was only one other thing that needed fixing, and that was our confidence level. Despite the efficacy of the "7 Habits," it was still lacking. To change that, I needed to change my employees' physical environment. It would be way too expensive to remodel all three floors of our offices, but on the other hand, I wanted to give a good first impression when a prospect got off the elevator. Back then, when you got off our elevator, you faced a blank wall with torn carpeting. As you approached the office, there was an old desk for a receptionist with a wall right behind. It was dark and dreary and gave the impression that we were struggling, so we decided to renovate.

On each elevator wall, we prominently displayed our key messages. On one floor, we posted our ethics and principles, so that everyone saw them each day. On another floor, we displayed our new vision and mission and how we delivered outstanding client service. Then we ripped out the wall behind the receptionist desk and opened up the view to our conference room and windows to the street. We moved the receptionist desk to one side and made the look professional. I always felt that the first person our clients and others met was the most important. We had Camille be our receptionist to serve that purpose. She was always smiling and happy.

Then there was my office. I was the third office managing partner (OMP) at this location and the office had yet to be updated from its original condition. It was very large and rectangular. It was intimidating. So we hired a decorator who reduced the size of my office and constructed an adjoining conference room that could be used by everyone, not just me. My executive assistant's area was also redone to make her more accessible to others. The result was a much more personable and comfortable appearance.

When all was said and done, we had changed the tone of the office, both physically and mentally. When our people got off the elevator, they now were proud to call the space home. The feeling was that this was a winning office with a winning team.

CHAPTER 20

Managing the Office

The mood of our office was greatly improved. I liked the swagger in our partners' strides, despite the contemporary partying con-notations of the term, but there was still one thing that was greatly troubling them. Ever since the firm broke up into two separate reporting entities: Arthur Andersen (consisting of audit, tax, and business consulting) and Andersen Consulting (consisting of the information technology group), all of us felt there was too much emphasis placed on EPU (earnings per unit or profitability) and less emphasis placed on our traditional core values. Yes, our profit-ability had increased significantly and we were all earning more than we ever had, but we were all brought up on the philosophy that profitability was the result of doing all these other things right and EPU was the end result. We talked a lot about this at our office partners' meetings, but there was a sense of frustration that there was nothing that could be done about it.

I felt we were wasting a lot of energy, and it was time to prepare a white paper that we could deliver and discuss with firm-wide management. Bob Merenda was the partner who was most articulate and passionate on the subject, so I asked Bob to draft a document that he could share with us. It was a risk, but one we were all willing to take. We knew the firm needed a change.

The white paper that Bob prepared was titled "The Need for Re-examining our EPU Policy," and it was extremely well written. The issue that Bob raised was that "when we set the standard (EPU) too high or apply it too uniformly, we encourage behavior that is parochial and short-sighted. We become preoccupied with controlling costs, shrinking the denominator (number of partners), and keeping score. We overlook the investment opportunities, both in people and in markets that will drive our future."

We suggested that the unit system (shares of stock that the partners owned) should be based on principles. "The first principle is that the success and value of the firm is derived not from any one or a small group of partners, but from the sustained collaborative efforts of all our people." The second principle is that "each partner's share of the firm's results should be based on his/her responsibilities and sustained contribution measured in the context of opportunity and not on the attainment of a uniform goal."

The paper concluded: "Our high and unyielding EPU standard is driving all our major business strategies and day-to-day behavior.... We need to rediscover those timeless principles that hold the partnership together."

We finalized the white paper after much debate. On March 25, 1996, all St. Louis partners signed it. In essence, we wanted to go back to a more principle-driven approach, similar to what we operated on before we started to compete internally with Andersen Consulting in trying to match its profitability performance. We felt this was not only the mood of the St. Louis partners, but of many others as well. The remaining question was, to whom do we deliver this white paper, and how do we deliver it? We put it on the shelf until we found the right person and appropriate time.

As time went by, my job as St. Louis OMP became more exciting and rewarding. We were all guided by our long-range plan, and whenever there were disappointments, I would think about our long-range goals and be comforted by the fact that we were on the right track. I no longer was disturbed if we didn't win every single opportunity. Everyone was committed to our long-term goals and to his or her respective roles in making that happen.

As for myself, as I empowered the rest of the organization, I was able to get involved in a diverse set of activities that kept me inspired and personally satisfied.

Client Service

I tried to be involved in serving our clients as much as possible by attending every audit committee meeting of each of our publicly held clients. I did this for a variety of reasons. First, it forced me to meet with our client's executive management and make sure we were delivering outstanding service. Second, it enabled me to see our partners in action and how they communicated with the audit committee. This helped me become a better coach to them. I always had a knack for communicating to boards in a creative way by following the firm's principles of "think straight, talk straight." I also prepared for those board meetings and tried to anticipate their questions. This was not always the case with my fellow partners, so I made sure that they improved the style and substance of their communications and encouraged them to rehearse for their meetings.

At first, most of the partners felt uncomfortable in preparing for these meetings. But as time went on, the partners saw and appreciated the favorable comments they were getting from their clients. The audit committee appreciated the value they were getting from these more effective communications and got comfort from our partners sharing sensitive topics in a direct way. The mindset became that we were serving the needs of the audit committee, as well as senior management. Although this was not always easy to do, it was important.

An example of how this philosophy came into play was at Venture. Venture was a discount store chain once owned by May Company and spun off as a separate entity. Julie Seeherman was CEO for many years before retiring. The board replaced Julie with a person who was a merchant from a regional department store chain who had never had a relationship with Arthur Andersen. His personality was quite different than Julie's.

Venture had trouble competing with Wal-Mart and Target.

Although Venture had a conservative balance sheet, its performance was on a slippery slide, heading south. The first time I met the new CEO, he asked me to meet him for dinner at The Ritz-Carlton in St. Louis. When I arrived, only a few tables were taken, but one was the booth that he said was his favorite. The hostess offered him any other table, but he wanted "his" table and made the hostess move the people sitting in it to another booth. When we sat down, he ordered his favorite bottle of wine. He did not ask me if I drank, let alone if I wanted wine. Instead, he said, "Just bring two glasses."

My goal that evening was to get to know him, but it was not very difficult to do. He proceeded to tell me that he knew all about me. He had already "checked me out" with his industry contacts. He said if it were not for me, he would fire Arthur Andersen in a heartbeat, but he had confidence in me. I told him that I was the advisory partner and that the audit partner, Mark Wuller, was another outstanding individual who had strong retail industry credentials.

The performance of Venture continued to erode despite the new efforts by the CEO. As we were wrapping up the job, I went to see where things stood and quickly saw the company was in trouble. It wouldn't last much longer. I asked Mark to get their plan for next year and compare it to their performance of the previous three years. When we looked at that analysis, it was highly unlikely that Venture would make it for another year without significant financial engineering. Mark and I put together an analysis of what it would take to keep them alive. We concluded that Andersen would have to give Venture a "going concern opinion," which means that we felt they may not be able to avoid bankruptcy the next year.

We knew the audit committee was not going to like what we would have to say, so Mark and I rehearsed our presentation. We thought we would show them the results that they would have to achieve in order to avoid bankruptcy (i.e., how much margin or sales growth and/or expense reduction), and then ask if they felt the company could achieve this performance. Following our presentation, the outside directors, who were current or former CEOs, thanked us for our candor and recognized it was unlikely that Venture could achieve such results. It was not long after that Venture disappeared. The firm was not subject to any litigation stemming from this association, but we did earn a lot of respect from the board of directors for being so insightful.

As managing partner, I was frequently involved with conflict. As stated earlier, when I got to St. Louis, Jerry Ritter, CFO for Anheuser-Busch (AB), greeted me with a lawsuit threat. Jerry had since retired and was replaced by Randy Baker. Reporting to Randy Baker was John Kelly, controller. Both these gentleman knew who the real "boss" was at AB: August Busch III.

August was also the chairman of the audit committee for Emerson Electric, whom I frequently met with directly as I serviced Emerson. His reputation as being tough was well deserved. When he gave me a stare, his eyes seemed to penetrate my body.

He could intimidate me without even saying a word. But, having dealt with tough clients before, as well as some of my leadership partners at Arthur Andersen, I was prepared to deal with August.

Randy said that they were going to give us one more chance to settle this dispute before they filed suit against us for the marketing blunder. He asked for $3 million. I replied that if that was what they wanted, then they would have to sue. Based on my discussion with our partners and our analysis of the evidence, we had done nothing wrong. Randy reminded me of the $25 million project that Andersen Consulting was doing for them and that if we did not come to a solution, they would "throw them out" and never allow them back in. I said I would think about it and get back to him.

I called George Shaheen (the same guy who helped me with copying at the Knickerbocker Hotel in Chicago some 30 years earlier), who was the head of Andersen Consulting. George suggested I talk to our partner, John Kelly (no relation to John Kelly, controller at AB), which I refused to do. I worked with John in Dallas and I thought he would believe their people were doing an excellent job and there would be no need to do anything to preserve their relationship. He would see this is an Arthur Andersen problem and not a threat to Andersen Consulting.

George then suggested I talk to Joe Forehand, who was the managing partner for the consulting practice in Dallas (Joe would later replace George as the CEO of Andersen Consulting). Joe always seemed reasonable, and we had a decent relationship, despite the hardship between the consulting and audit divisions. Joe asked that I involve some of his other partners who worked on the AB account. At first, they evinced the typical Andersen Consulting (AC) bravado. They said they had a great relationship and there was no way that AB would dismiss AC. AB could not survive without AC!

I then discussed things with the head of our U.S. operations, Jim Edwards. Jim was not interested in writing a check for one penny, let alone $3 million. He was open to the idea of offering AB discounted services. Jim felt that if we offered $2 million of services at 50% off, it might be a win-win situation. We would not make any money, but we would develop a working relationship with AB. They could then see the quality of service we could provide. Who knew where that could lead?

I felt that AB also would want some cash before they would agree to our proposal. I called Joe Forehand and told him to talk to his Andersen Consulting partners. If they did not come up with some cash, I guaranteed him they would lose a $25 million account. After further consideration, Joe reluctantly agreed to contribute $1 million.

I got back to Randy Baker with our counter offer, $2 million of discounted services with no cash. I needed to present something that we could negotiate from and, as expected, he declined and threatened again to sue and kick Andersen Consulting out of the building. After much discussion, he then said he would think about our proposal.

My visit to AB was a classic. I met with Randy in the conference room next to August's office and reiterated our proposal of $2 million of discounted services that had to be performed within the next three years. Randy wanted to know if this was our "best" offer, which I confirmed. He then went into August's office. After 30 minutes, Randy and August came out and asked if I had final authority to cut a deal. I said, "I do."

They then presented a counteroffer: $1 million in discounted services and $1 million cash. After much discussion, I agreed to their offer.

I returned to the office and called Jim Edwards, partner in charge of our U.S. operations, and Joe Forehand with the good news. However, Jim said he would write the check. "I don't want you getting one penny from AC. I don't want to owe them any favors." I couldn't believe what I had just heard. Here, I had been working for months to get AC to pony up the $1 million in cash to preserve their $25 million account. Now, Jim wanted to write the check from the Arthur Andersen budget! He said we needed to deliver the check by August 31 so we could get it into our current fiscal year. And so, after years of negotiation, we finally got it done. We now had a new client, but it was costly. AC retained its $25 million client and it cost them nothing.

My involvement with Emerson Electric accelerated during the late 1990s. I made multiple trips to Asia with Bob Cox, Senior VP for Emerson Electric, to make sure our people understood the scope of their work and were delivering it in an outstanding fashion. Hong Kong and Singapore were regular stops on these visits, but we also went to Bangkok, Shanghai, and Beijing, among other cities. My involvement in helping develop the firm's international strategy also helped me respond to the needs of Emerson Electric.

Our relationship with Emerson continued to grow. Walt Galvin, CFO, was pleased with how our people were performing and how things were being communicated back to him and his people at corporate. As time went on, we gained additional assignments. Our team that included David April, an experienced manager, and my partner, Mark Wuller, was totally engaged in trying to exceed client expectations.

Client Entertainment

Our firm sponsored a number of events for our clients and friends. As OMP, it was my responsibility to participate in these events to get to know our clients better and to show our appreciation for their business. Today, some might view this as a conflict of interest that would impair independence, but I disagree. Participating in these activities helps you develop a trusting relationship, which becomes key to improving the quality of audit work. It enables you to get more information about the key decision-makers of the client and to better understand how they think. It also enhances timely communication.

When I came to St. Louis, Andersen had four seats for Cardinal baseball games, but when I saw where they were, I cancelled them. In those days the Cardinals were owned by Anheuser-Busch, and I called Jerry Ritter to tell him we were cancelling our seats, unless we could get better ones. Not long after, the Cardinals added field box seats. Jerry called to tell me that he was holding four seats for us in the front row right behind home plate. From that point forward, all our partners and managers wanted to take their clients and friends to a game. The seats were always in great demand.

By observing someone play golf over four hours, you get to observe their ethics and values, and learn more about them as individuals. This helps you evaluate their character while building trust in your relationship, which in turn enables you to be a more effective auditor.

Civic Activities

As an OMP, I was expected to be active in the community. Our office was always looking for ways to make St. Louis a better place to live and work. One of the facilities we backed was the Sheldon Theater. This was a historic, small theater with wonderful acoustics. However, it needed a complete remodeling. After it reopened, they needed sponsors for concerts. That's where we came in. We were influential in getting them to bring Willie Nelson to the hall. Our partners invited clients to the show. We had a special dinner beforehand and then pictures with Willie afterwards. Another year, we did the same with Art Garfunkel.

I was active in a number of civic ventures. One was the St.

Louis Regional Commerce and Growth Association (RCGA), where I was a member of the executive committee and served as audit committee chairman and membership chairman. Each year they had an annual event where they gave the "Right Arm" award to a leader of the community. One year I introduced Jack Buck, the winner of the Right Arm Award, who was the famous announcer for the St. Louis Cardinals. Jack was coping with Parkinson's disease. The disease affected his physical abilities, but certainly did not impact his brain. While I was introducing him, I saw him take out a small piece of paper and pencil and barely have enough motion to scribble a few notes. However, that was all he needed to give a brilliant 30-minute talk that had everybody laughing and in tears. A few years later, Jack died from this dreadful disease.

I also participated in an RCGA study of other cities with a cross section of people from St. Louis. The first year, we went to Cleveland, where we came back with ideas on how to make St. Louis a better place to live. Later, I participated on similar journeys to Baltimore and Toronto. This has become an annual event for the RCGA.

St. Louis has one of the largest and most successful Boy Scout chapters in the U.S. The leaders of the business community get deeply involved with the organization. I was surprised one year to be honored with the Silver Beaver Award, which recognized those individuals who contributed distinguished service to youth.

Jerry Loeb of May Co. was the president of the local chapter of Junior Achievement (JA) and later became an officer of the JA national organization. Jerry got me involved. I helped them raise money and taught classes for young enterprising students.

I was a member of the Board of Trustees of Drake University since the mid-1980s. I served on the search committee for a new chancellor, was chairman of the audit committee, and chairman of the investment committee. It was a great experience to be part of this wonderful institution.

These are just a few of the organizations with which I was involved. As the OMP for the St. Louis office, it was important to give back to the community. To some, this may seem like a chore, but to me it was a rewarding change of pace and an opportunity to meet and work with many wonderful individuals.

Training

The Arthur Andersen culture of learning did not stop for OMPs. Every five years, the partners were required to attend a five-day executive development course (or, as we called it, "The Partner Retread School") specifically designed for Arthur Andersen and Andersen Consulting partners. The faculty came from such prestigious institutions as the University of Chicago, Michigan, Harvard, Wharton, Stanford, etc. The retread school did not cover technical topics of our trade, but was meant to broaden our overall abilities. It covered the arts, politics, world cultures, the economy, and other vast subjects. As the OMP, I attended two retread schools, the second in Montreal.

Jim Kackley (who had taught me at the first training school

I attended with the firm) was managing partner for the Central Region. He was market and client-focused, yet very people orientated. Jim, with the help of Bob Allgyer, started the "Master's Program," which was designed to have our younger partners broaden their perspectives to help them become trusted advisors to their clients. It also taught them how important it was to have a balance in life and to spend time with their families. We rotated these sessions across our offices in the Midwest.

The program ran 18 months. It concluded with a session at a special place with wives invited. Robert Cooper, noted outside facilitator, ran the program and was assisted by Deb Kiley, a psychologist who worked in our Chicago Office. Jim Kackley, Bob Allgyer, and I were facilitators and mentors to the participants. Many of today's leaders at other accounting firms previously graduated from this program.

Meetings

One of the obligations of an OMP is not only to attend a whole bunch of meetings, but also to lead them. Some thought there were too many meetings. I couldn't disagree. But as I look back, when done properly, meetings were a very effective way to get all our leaders to understand and connect with one another.

When I was first appointed OMP for St. Louis, I admired the turnaround of the Minneapolis office, led by Steve Hemsley. Steve later became a leader in our firm-wide initiatives. Today, he is CEO of United Healthcare. Steve had a completely different style than mine, but I was impressed by how he thought and how he was able to get everyone focused in a new direction. I went to Minneapolis with Steve Riek, our office administrator, and Bill Scheffel and Bob Merenda, our audit and tax division heads. We wanted to understand how Steve turned the Minneapolis office around. That visit gave us fresh ideas and confidence that we could implement something similar in St. Louis.

I also attended monthly Central Region meetings, where I was joined by OMPs from across the region to focus on our resources and client needs. We talked about how we could better serve our clients and develop our people. It was always enjoyable to attend Jim Kackley's meetings, where he taught me a lot about how to facilitate them.

Later, I attended a number of U.S. OMP meetings and, later, U.S. manager meetings. These were held around the country and normally lasted a few days. They helped us understand the direction of the firm and keep us all on the same page. It was also beneficial to pick up good ideas to bring back to our respective offices.

Family

In addition to my commitment to the firm, I had strong family ties. During my term as OMP for St. Louis, all of my kids graduated from college and started their own careers. My daughter, Laurie, graduated from the University of Arizona and then attended graduate school at the University of Chicago. While in

Chicago, she met Patrick Solberg, who later became her husband. Laurie became a social worker in the Maywood public school system. Today, she lives in River Forest, just west of Chicago, and is mother to Zoe and Ryan.

My son Jonathan graduated from the University of Arizona in May 1997. Jon went from there to San Francisco, where he is now an entrepreneur in direct marketing.

Shortly thereafter, my son Brian graduated from the University of Texas, which is also where he met his future wife, Ali.. Brian traveled the country with Ali on the $1000 graduation present I gave him. Afterwards, they settled in Portland, where they still live today. He and Ali now have two daughters—Mazzi and Nico—and Brian is a successful graphic design manager for an advertising firm.

A year later, our son Jeremy graduated from the University of Arizona. After graduation, Jeremy settled in Los Angeles, where he worked at a post-production company, editing film for the movie industry. Today, Jeremy is a personal trainer and nutritional coach and is married to Paola, who was born and raised in Bolivia.

Then, there was my lovely and understanding wife, Susan. In 1997, Susan turned 50 years old. We had agreed to celebrate her birthday in Hawaii. Our plane first stopped in Dallas. This enabled us to meet some of our Dallas friends, who took us out to our old country club, where other friends and family surprised Susan on her 50th birthday. The next day, we were off to Hawaii, where

Susan was surprised by three St. Louis couples to help celebrate her 50th all over again.

Susan and I also had the good fortune to travel together during my term as OMP. We would take an annual 10-day vacation to Acapulco each January. But I would also take a business/vacation every October.

One of my responsibilities as OMP was to conduct an annual partner review and to recommend unit recommendations (i.e., salary recommendations). This took a lot of time and it was hard to do while in the office. So, each October we went to a different resort, where I worked on partner evaluations in the morning, before having lunch and playing golf in the afternoon. After dinner, I completed more evaluations, until they were all done by the end of the week.

Celebration

One of my favorite events as an OMP was our annual August 31 New Year's Eve celebration. While the timing may seem awkward, that was the end of our fiscal year, and we always closed the office early and had everyone meet in an auditorium by Barnes Jewish Hospital to celebrate our success and review our plans for the coming year.

Our marketing group, headed by Mike Raymond, never allowed me to just go up and speak. They told me what to do and what to wear. They always designed a costume that could get everyone laughing to lighten the mood. I'll never forget the year we were hosting the Willie Nelson concert, and they had me dress up in braids and a Willie Nelson bandana. It was so far from how I usually dressed. Everyone had a good laugh. The meeting always involved an outside speaker, to enlighten and motivate us, and ended with a champagne toast.

We also conducted annual partner/manager retreats sometime after the end of the fiscal year to review the results of the office and make plans for the coming year by industry and functional segment. Each retreat had a different theme and was meant to help everyone get to know one another on an informal basis.

Managing an office was complicated. It involved a lot of different facets. I had to wear a lot of hats, so to speak. I needed to be concerned with a lot of things—to be an active client service leader for key clients of the firm to lead by example; to help other partners develop and maintain great relationships in order to have them deliver great service; to be a gracious host for key executives in the business community; to be engaged in civic activities and to give back to our community; to continue to expand my knowledge and skill sets; and to be engaged in attending and effectively conducting many meetings. I also had to find the quality time to spend with my family, outside of the office. Finally, I needed to celebrate my work's successes.

The firm must have seen that I enjoyed my role as soon thereafter, a new opportunity arose.

CHAPTER 21

War of the Roses

In any divorce, there are different perspectives as to why it happened: the father's, the mother's, and the kids'. Since I was not part of the senior management of the firm in the 1980s, when it split into two separate operating units—Arthur Andersen and Andersen Consulting—my perspective was more like that of a child. I witnessed it, I experienced it, but I did not entirely understand it.

In order to begin to understand the separation, you need to go back to 1978, the year I made partner. That was the year our CEO, Harvey Kapnick, gave a brilliant speech at the partners' meeting in Chicago. His thesis was that it would be in the best long-term interest of the firm to split into two separate firms. He believed that even if we didn't do it now, one day the SEC would make us do it later. As mentioned in Chapter 11, the partners (especially the consulting partners) did not favor his recommendation and forced him to resign.

But over the next decade, sentiments changed, and the consulting partners wanted out.

Two things caused this seismic ideological shift: the personality dynamics of our leadership and the macroeconomic events that took place in the market.

Personalities of Leadership

After Harvey resigned, a special partners' meeting was called to elect his replacement. The quietest man won: Duane Kullberg. Perhaps it was because Harvey was so aggressive and vocal; the partners thought the opposite would be safer. They wanted someone who could listen and bring the firm together.

Soon thereafter, Duane assembled his team. Ed Jenkins led our audit division, Dave Bucholtz our tax division, and Bill Mueller the consulting division. All three performed admirably, but Bill Mueller left the firm soon afterwards to become an executive at a health care company. He was replaced by Vic Millar.

A very cerebral man, Vic Millar had a quiet leadership style that opened our eyes to innovative thoughts and ideas. One of his most impactful contributions concerned the firm's presentation style. For the most part, up until Vic's leadership, presentations were comprised of words or numbers plastered on slides. Vic changed that. He gave presentations that were clear, simple, and picturesque. He may have been quiet, but he was an effective communicator.

All was going well, but soon the winds would change. Vic Millar left to run Saatchi and Saatchi, a large advertising firm, and appointed Si Moughamian as his replacement. Unlike Vic, Si was a hands-off manager who delegated authority to his subordinates, many of whom had different operating styles than he. Chaos was brewing. Soon, it would take hold.

Around the same time, Duane created a new position called COO—Chief Operating Officer—and assigned it to Frank Rossi, my former boss in the Dallas office. As our first ever COO, Frank was responsible for our worldwide office operations in all three divisions: audit, tax, and administrative services, i.e., consulting. Frank was a rising star in Arthur Andersen largely due to his performance in Dallas. When Frank took over the Dallas office, it was underperforming and floundering. When he left, it was on a fast growth track. He completely turned it around.

But his leadership was not without its flaws. While Frank seemed to get along with everyone—particularly when he felt he was in charge—he could also be extremely intolerant of people who disagreed with his viewpoint. In those situations, he would revert back to the Marine-style leadership the firm had employed in the past, sharing his opinions of others in a less than tactful way. For example, when we finished the third audit of Zale in May 1979, it was so complex that we had more than 40 people serving them. It was customary for the client service team that had just finished a big tough assignment to celebrate its completion with cocktails. I was the lead partner on Zale and asked Jim DeLoach, one of our young managers on the engagement, to organize the event. Jim sent a memo to all 40 people, inviting them to the City Club for cocktails from 4–7 p.m. for this "annual event." Jim used a poor choice of words. He meant to say "year-end event," but a few days later, Frank forwarded a copy of this invitation to me and our audit division head, Dale Kessler. He marked the following comments in red ink:

> **"Who decides this will be an annual event?"**
>
> **"Who is paying for this because the firm is not going to?"**
>
> **"I thought we cut out this garbage!"**
>
> **"I am not prepared to absorb an hour of this time and the Zale job can't afford it."**
>
> **"4–5 p.m.—what do they charge their 1 hour to... vacation or what?"**
>
> **"40 people is a field trip!"**
>
> **—FAR (Frank Rossi)**

Now, Frank was probably right. We probably did go too far, but he also didn't have to react so vehemently. But that's just how Frank was. If you caught Frank the wrong way, he could be tough to deal with. Fortunately, most of my experiences with Frank were cordial.

However, I couldn't say the same about everyone in the Dallas office. In those days, the client service team always included a consulting partner, and the audit partners were never reluctant to introduce a consulting partner to a client. It was part of our "One Firm" culture. Our industry programs were all combined. We would go to market together, help each other and even go on vacations together. When I was running the retail practice in Dallas, this cordiality began to break down after Dave Ewing, the consulting head, unexpectedly passed away. His replacement was less than cooperative.

After Dave's death, John Kelly came in to run the Dallas consulting practice. John came from a different perspective. He didn't like his consulting people relying on the audit folks for work. He felt that his consultants were better than the stodgy, old auditors and that the consulting people needed to operate more independently. So, he began to emphasize different things. Whereas David had been happy with completing smaller consulting projects for audit clients, John put pressure on his people to sell bigger and more complex jobs to non-audit clients. The rift between auditing and consulting was widening.

John Kelly viewed Arthur Andersen as a consulting firm. He was not concerned how his consultants' performance impacted the audit division. I remember, once when we were helping install some systems for Zale. Dean Liles, the Management Information Services Director, called to say the company was having problems with our consulting work and, in particular, the person in charge. Dean asked me to get more involved. So, I spent some time with the project's quality control partner, Steve Zimmerman, a consulting partner from our New York office. Steve corroborated much of Dean's concern and said we needed to talk to John Kelly. However, when we talked to John, he was far from helpful. He told us that he felt that the partner was doing his job, and the problem was with the client and not us. He didn't care about the audit relationship. This was a consulting job and he didn't want me to interfere. Eventually, Arthur Andersen was replaced on the project. This divisive "Us versus Them" attitude was part of John's DNA.

As the decade continued, the friction between the audit and consulting group grew more intense. The consulting group started to ride a wave of growth, landing bigger and bigger projects. Its management team derived more pleasure from selling work to a non-audit client than to an audit client. They had less red tape when they were in charge of the relationship and could be more independent. The consultants didn't have to worry about getting approval from the audit committee or deal with the audit relationship. So, from the top of the organization down to each office, the consulting partner's management would make its message loud and clear. "We do larger and more profitable engagements for non-audit clients." As a result, our audit clients were not being properly served, particularly on small consulting projects, such as cost reduction projects, organizational reviews, data processing reviews, etc. To fill this void, the audit division started hiring and training its own people to perform such projects. In turn, the consulting division started talking about the auditors being the "bad guys" who were doing consulting projects and competing against them.

But we weren't. These projects were much smaller than Andersen Consulting projects. They were the types of projects Andersen Consulting wouldn't waste its time doing. Andersen Consulting wanted to do the larger projects for non-audit clients, yet consulting management continued to whisper tales of Arthur Andersen's nefarious misdeeds. They told their partners that we posed a competitive threat and would ruin the Andersen Consulting image in the marketplace. The petulant teenagers had finally grown up and gotten the keys to the car. They weren't going to listen to their parents anymore.

The situation was extremely uncomfortable for audit and tax leaders. The audit partners were getting frustrated that the consulting partners were no longer paying attention to their audit clients. The consulting partners were told to focus on non-audit clients. Further, if they did work on audit clients, they would no longer cooperate with the lead relationship partner, who was typically the audit partner. They wanted to play by their own rules.

This independent thinking was in direct conflict with our "One Firm" culture and drove the audit management team crazy. Despite his best efforts, and although he was in charge of the firm's worldwide operations, Frank Rossi had a tough time resolving conflicts to the satisfaction of the consulting division management. He spread himself thin trying to hold the firm together, flying all over the world. But he was not always able to get consulting to follow his instructions. The rift was too deep. The leaders of each division were locked in a bitter conflict that would soon pollute every strata of the organization.

Macro Economics

During the 1970s, the auditing industry was booming due to new SEC registrants and changes to accounting rules. When I started with the firm, Accounting Principle #8 on pension accounting had just come out. By the '70s, hundreds of new rules, regulations, and accounting interpretations had come into force. As accounting became more complex, audit fees went up. As fees went up, the auditing profession grew exponentially. However, this was soon to change.

At one time, accounting firms were not allowed to advertise, thereby discouraging cutthroat price wars. When these prohibitions were eliminated though, firms started to cannibalize each other's clients. Pricing pressures increased; rates became intensely competitive. It was no longer easy to pass off cost-of-living adjustments to clients once they started demanding fixed fees from the outset. If we exceeded our cost expectations, it was difficult to pass the overage on to clients. That put unprecedented pressure on margins.

At the same time, the profession was becoming riskier. Times were changing and we sometimes had a hard time adjusting. As judiciary trends changed, plaintiffs started focusing on accounting firms whenever there was a restatement of financial records or the company's stock prices suddenly dropped. Accounting firms didn't want to take the risk of going to trial, so they started settling suits before they went to court. As a result, insurance premiums skyrocketed. The cost of doing business rose significantly, and firms were not able to increase rates fast enough to cover the increased costs. All auditing firms faced the same situation, but it was not as major an issue for the consulting practice.

Consultants started to realize that they were paying some of this cost, even though litigation was not due to their consulting engagements. They felt they were getting a bum deal and were being forced to partner with a group that had a much higher risk profile. The consultants grew more fearful in the mid-1980s when Ernst & Young made headlines following significant litigation with its real estate and savings and loan clients, such as Charles Keating of Lincoln Savings and Loan. There was even talk of E&Y failing. This sounded alarms in the consulting division of Arthur Andersen. What if E&Y's fate was a harbinger of things to come? Consulting management told their partners that being associated with an auditing firm was now too great of a risk. They needed to split away to minimize that risk.

The effects of all this turmoil were amplified by Andersen Consulting's simultaneous wave of success. Like auditing in the 1970s, Andersen Consulting was in a sweet spot. Technology was surging to the forefront, and all major companies were turning to consulting firms to help them figure out how to best apply technology to their operations. Andersen Consulting could not hire people fast enough to meet demand. While auditing and tax growth rates stalled, Andersen Consulting was growing by leaps and bounds. The consultants grew restless.

The Day of Reckoning

In 1988, Duane formed a committee to make recommendations on the issue. The committee recommended breaking up the company into two loosely connected business units with a holding company on top. Under this plan, each business unit had their own back office support, so they no longer shared the administrative costs. Each unit had its own systems, accounting department, recruiting department, etc. Each business unit was also tasked with the job of determining its profitability, which was still shared between the two units. However, to placate the consultants' grousing, a compromise was reached. Should one business unit earn more than the other, the higher performing unit would subsidize the lower performing unit based on a very complicated formula that had certain limitations. I'd try to lay it out for you, but the formula was so complicated that only a few people in the firm could understand it, let alone explain it.

The partners met to hear this recommendation and vote, but the debate surrounding it was hardly a fair one. It was presented to the partners as if this were the last hope of keeping the firm together. I strongly objected to the proposal and wrote Dick

Measelle, our U.S. audit division head, a long letter articulating my five concerns about this income allocation formula.

First, it threatened the firm's unity. It was all about earnings and who earned the most. It did not bode well for the firm's "One Firm" approach. If we started this with consulting, where would it end? Would the tax department be next? Would certain countries follow? Certain offices? I also felt the new system would adversely affect the way we serviced clients, particularly large international clients. Would the consulting people want to do work for our audit clients? What would happen if a consulting client wanted us as their auditors? Would consulting allow this to happen? Andersen's strength was in its unity, and now that would be taken away.

My second concern was governance. I felt the new organization would make the CEO role impotent. With each organization developing its own strategies, and with profitability being measured at the division level, what was the purpose of the home office and the CEO? Yes, overall we had a vision and strategy, but it was broad. Our vision was "to be the premier professional services firm," and our mission was "to provide quality professional services that met the information needs of the global marketplace." Under this system, there would be no overall strategy. Instead, the strategy would be developed by the two respective business units.

My third concern was the overall direction of the firm. At that time, we had no comprehensive long-range three-to-five-year business plan. This new divisive structure would only amplify the issues inherent to this structure. We would live by the EPU (earnings per unit). We would focus on annual goals and short-term thinking, with profitability being our driving force. Each unit would be solely focused on earning as much as possible in the short term in order to survive this new formula. It would destroy our organization's integrity from the inside out.

My fourth concern was overhead. By dividing the firm into two business units, our overhead would dramatically increase. What we did once (accounting, payroll, recruiting, etc.), we would now do twice: once for audit/tax and once for consulting. Furthermore, firm-wide overhead costs would be divided between the two business units. While this may not seem like an issue, it could quickly degrade into each unit complaining about and protesting against costs and services that did not directly benefit its unit. Each could say it could do without this or that cost being allocated to them. This would create more friction and make the home office even more irrelevant.

My fifth concern was that the formula did not take into consideration the relative capital needs of each business unit. Yes, the consulting division was starting to earn more than the audit division, but it also required a lot more capital to continually develop new products and services. Yet, the interest expense of the firm was allocated by the home office to each business unit without considering the discrepancies in the two units' capital requirements. Auditing was bearing some of the burden when it shouldn't have to.

I knew the firm could not survive over the long haul if it operated as two separate organizations. I knew it would slowly tear us apart. Instead, I felt we should explore a leveraged buyout exercise, in which we would evaluate spinning off or selling one of the units. Needless to say, I did not get much support for this recommendation. It was quickly deemed too radical.

Sadly, the resolution was easily passed by both business units. I and my non-voting peers begrudgingly accepted this solution. The new arrangement was troubling to us. For its first 20 years of existence, the administrative services division (Andersen Consulting) had not made much money, if any, and we had supported them. Year in and year out, its losses were absorbed by the audit and tax partners. Now, in the last few years, the consulting division was growing faster than the audit/tax division, and it wanted caps and limitations on sharing. It seemed ungrateful.

From this point forward we operated as two separate firms. Our audit/tax division immediately began to develop its own strategy.

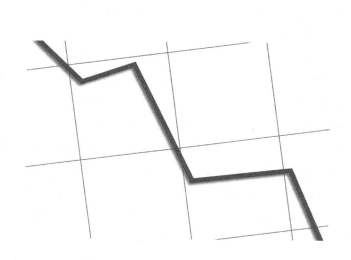

CHAPTER 22

Sibling Rivalry

Larry Weinbach was elected the new managing partner of Andersen Worldwide in 1988. A real gentleman with remarkable communication and negotiation skills, Larry was charged with implementing the new organizational structure. I knew Larry. I liked Larry. He was my instructor when I attended the New Managers' School in St. Charles after my initial promotion to management. He was a great guy, personable and well-liked by everyone. I thought if anyone could manage our new organization, it would be Larry.

Larry appointed Dick Measelle to lead the audit/tax business unit and George Shaheen to lead Andersen Consulting. Each unit set its structure and picked its leaders within 60 days of the announcement.

The two of them were more than qualified. Dick had already helped start an office in Spain and worked as the managing partner in the Detroit office. Later, Dick was appointed the head of the audit practice and reported directly to our CEO, Duane Kullberg. Dick seemed to have a collaborative style that was compatible with Duane's. Like Duane, he was very cerebral and an excellent big-picture thinker. He was quite different from Ed Jenkins, the former audit division leader. Dick's major emphasis was on how we could grow the practice. He wanted the auditors to be "trusted business advisors" for their clients, not just good auditors. This meant identifying other needs and services that could benefit our clients, some of which could slightly conflict or overlap with those performed by Andersen Consulting.

George was also a big-picture guy and very personable. He started in the Chicago office, but several years later, he lost his wife to cancer. George had young children at the time and was thinking of resigning from the firm to be with them. To accommodate him, Jim Brice, the managing partner of Chicago, convinced George to take a leave of absence for a year or two. When George returned, he wanted a change of scenery, so the firm transferred him to Charlotte, where he ran the consulting practice before being transferred again to San Francisco, where he was put in charge of the Western Region. As the story is told, George was forever grateful to the firm for being patient and understanding during his tough times. But George was young and ambitious. He wanted to take the consulting practice in a different direction than his predecessor had.

The audit/tax business unit was comprised of five regions in the U.S.—Northeast, Southeast, Central, Southwest, and West. Jim Edwards, the former managing partner of the Atlanta office, was named the head of U.S. operations. Frank Rossi's COO position, as head of the worldwide operation, was eliminated. To placate him, he was made head of the Central Region. Frank was not a happy camper and would soon leave the firm to start his own private equity firm. Soon after Frank's departure, I talked to him about how to plan a retirement strategy. He had very simple advice.

"You don't plan it, but you know when it's your time."

Those words stuck in my head and would one day come front and center for me.

Each business unit reported to Andersen Worldwide, run by Larry Weinbach, who believed that with modern technology, there would be no need to have a physical home office in one location. He felt the home office could operate virtually and, as a result, he abandoned the home office in Chicago and ran the firm from his office in New York. That made Larry happy, but in my opinion was a critical mistake. In Chicago, our home office was contained on one floor. It forced our executive team to have personal interaction and communication. When the home office became virtual, it cut off communication between the leaders of the firm. It created a disjointed and disparate firm. Larry made a grievous mistake.

As the U.S. branches of the firm reorganized, so did its operations worldwide. Europe and the Middle East (EMEA) named separate leaders for each of their units, as did Asia Pacific. The firm was now carved into consulting and audit/tax units throughout the world.

Larry Weinbach's first term in office was a success, if one measured success based solely on profitability. From 1989 to 1993, earnings increased 21% per year while revenues increased 18%. But those numbers obscured the conflicts, problems, and bitter relations between the two business units. As I feared, there were rumblings in EMEA and Asia Pacific that they were not well represented on the board. They complained that their voices were not being heard. The tax division—now led by Harry Ruffalo—complained that it needed more say and authority in the new organization. Putting further stress on the company's financials, to accommodate our new structure, we needed to replace all our systems. We assigned a number of consulting people to a project called FS 90 to undertake this expensive initiative.

Despite these concerns, in 1993, Larry was nominated for a second term in office. He shared some of his concerns in a memorandum to the partners. One of his biggest concerns was partner insecurity. He recognized that in order for the audit and tax business unit to maintain an earnings level equal to that the consulting division, it would have to prune the number of partners. One way to increase EPU was to decrease the number of partners. The idea was disconcerting to many, who knew that if they didn't achieve certain results, their careers were at risk. It was damaging partner morale, fostering an environment of selfish hostility rather than amicable cooperation.

Another concern was business unit cooperation and scope of practice issues. Larry called for us to develop mutual trust and respect among all partners and employees. This issue could become our "Achilles heel if we let it divide us into two separate firms." But Larry didn't offer a viable solution. All he said was that our job as partners "…was to continue to make the pie bigger so that we and all our people could enjoy the fruits of our larger pie. This means that the business units must be flexible in determining the proper protocol to resolve the present differences." This plan was not sustainable. Obviously, the basic relationship between Andersen Consulting and rest of the organization was not getting any better. In fact, it was getting worse.

Nothing was being done to force the two units to work better together. At this point, every partner in each business unit was making more money than they could ever have hoped to make when they joined the firm, yet they ignored this fact and instead focused on the "transfer payment." That was the amount that one business unit reimbursed the other business unit, based on the new complicated formula that nobody fully understood. Each year, when we announced our earnings, we were shown the earnings of each business unit, plus or minus the transfer payment in order to equal the net earnings of each business that was to be allocated to each respective partner. Since Andersen Consulting usually earned more than Arthur Andersen, it contributed the transfer payment to Arthur Andersen. This angered the consulting partners. Instead of being thankful that they successfully negotiated this new arrangement that limited the amount of their transfer payment, they looked at it as money out of their pockets. Their view was that if they operated as "One Firm" by themselves, they could earn much more money. They did not credit the many opportunities handed to them by the partners in the other business unit or the fact that Arthur Andersen had borne the burden of their losses for many years.

I feared the day this selective amnesia would extend throughout the whole firm. If that happened, collapse was imminent. Soon, it did. It was no longer auditing vs. consulting. Soon, it became office vs. office, partner vs. partner, etc. I remember when the Houston office was making more money than all the other offices. It felt, "We need to receive more since we produce more." Offices in Europe also felt that way. We overcame those objections when we acknowledged that the strength of the firm was the "One Firm" concept. That concept allowed us to share our profits ratably throughout the world. At one time, we wanted to help underperforming locations and were not hesitant to make investments to do so. But now that we were measuring profits at a more detailed level, offices would not cooperate with each other if it affected their EPU. Historically, if a particular office needed help, another would send a specialist there to help them out. Now, before an office was willing to help another, it would ask, "Who pays?" Instead of the decisions being made on the basis of what is best for the client and the firm, they were being made based on "What is in it for me?" The "One Firm" concept was no longer working.

Another concern mentioned by Larry was culture. "As we become increasingly diverse, it will be a challenge to maintain the culture that has enabled us to achieve the success we are enjoying."

Instead of emphasizing the preservation of our culture, Larry went on to say it must change. "Our culture, like everything else we do in this organization, must adapt to the new changing realities in the marketplace." In my opinion this was another mistake. The strength of the firm was our culture. Without it, what would be the glue that would hold us together?

From 1993 on, by any financial measurement, the two business units operated successfully. Each was making considerably more money than ever before. Each unit continued to pressure their partners to earn more money. Despite financial success, the partners in each business unit were less content. They felt enormous pressure to produce and supervise more hours of work, or their careers would be in jeopardy.

I remember when, just before I left our Dallas office in 1993, Dale Kessler, our managing partner, issued a memo asking each partner to prepare a "personal value statement," which forced each to document the financial value he or she was delivering to the partnership. There was a section titled "Target Opportunities and Revenue Generated." Another was titled "Client Involvement and Revenue Generated." There was nothing on leadership, teamwork, quality of work, or other factors that go into making someone an effective team-oriented partner. It was all solely about your own personal contributions and value.

It was not surprising that these fractures did not diminish between 1993 and 1997. The spark had been lit, and the fire was spreading. In fact, things got so bad that Larry Weinbach investigated the possibility of splitting the firm in two. The consulting firm would leave Andersen and, in accordance with the partnership agreement, pay an exit fee to the firm. We discussed the concept at the annual partners' meeting April 27–30, 1997, in Paris, France. The stage was set. Spouses attended this meeting, but few partners spent much time with them. This would be an intense meeting, one in which the future of the firm was to be decided.

Larry started the meeting by saying he didn't know if the firm could survive in its present state. There was too much animosity between the two business units. He hired an investment banking firm to value each business unit. He then presented an alternative, whereby Andersen Consulting could buy its "freedom" by paying a fair market value to Andersen partners. That fair market value was an estimated $3 billion. Both business units were upset. The audit/tax group felt the price should be at least $5 billion. The consulting partners felt like it could be less.

If the firm were to stay together, it would not be under Larry, as he was completing his term as CEO. The board nominated two candidates to replace him. One was George Shaheen from Andersen Consulting, the other Jim Wadia, a tax partner from London.

Jim was on the board of partners and also ran the London office. He specialized in transaction services that involved things like litigation support, arbitration assistance, and mergers and acquisitions. Unlike most other partners, Jim had not begun his career in the firm.

Each candidate made a presentation to the partners. Later, in a joint session, Larry asked each of us to comment on various questions submitted by the partners.

This was the first time I, like many others in the room, had any contact with Jim Wadia. I had no idea of who he was or what he did. Jim was raised in India before moving to the UK as a child. He delivered an effective speech in his British accent, but you could see he was not raised in the firm culture. His background and experience seemed light for a CEO who would be inheriting serious problems. His leadership persona was also a handicap.

George Shaheen, on the other hand, had a lot more presence and stature. His talk was sincere. His vision was of a new firm that could work together in harmony. He delivered it with grace. The problem for George was that the audit/tax partners did not trust him. They felt he would spin off and sell the audit practice.

The partners met in groups to discuss the candidates. Audit and tax leadership was concerned that their partners would not vote for Jim Wadia due to his lack of visibility to the U.S. partners. They were worried that the U.S. partners would vote for George with the hope that he could bring the firm back together. To counteract this, Steve Hemsley, an audit partner, and Barry Wallach, a tax partner, arranged "white papers" behind the scenes and then met with the managing partners and other leaders to tell them why we needed to support Jim. They shared questions and the related "Andersen Response." We were asked to enlist the support of the partners in each office to "vote the right way."

The process turned me off. I grew up with the culture of "think straight, talk straight." I didn't see the need to convince my partners to do anything. They all had minds of their own. They were listening to the same things I was listening to and could make their own decisions. In disgust, I walked out of the management meetings.

When our meeting reconvened, we then voted on Larry's successor. I voted for George Shaheen for a number of reasons. First, I didn't have confidence that Jim Wadia could solve the firm's problems, and thought he might actually make things worse. Second, I knew George, and felt that his background and skills were better than Jim's. If the worst thing that happened was that George spun off Arthur Andersen or sold it to another firm, so be it. We would end up with a stronger organization. Further, we would all be financially better off. I felt the risk was greater with Jim than with George.

Before we voted informally (since not all partners were present, we would have an informal vote of confidence before having a formal vote later), the partners were summoned to the hall to hear the candidates answer the questions that had been submitted. George did a fantastic job and said all the right things—until the very end. The last question was, "If you lost the election, how would you support the other candidate?" Jim answered by saying he would give George all the support he wanted. When George took the microphone, at first he stared in silence, then looked up at the ceiling, reflected some more, and then said in so many words, "I have strong beliefs and philosophies and could not work with someone who had different beliefs and philosophies." The election was close, with neither candidate receiving a strong majority. To this day, I believe that if George had given an answer similar to Jim's, he would have been the next CEO.

In between this and the final vote, I called George to share my perspective. I told George that in the U.S., most of the vote would be controlled by our larger offices: New York, Chicago, Houston, Washington, Atlanta, and Los Angeles. He should visit with the audit and tax partners in those offices and let them ask questions that he could answer spontaneously and from the heart. His sincere and open communication would give them comfort and confidence. But George said he did not have the energy to do it. My response was that, then, it didn't appear he had the energy to be our CEO. George raised the white flag. He was done.

A formal vote was later held among all the partners. To be elected, a candidate needed the support from two-thirds of the partners. Although George had more votes, he could not come close to the required two-thirds support. Since neither candidate received the required majority, the firm nominated Bob Grafton as the interim CEO. Bob was the former partner of the Washington, D.C. office and was well liked by all. But he was close to his retirement. Although Bob was the interim CEO, he had no real power. Each division was in charge of doing its own thing. The consulting division was led by George, and the audit and tax divisions by Jim.

It was not long thereafter that Andersen Consulting requested a divorce from the firm without any payment to be made. Arthur Andersen responded with a promise to sue the Andersen Consulting partners. The partnership provided that if a group left the firm, it would have to pay fair value to the firm based on a formula specified in the partnership agreement. However, Andersen Consulting said it was splitting up for cause (i.e., Andersen was now performing consulting projects and in effect competing against Andersen Consulting). The partnership agreement called for disagreements to be settled by an impartial international arbitrator. The arbitrator had to come from a country in which neither business unit had operations. This meant the arbitrator had to be selected from a small country outside the U.S.

Jim Wadia immediately worked on putting together his own management team. Since he did not know many of the U.S. partners, he traveled to the U.S. to meet with partners from each region to decide who should run the U.S. operations. Our Central Region, which was the largest in the firm, was meeting in Kohler, Wisconsin, and Jim Kackley, our regional OMP, arranged for Jim to visit. He also arranged for Jim to meet one-on-one with certain partners. I was one of those whom Jim selected.

When I met with Jim Wadia, he asked who I thought was capable of leading the U.S. and whom I would select. That caught me off guard. Up to then, I really hadn't focused on that position. I suggested he pick someone who was young and energetic, someone who could bring fresh thinking to the firm, yet uphold its traditions and values. We also needed someone who would have the respect of Andersen Consulting and could be visible in the marketplace.

Jim asked me who in the Central Region could be considered. I named Steve Samek, who, at the time, ran the audit division for the Chicago office. I worked with Steve when I was in Chicago 25 years earlier. At that time, I thought he had so much talent that one day he would run the firm. He was smart, creative, and had great presence. I don't know if my recommendation made any difference or not, but Steve was selected to run the U.S.

One of the first things Steve did was to reorganize the U.S. operations from six regions into eight: Northeast, Mid-Atlantic, Southeast, Great Lakes, Central, South Central, West, and Great Plains. The Great Plains comprised the offices that did not fit into any of the other regions, namely Milwaukee, Minneapolis, Kansas City, Omaha, and St. Louis. Our Milwaukee office was the second oldest in the firm and had significant market share but didn't want to be part of Chicago. It wanted to remain separate, so it wouldn't be dominated by the largest office in the firm.

As Steve was finalizing these arrangements, he visited with me and the St. Louis office. We thought it was time to show him our letter, "The need for re-examining our EPU policy," mentioned in Chapter 20. Surprisingly, Steve embraced our paper and thoughts. I say "surprisingly," because after Steve was put in charge of the U.S. operations, there was even greater pressure for increased earnings.

When Steve met with me, he said he was thinking of putting me in charge of the Great Plains Region. He thought I would be best suited to get these fragmented offices working together. However, he warned it would not be easy. In fact, he thought this would be the toughest regional job, as it had the least synergy among its offices. All other regions had one dominant office. The Great Plains region would be made up of offices of approximately similar size. I was pleased that Steve gave me this increased responsibility and thanked him for his confidence in me.

In May 1998, Jim Wadia assembled the U.S. audit and tax

leadership group and shared his management principles. Jim indicated that he and Barry Wallach were going to take the lead in running the arbitration against Andersen Consulting and that the rest of us needed to focus on the marketplace and our clients. Jim said he had plenty of experience in international arbitration proceedings and that Andersen Consulting would pay dearly for leaving the firm.

Soon, I visited the office leadership of each of the offices in the Great Plains: Minneapolis, Milwaukee, Kansas City, and Omaha. During these visits, it became apparent to me that not one of the offices was in favor of regionalization. Each of the offices was successful in its own way and saw no need to regionalize. I tried to explain how the whole could be worth more than the sum of the parts, but my thoughts fell on deaf ears. I needed a plan.

To deal with this, I had leaders from each office meet in Minneapolis. Steve Polacek, the managing partner for Minneapolis, hosted our meeting. After a cool opening day, we went out for a big feast with plenty of good wine. Everyone seemed to loosen up and started to let their hair down—until the next day.

The next day, Tom Fischer led the charge against regionalization. He saw no benefit in regionalization and was not prepared to change his ways. Steve Polacek had his support.

It was not long after that I flew to Milwaukee to meet with Tom in private. I shared how we could service our clients better by using the best resources from the region. Tom replied, "You may be good at growing a market, but I could not stand in his shadow when it came to motivating the troops." I responded, "Great. Why don't you take the lead on our HR initiatives, and I will take the lead in developing our growth strategies." We would split leadership responsibilities. If he agreed, we both must trust and share everything with each other.

Tom was surprised I was willing to give up this responsibility, but he agreed. We had a deal! The ice had been broken. From this point on, we worked together as a team and trusted each other. It was the beginning of great times.

Steve Samek had his U.S. regional leadership team meet in January 1999, in Phoenix, Arizona. I had mixed emotions about representing the Great Plains at this meeting. Prior to the leadership change, Jim Kackley was the managing partner for the Central Region. The St. Louis office reported to him. Dick Measelle had previously introduced a partner sabbatical program, and Jim encouraged our leadership group to take a three-month sabbatical. I told Jim I was eager to take him up on the offer. Susan and I were going to rent a place in the Palm Springs area and use the time to investigate various communities where we would eventually like to retire. However, now that I was taking on additional responsibilities, I did not feel it was right for me to be away three months. So we cut it to four weeks. Tom Fischer led the Great Plains during my absence. I had complete confidence in his abilities to do so. Further, I thought he would gain a greater appreciation for my role.

Steve had his U.S. leadership meet in Phoenix on January

7–8, 1999. From there, Susan and I visited with our friends, W.R. and Judy Howell at Desert Highlands, just outside of Phoenix, before driving to Palm Springs. Our sabbatical ran from January 10 to February 8. During that time, Susan and I visited many real estate developments to decide where we wanted to buy. We finally decided on buying a home at Mission Hills in Rancho Mirage, California.

With that, our retirement plans were set. In the meantime, there was heavy lifting that needed to be done at work. I had to unify the region, make sure that our five offices in the Great Plains region worked together to use the best resources for our clients no matter where they were located. I needed them to cooperate with one another to develop strategic growth strategies on an industry and functional basis. This was no easy task, but all I could do was devote myself to it as we waited to hear the results of the dispute with Andersen Consulting.

Our hopes were high that Andersen Consulting would eventually have to pay a nice price for its freedom. Our meeting in France set $3 billion as the minimum of our expectations; Jim Wadia was confident that the final settlement would be considerably higher.

CHAPTER 23

The Calm Before the Storms

The new millennium started with a heavy, sometimes tedious, workload. I'll never forget the minutiae of the regional managing partners' meeting in Sarasota, Florida, where we spent virtually the entire first day talking about controlling cell phone expenses. Yes, cell phone expenses. Steve Samek introduced the topic. Then, we heard from Barry Wallach, a Chicago tax partner. Then, we heard from Steve Goddard, the Houston office managing partner. I thought it would never end. As you looked around the room, you could see everyone's eyes roll. As if that was not enough, Steve said the next day he was getting the other office managing partners on the phone, and he was going to give the same presentation to them.

There was no way we could let that happen. Why waste our time on such a relatively unimportant topic? That evening, Lou Salvatore, the managing partner from our New York office, shared his frustrations with me. Lou and I wanted to shift the meeting's focus to talk about our strategy, our people, and our clients, and how we could improve our service to them. We felt this was an excellent opportunity to convey to Steve our frustrations with the way things were going. We approached Steve and suggested that he ask each participant what he or she liked or didn't like about his management style and the first meeting. Lou agreed to set the tone and lead this constructive criticism. I agreed to meet with Steve to coach him on how to listen carefully to what was being said, rather than simply assuming the defensive. This would be difficult for Steve, but we really did want to help him become a more effective leader of our U.S. operations.

Thus, each regional managing partner briefly aired his or her grievances while Steve followed my advice and listened intently. The meeting went as well as could be expected; however, I made two mistakes. First, I participated like everyone else, repeating advice and comments I'd given to Steve a few months earlier when I had flown out to Chicago to talk to him about his leadership style. During that visit to Chicago, I had already told Steve that I thought he needed to be a better listener and solicit input from others. I had already told him that he needed to do a better job of prioritizing his tasks and ideas. All of them may be important, but they weren't all urgent. I did not need to repeat my comments in front of the group, especially when Steve had been receptive of my input all those months ago. I should have just kept my mouth shut.

The second mistake I made was to mouth off to Barry Wallach. Barry could not sit still and listen, like everyone else. Instead, he went to a board and started writing down people's comments. So, I challenged him. I found it distracting, a sign of Barry's inability to control his own nervous energy. When I challenged Barry, he refused to stop. He said writing was how he learned. But on that day, I didn't have the patience or understanding to tolerate it. I couldn't let it go. Barry and I were good friends until that meeting. As soon as I confronted him, things were never the same.

Despite my mistakes, we all left this meeting hoping things would change. We hoped that Steve and Barry would solicit input from the other leaders, be less verbose and dictatorial, and focus more on our strategy, our people, and our clients. But things didn't change.

When I returned to St. Louis, I met with a number of our partners, who were in the process of planning our Great Plains market circle leadership meeting. Each of our offices in the region was doing well, but we were still not integrating all our services. I believed we needed to organize by industry and service line in order to empower those departments to better service our clients and grow the practice. This was quite a change from how each office operated. I held the meeting at a conference room near the airport in Dallas to encourage the image of interoffice equality. By meeting on neutral ground, every office was on equal footing. We all had a say. We all had power.

At this meeting, I brought in several strategic and motivational speakers, including Jim Loehr from Florida, to boost morale and unify the region. This was a key meeting for the Great Plains

Region. The partners from each office left feeling more comfortable working with each other. We trusted each other more. Each of us was committed to our new strategy and left with a renewed sense of hope regarding the firm's future.

Other segments of the firm added to this wave of optimism as they continued trying to improve Arthur Andersen as a whole. Around this time, Steve Samek asked Jim Edwards, a senior partner of the firm, to head our Global Managing Partner (GMP) Program. As part of the program, each office identified the largest companies in its marketplace and developed plans to improve their relationships and work quality for each of these clients. In March of 2000, the partners assigned to these clients met in Arizona to discuss and improve each other's plans. Unlike some of my peers, I felt entirely comfortable with the approach. Essentially, it was what we were doing in St. Louis and in the Great Plains Region, sharing ideas and working together for the betterment of all. It formalized the process a little more, but we were all focused on these activities anyway.

In May, we had another Global Managing Partner meeting, this time in Chicago. Each partner who handled a large company shared what was working and what was not. Our focus was to make sure we were serving our larger clients well and had started applying the previously developed methods to our larger targets and accounts. To facilitate accountability, the firm developed an elaborate reporting mechanism to measure the success of the program by monitoring improvements to client service.

That summer, the Great Plains Region spent a lot of time figuring out how to make each of our offices work better together. We all met in St. Louis to review and approve each other's newly re-organized and streamlined business plans. Our efforts paid off. As a result of this increased interoffice communication, our effectiveness had markedly improved. We were helping each other. We were making sure each major client in the region was getting the best service and ideas available. Our clients were pleased and each of our five offices was growing significantly. Our strategy was working.

In July, one of my friends in St. Louis invited Susan and me to their son's wedding in Peoria. The son was marrying a Shaheen, George Shaheen's identical twin brother's daughter, to be exact. This was the first time I'd seen George since he had left the firm. Although he no longer was associated with the firm, George weighed in on the arbitration issues. He thought Andersen Consulting would win its arbitration. Alarmed, I told George that our new CEO, Jim Wadia, and Barry Wallach were spending virtually all of their time on the arbitration and felt confident that we would win. George took a sip of his drink and replied, "Soon, time will tell."

There was nothing any of us could do, though, except keep doing our jobs, so that is what the regional managing partners did. Over the rest of the year, I visited all of our offices within the region to see how things were working and to listen to any concerns. The management team in each office was doing a magnificent job.

Each office was exceeding its goals and growing its practice. We were grooming a great group of young leaders who were ready to take on more responsibility. Things couldn't have been better.

Towards the end of January 2001, Susan and I returned to Acapulco for our annual vacation. We rented a bungalow facing the ocean at the Hotel Pierre Marques and spent our days playing golf, relaxing by the pool, playing gin rummy, reading, and going out to dinner. It was a perfect break from all the hard work and chaos. But all good things must come to an end.

CHAPTER 24

The Storms

While on vacation, I thought about my last visit with George Shaheen. He seemed as confident as Jim Wadia that they would win the arbitration. I was not so certain. The arbitrator was from South America. Who knew how this one person could rule? It was like playing Russian roulette.

I remembered the process I was involved in years earlier when the May Company was in arbitration with Federated Department Stores over the final purchase price of the Filenes and Foleys department stores. I recalled how both sides presented information that surprised the other and how both sides thought they would win. In the end, both were disappointed. An arbitrator seeks a middle ground; neither side gets exactly what it wants. Perhaps it would be better if we settled out of arbitration. Both business units felt they could win, but both also recognized they were taking big risks by putting it all in the hands of an unknown arbitrator from

South America. With all these risks, perhaps both sides could be convinced to seek their own middle ground.

When I returned, I called Jim Wadia and shared my thoughts on and experiences with arbitration. Jim strongly disagreed and said international arbitration was very different from arbitration in the U.S. He said, "There is no way we will lose this arbitration." I asked him whether it was worth the risk, but he replied, "Don't worry. I have this under control."

I'd done all I could do.

Not long after the conversation, I was driving to my office, listening to a voice mail from Jim Wadia. The arbitrator ruled in favor of Andersen Consulting. The results were extremely disappointing. The fallout was monumental. Jim announced his immediate resignation from the firm. He had tried and failed, so he fell on his sword. The firm was without a leader, and the Andersen partners were in shock that they were not going to receive as much as they had originally thought. I arrived at the parking lot, but I didn't get out of my car. I just sat there, lost. I had no idea what I would say to everyone. There was nothing I could do to placate their concerns.

But I had to try, so I pulled my keys out of the ignition, grabbed my briefcase, and went inside, waiting for the chaos to begin. Sure enough, one by one, the partners came to my office to press me for details. But I didn't know any more than they did.

Soon, we got updates from our management team. The arbitrator had ruled that the Andersen Consulting partners had to pay for splitting from the firm, but it was a fraction of our asking price. Further, most of the proceeds from the settlement needed to be used to shore up our operations. Whatever funds went to the individual partners was added to their capital accounts and not distributed outright. Only when they left the firm and gained access to these accounts would they also gain access to these funds.

The audit and tax partners had been fooled by Jim's unrealistic expectations. We had turned down $3 billion in hopes of getting considerably more. Now, we were getting considerably less. I could see why Jim resigned, but I couldn't shake the inevitable guilt I was feeling. If only I'd been more argumentative and forceful with Jim or perhaps if I had shared my thoughts with others, none of this would have happened. Perhaps, I could have convinced the partners to settle outside of arbitration. Nevertheless, we were where we were. We had to accept the state of things and move on.

Life had to go on, and with it, business as usual.

The board selected Lou Salvatore to be our interim CEO. Lou inherited a mess, but managed to do a tremendous job. Lou increased transparency and communication between him and the partners and quickly settled everyone down. The partners enjoyed his leadership so much they tried to convince him to be the permanent CEO. But Lou rejected their overtures. He had no desire to be. The board had to look elsewhere.

In the interim, each of the offices in our region continued to perform well. The firm and its partners showed great resiliency. We kept moving forward. The Central Region soon submitted another group of partners for the Master's Program. Once again,

Bob Allgyer and I facilitated the group. We kicked off this session on May 6 with a meeting in Detroit. The session was a success, and we decided to meet next in Chicago and, later, Cincinnati, Ohio.

But my attention was soon diverted from the firm. My personal life didn't stop in times of professional crisis. My daughter, Laurie, was getting married on June 2, 2001, in Chicago. Laurie wanted a small family wedding, particularly since her husband, Patrick Solberg, came from such a large family. She wanted to keep it intimate, so the people she invited were truly special. Nearly everyone she invited came to the wedding, except for Susan's parents. Susan's mother was suffering from Alzheimer's, and her husband had a hard enough time caring for her in the comfort of their familiar Florida apartment. He didn't want to brave the confusion and exhaustion that would come with traveling to Chicago. We tried to convince him to come, but try as we might to persuade him, he repeatedly reminded us that when he married Marian, he had vowed to be by her side in sickness and in health. He wasn't about to leave her now.

For some reason, it was the year of weddings, as several of my personal and professional contacts tied the knot. On September 1, 2001, Susan and I attended another wedding. Bob Cox, the executive vice president of Emerson Electric, with whom I'd travelled to Asia on many occasions, was getting married at Bellerive Country Club. It was a large wedding with much of the Emerson Electric management team in attendance. While the wedding itself was beautiful, it was not what made it so memorable. I also had an enlightening conversation with Mike Barry.

A friend of Bob's, Mike was an audit practice director in the firm and had just recently retired. At the wedding, Mike told me that when he retired, he took all his money out of the firm. I was surprised. Most partners left their retirement account in the firm and earned an attractive return over a 10-year span. It was what I'd always assumed I would do. Waiting brought a steady stream of income from ages 56 to 65 and spread out the income tax burden over a decade. I asked Mike why he did that. He told me he was troubled by the firm's new management team and direction and no longer had confidence that the firm would still exist in ten years.

Our office's fiscal year-end New Year's event was held at Barnes Hospital auditorium. Once again, it was a big hit. By now, it was tradition for me to dress in a costume and make everyone laugh by acting silly. We celebrated our success and enjoyed clever skits put on by others in our office. Never did it enter my mind that this would be our last New Year's Eve party.

Around this time, Steve Samek had his regional managing partners' meeting at our training facility in St. Charles. It was a multi-day meeting. We covered a lot of topics, including the future direction of our U.S. practice. As I looked around the room, I sensed very little energy. Steve led the discussion. There was very little participation from the group. I thought: If this is the leadership of the firm, how will we energize the organization to support this new direction?

At the end of the session, Steve asked for comments. The room was silent. I stood up and said that what I was about to say stemmed from my love for the firm, and if anyone viewed my comments the wrong way, I apologized. I commented that there did not seem to be a lot of energy or support in the room for our new strategy. We were the ones who would be counted on to execute it and lead our respective offices. I suggested that we consider merging with another firm. Since we no longer had Andersen Consulting, there would be several firms who would love to merge with us. We could end up in a dominant position.

I initially got the same reaction as Steve got from his presentation—total silence. Finally, two senior partners responded. Both felt we should not seek to merge now, but wait to see how the strategy played out. There would be no risk in waiting. I responded: "What happens if we get involved in major litigation?" Then we would be acting out of weakness, not strength. I suggested we explore the possibilities now, while we were strong. However, I could not get any support for my position.

The firm went on to elect Joe Berardino as our new CEO, replacing Lou Salvatore. Joe Berardino was the audit division head in New York and had worked in our consumer practices division, serving large multinational accounts. I worked closely with Joe in that capacity. He was a great guy. I was glad to see Joe get the opportunity and thought he would do well, assuming we had no more unforeseen crises. It would take time for Joe to grow into the role, but I had no doubt that he would be a great CEO.

Bob Allgyer could not attend the Master's Program in Cincinnati on September 11, 2001. I felt comfortable leading the group for that session. Robert Cooper, our outside facilitator, was handling most of it. Before we broke out in discussion groups, Robert lectured the group on leadership. It was time for a break. Most people went into the lobby of the hotel only to return declaring that the United States had just been attacked!

I couldn't believe what I had just heard and went to the lobby to watch the large TV screen, when I saw another plane crash into the second tower. What on earth was happening? I listened for a few minutes and got everyone back in the room. I said it was time for us to end the meeting and for everyone to return home. Certainly the airports would be closed, so I had different groups go down the street and rent as many rental cars as they could. We got a bus for the people from Chicago. They left first. We broke the rest of the people into groups and instructed them to drive home. I went with one St. Louis partner and two Kansas City partners, who dropped us off in St. Louis before heading home. It would be a day that would change America forever. It would also be the beginning of the end for the firm.

Joe Berardino set up his new management team. Terry Hatchet, a former Houston office partner who was running the Dallas office, became the new U.S. audit leader. I now reported to Larry Gorrell, who became Central Region managing partner, located in Chicago. Larry started in the Chicago office about the same time I did and specialized in the financial services industry. His most recent position was managing partner of the San Francisco office and head of the Western Region.

Larry was very smart, a numbers guy, and somewhat introverted.

Unlike his predecessors, he did not have much interest in meeting new clients or seeing new faces. He was more interested in statistics and things that affected profitability. He was not interested in investing in initiatives that did not generate a quick and measurable impact. This was quite an adjustment for me and the other office managing partners in our region. Before any meeting, we would get large binders full of statistical reports and then be expected to review all the material before the next day's meeting. Invariably, he would never ask for anyone's input at the meeting, but instead shared his interpretation of the numbers and what needed to be done to make them better, no matter how good or how bad they were.

The first worldwide partners meeting under Joe Berardino was held in New Orleans with spouses. The partners were scattered in various hotels around town. We all met in the convention center.

Before the meeting, the global managing partners met with Jim Edwards to discuss our progress on serving global clients and introduced a young partner from the Houston office who talked about his service to one of the largest clients of the firm, a company called Enron. I had never met this partner and did not know much about Enron. He proceeded to get us up to speed.

At the general session the next day, Joe Berardino gave his first speech as managing partner and introduced his executive team. Between sessions, he brought in actors from Cirque de Soleil, who entertained us to dramatize key messages. One was on strength, another on teamwork, etc. As I watched these acrobatic acts, I reflected on what Frank Rossi once said. "You will know when it is the right time to retire. It is not something you plan." I suddenly felt this was the time.

Joe was a relatively young partner with a new team. Perhaps this was the time to pass on leadership in the Great Plains Region to younger partners. We had so many ready, willing, and able partners who could take over my role. Additionally, Tom Fischer, the Milwaukee office managing partner, had been asking me for months when I was going to retire. He wanted to leave the firm when I did. He did not want to work for someone else. I always said I would let him know when I felt the time was right. I had a strong feeling that the time was now.

At the break, I met with Larry Gorrell. Larry had always been eager to talk about my succession plan. I grabbed Larry and told him that I was ready to retire next February on my 56th birthday. I told Larry that with new national leadership, it made sense to have new leaders in our region as well. Larry said he would accommodate my desires and asked whom I recommended as my replacements. "Replacements?" I asked. Larry said "Yes, replacements." He wanted to break my job into two: one for St. Louis managing partner and the other for regional managing partner. I told him I had several candidates, most of whom he had never met. I encouraged him to meet them and select two from the list.

Later, Larry grabbed me and said he had given my request more thought. He said February was not the best time to leave the firm, since it was in the middle of the busy season. He requested I leave in May, not in February. I replied, "No problem. I've been here for 35 years. A few more months will make no difference." Larry asked that I keep this between him and me. He would inform the leaders of the firm. Once again, I replied, "No problem."

When I got back to the room, I was excited to share the news with Susan. She was glad to hear it. After the meeting, I went with friends from St. Louis for a long weekend in California, where I played the course I played on my very first round, Cypress Point, as well as the course I played on my second round, Pebble Beach. Life could not be any better!

When I got back to Chicago, Larry asked if I could meet with him the day before our regional managing partners' meeting. The purpose of the meeting was to talk about my transition. We were to meet at 4 p.m. and then go out for dinner. I arrived at his office early and waited to meet with Larry. I waited and waited and waited. It was 6 p.m. before Larry rushed out of his office and said we could talk in the cab as we rode to the restaurant. We discussed some of the candidates for my replacement, but when we reached the restaurant, he surprised me by saying that his wife would be joining us for dinner. How are we going to talk about this subject with his wife there?

We had a nice cordial dinner. Larry and his wife were talking freely after each had a number of cocktails and wine. They talked about a lot of things, but not about Arthur Andersen or my retirement. The next day, Larry apologized and asked me to simply pick a replacement for each position. I told Larry that he needed to meet these people and pick his best match. I thought it was important for him to do so. Larry never did pick my replacement.

Weeks passed, and I felt it was necessary to share my plans with a few of the partners in our regional offices. I advised them that Larry Gorrell would be meeting with them to consider my replacement. Tom Fischer pleaded with me for the two of us to leave immediately. "Why wait?" he asked. I replied that we could leave together, but on a timetable that makes the most sense for the firm. It will happen soon.

At the end of our monthly meeting for St. Louis office partners, I told them my news and asked them to keep it quiet. It was important that our clients find out at the proper time. My partners understood. I got a warm and caring response. I was embraced by a few of them and tears came to my eyes. I knew I would miss them terribly.

A few weeks later, a second storm hit the firm (the first being the Andersen Consulting arbitration). I had my quarterly meeting with Randy Baker, CFO for Anheuser-Busch (AB), to make sure that he was satisfied with our services. Randy said he was most pleased with the Andersen work and AB was thinking about expanding our service level. But he had a question for me. The question was what I knew about Enron. I told him that I knew it was a client of ours, but not much more. Randy asked if I had read the *Wall St. Journal* that morning, which I hadn't. He shared with me an alarming story regarding the accounting for non-consolidated subsidiaries of Enron. I said I would be happy to have him talk to partners who knew more than I.

Randy was to give a presentation to his board. They wanted him to comment on what he thought about Andersen and Enron. He saw it as a non-event, one that he would be able to handle without further questions or information.

The following day, Randy called to say that we were fired from all work at AB. All projects were to be terminated immediately. I was in complete shock. After all, had it not been just yesterday when he told me he was immensely pleased with our work!?!

Randy told me several directors were not interested in his opinion about us. They believed Andersen shouldn't have been involved with Enron. They wanted to make sure that AB had no relationship with Andersen. I asked Randy if he would meet with me and Terry Hatchett, our audit division head who used to be from Houston, and learn more facts. Randy said he would, but it would not change his mind.

Terry flew in to meet with Randy. Terry did a great job of responding to Randy's concerns. We asked if we could meet with August Busch III. Randy asked us to wait, while he approached August III. When he came back, he replied that August was going to Hawaii for vacation and had no time for us. We offered to fly to Hawaii and meet with August for 30 minutes. Randy said he would discuss our offer with August.

The next day, Randy called to say August did not want to

see an Arthur Andersen person ever again. He further instructed his managers that if any of them were on a board where Arthur Andersen was the auditor, that he or she must resign from the board or resign from AB.

Things went from bad to worse. Each day, there was another story about Andersen and Enron. Our people and clients started asking more questions and requesting more information. I met with all our major clients and shared with them what I knew. For the most part, our clients were supportive and understanding. They loved the firm and the people that were serving them. They reaffirmed their support and loyalty. But there were a few exceptions.

David Farr, CEO of Emerson Electric, and Walt Galvin, CFO, asked to see me. They started by saying how pleased they were with our service. However, August Busch III, their audit committee chairman, felt uncomfortable doing any work with Arthur Andersen. Reluctantly, they needed to sever our relationship. This was heartbreaking to me as I enjoyed working with Emerson and its entire first-class team. I put myself in their position and didn't even try to persuade them otherwise. I knew August and his style. I told them I understood and wished them luck. I left the building with tears in my eyes. I had just lost a great client and wonderful friends.

It was January 2002, the time when Susan and I always went to Acapulco. I debated whether or not to go, but felt I would be fresher when I returned. I knew we were in for difficult times but did not expect events to unfold so quickly, nor so dramatically.

We arrived at the same bungalow in which we always stayed, and Susan and I discussed my upcoming retirement and whether to keep our money in the firm or take it out. At this point, I had no idea that the firm was being threatened. Our involvement in Enron would result in lawsuits, but lawsuits usually took years to resolve. Back in the 1980s, many thought that Ernst & Young would not survive the real estate and S & L crisis. Later, rumors were rampant about the survival of KPMG.

Each day, Susan and I would take walks on the beach and discuss the plusses and minuses of taking my retirement money out of the firm. Then, my trusted, efficient, and reliable executive assistant, Rozann Steinkoenig, started to send me daily FedEx packages. I was on the phone constantly with clients and non-clients who wanted to talk about what they were reading in the papers. Soon, all my time was being devoted to the firm. There was no sense in staying in Acapulco. This was not a vacation.

I remembered my discussion with Mike Barry at Bob Cox's wedding. Mike said he took all his money out upon retirement. I thought, if I were an investor, would I put all my money in Arthur Andersen, knowing all the risks? I decided I would be like Mike and take all my money out upon retirement. It was now time to get back to St. Louis and get my retirement paperwork in motion.

CHAPTER 25

Living Hell

When I returned from Acapulco, there was a pile of work for me and I had more than 20 calls to return. I had to get caught up on the latest developments, but I still naively believed that the Enron situation was a long way from being settled and would have no impact on my retirement.

When I received an update on how much I would receive upon retirement and how much I would get each month for the next 10 years should I elect to defer, I called Larry Gorrell. He said he still had not discussed my retirement with anyone. That was alarming to me. It had been over two months. He should have talked to someone by now.

I was worried. Virtually every day, our Houston office client, Enron, was making headline news about its sliding stock price, potential financial misstatements, and the dubious character of its senior management. Frequently, Arthur Andersen was mentioned, even though we did not audit the two subsidiaries where the accounting irregularities had occurred. These two entities were audited by two different accounting firms.

Much of my time was spent meeting with our people and our clients to explain what was happening to Enron. Compounded by the fact that it was also busy season, I spent longer and longer days at the office. If that were not enough, I got a call from Tom Fischer. Tom said he was in a car heading to a client and that he was not feeling well. He was having chest pains. I tried to convince Tom to pull off the road and call for help. Although he refused to do that, I did convince him to go to a hospital and not go to his client. Later that day, his wife, Vicky, called to say that Tom had a heart problem. He would be in the hospital for an extended period of time. Further, his doctor advised Tom to retire ASAP. She said if it meant he forfeited retirement pay he would otherwise get, so be it. He needed to leave the firm immediately. His life was more important.

I now had another crisis to deal with. I assured Vicky that I understood their situation and said I would see what I could do about Tom's financial affairs with the firm. I called Larry Gorrell. Larry suggested a "wait and see" approach on how Tom progresses before we make any decisions. I talked to Vicky every day to find out how Tom was doing, and every day, she asked about getting their retirement money. She said that the doctors strongly advised him not to return to work. He was retiring no matter what. He needed a clean separation.

Normally, our full early retirement pay did not go into effect until a partner reached 56, but Tom was too young for that. A partner could receive partial early retirement pay between the ages of 50–56. Since Tom fell into that age category, I called Larry again to plead his case.

Larry said he had a better idea. Why doesn't Tom take disability and then in two years he would get full retirement benefits? I told Larry that Tom wanted a clean separation for health reasons. I begged him to give him what he deserved. Larry was still hesitant. Finally, I told Larry that I had used up all my persuasion. If this is what Larry wanted, so be it. But if something happened to Tom, it would be on Larry's conscience, not mine. A week later, our home office called to say they would be sending a check to Tom. Hallelujah! He was getting his money!

From then on, I harbored distrust for Larry Gorrell. Even though he knew about my retirement for three months, he had not communicated anything new to me. I called Kay Priestly. Kay was on the board of partners and in charge of partner HR matters. I asked if she knew about my retirement. She did not. I told her my story. She advised me to send my retirement letter to Joe Berardino with a copy to her. She said to do it that day, as the firm was considering freezing all retirement benefits after the next board meeting. She assured me that my retirement would not be affected if I sent the letter right away.

I sent my letter to Joe Berardino, and copied Kay and Larry Gorrell. When Larry received it, he was furious. He reminded me of his previous instructions. When I informed him of what

Kay had said, he still could not give me a reason why he had not shared my retirement plans. I knew I had made the right choice. Joe Berardino called and said he was surprised I was retiring, so I told him my story. He was surprised Larry had not communicated my intentions, wished me luck, and thanked me for my years of service. I told him I would be at my post until my retirement took effect in a few months.

On February 19, 2002, I turned 56. A while back, I had arranged for my kids to fly to St. Louis that weekend. The firm normally sponsored a retirement party and I thought this would be the best time for mine. However, there would be no retirement party. This was not the time for celebration. Instead, Susan made a great dinner and we enjoyed a nice quiet evening together. It was nice to be with my family. I certainly needed their support. Susan and I were worried about our future, so it was nice to be surrounded by the love and support of my kids. I tried to hide my troubles from them as much as possible, but they could see how much weight I had lost. They were worried.

Considering what I had just gone through and what was being printed in the newspapers, I was worried, too, only not for myself, but about the survival of the firm in general. I also learned of contingency plans that were being made in case the government indicted the firm. It seemed inevitable after the government learned that the audit staff on Enron had shredded duplicate and draft documents in accordance with firm policy. We had done nothing wrong, but the government didn't care. If our PR was bad before, it was getting worse.

I met with our public companies to tell them what I knew and to assure them that we would continue to act in their best interest. Most assured me that they were sticking by our side. I encouraged them to develop a contingency plan of their own. As much as I appreciated their kind remarks about the firm and the partners serving them, I wanted to make sure they weren't harmed by anything that might happen to the firm. I still maintained that clients came first, down to the very end.

I also met with our people, trying to placate their concerns. Everyone was worried, for the firm, for their clients, and for themselves. There was little I could do but encourage everyone to continue serving their clients in an outstanding fashion. I told them not to worry about things they couldn't control. The rest would take care of itself.

All was well until March 14, 2002. On that fateful day, the government indicted Arthur Andersen. For a professional services firm, this is the kiss of death. Clients now had to protect their interests and select another firm to audit their future financial statements.

We all felt we did not deserve the indictment and did our best to convince the government. As I understand it, we had an agreement with DOJ, but they could not convince their boss, Mr. Michael Chertoff, the head of the Justice Department. Our future was no longer in our hands.

Coincidentally, on Saturday, March 16, our office held a previously scheduled office meeting for every employee. Just about everyone showed up. In retrospect, the timing could not have been better. Partners, managers, staff, and office support all talked about how great the firm was and how our clients were continuing to give us support. We gave ourselves a round of applause. Everyone hugged. Everyone cried.

We could not believe this great firm was dying.

We all wondered how it was possible for so many people to lose their careers when each of us was lauded for doing outstanding work. I had been with the office for almost 10 years, and over that span and as long as anyone could remember, our work had been continuously recognized for its exceptionally high standards and excellence. Our office had nothing to do with Enron, but the government could still bring us down.

Towards the end, our office became closer than ever. We completed our audits as if nothing was wrong. Clients could not believe how our team could perform so well given the circumstances. But every person was doing what he or she had always done: putting clients first.

Behind the scenes, things were a bit more chaotic. Arthur Andersen was doing everything possible to corral support. Bob Merenda was able to get a meeting with the U.S. Senator from Missouri, Kit Bond. He met people from all aspects of our business and all colors and ethnic groups. Each talked to Senator Bond about the firm in his or her own words and what it would mean if Arthur Andersen went away.

But Kit ignored their pleas.

He said there was nothing he could do.

We decided to take matters into our own hands. We staged marches in downtown St. Louis to make people aware of the severity of the situation and what it would mean to St. Louis to lose our organization. I made pleas to the St. Louis Regional Business Council for its support. I even called my friend, David Maxwell, Chancellor of Drake University, who wrote a letter on our behalf.

John Bachman was CEO of our client Edward Jones and chairman of the U.S. Chamber of Commerce. I also worked with John as a member of the executive committee for the St. Louis Chamber. John was willing to do anything to help us and he lived up to his word. He appeared on CNN with Lou Dobbs to talk about the injustice befalling the firm. He said he would not leave Arthur Andersen until there was absolutely no other choice. John will always be remembered for his great friendship during that most difficult time.

Despite all our efforts, nothing changed. The government was not going to be satisfied until Arthur Andersen was gone. Our firm tried every strategy. We even tried merging with other firms, but it was too late. The risk was too great for other companies to take it. The only alternative was to sell ourselves off piecemeal, office-by-office, to other firms.

This was a very stressful period for all Arthur Andersen personnel. The stress was getting to me. One day, I came home and went to bed. I felt like I had a good night's sleep, so I got out of bed, showered, shaved, and got dressed. I looked at the clock. It was only 1 a.m.! Since I was already up, I worked until sunrise before going to the office to deal with all this stuff again. Susan was frightened. I had lost a lot of weight and looked extremely pale. Concerned, she suggested I talk to someone. I had my friend Bob Lefton, CEO of Psychological Associates, visit so I could vent to someone and get his perspective. Bob suggested I meet with a doctor.

The doctor put me on medication so I could sleep better and get through the days. He also tried to convince me to leave the firm immediately, just as Tom Fischer had been advised by his doctor, but I knew I couldn't. This was not the time to abandon ship. Instead, I just delegated more of my responsibilities to other partners as we negotiated the sale of our offices. After all, they were the ones who would move on. I would not work for a competitor after spending 35 years at Arthur Andersen. I was done.

Rick Seibert was our audit division head, and I asked him to take the lead in negotiations to sell the St. Louis office, and to play the nice cop. I would get involved on the thorny issues and play the bad cop. This way, his career would not be put in jeopardy and I could also help strategize the deal. The first firm to approach us was Ernst & Young. Its managing partner, Jim Havel, came to my house and explained that he did not enjoy his role and would make me managing partner of our combined offices. However, Jim's interest was short-lived as his regional managing partner in Minneapolis vetoed the idea.

I thought there were two workable alternative merger

possibilities. One was Price Waterhouse. I always enjoyed and admired working with its managing partner, Steve Swyers. They were a tough but good competitor, and I thought our offices would blend well. I met with Steve and his audit division head. They expressed an interest; however, the New York office would not allow a merger with our entire office ... segments of our practice, yes, but the whole office, no. There was too much legal exposure.

My other candidate was a local firm called Rubin Brown. Years earlier, we had the Rubin Brown management team visit our St. Charles training facility. We had considered acquiring them, but for a variety of reasons, we had not. However, Rubin Brown had good critical mass in St. Louis with several hundred professionals and could easily grow into other markets if it had the right leaders for those markets. Our people could help them do that. Our firm frequently started up new markets, both in and outside the U.S., by sending a leader to develop and grow a practice.

I asked Rubin Brown chairman, Jim Castellano, who at the time was head of the American Institute of CPAs, to come to my house. I described my vision of Rubin Brown becoming a player in the Midwest and eventually a national player. I described how the firm grew in the 1960s and how Rubin Brown could do the same, particularly in this tumultuous environment. Jim was receptive to the idea. For a variety of reasons though, Rubin Brown elected not to move forward. There went my second choice.

I turned my attentions to my next option. I was not high on Deloitte & Touche (D&T) for a variety of reasons. For them, a St.

Louis merger would not make much strategic sense, but I knew we had to pursue all avenues. We had discussions, but to no avail.

That left one firm, KPMG. Fortunately, KPMG was eager to take on many Andersen offices, including St. Louis. Rick Seibert played a key role and handled some of the more challenging negotiations. Initially, I thought our discussions involved the entire office, but KPMG was organized differently than Arthur Andersen. Ralph Cleremont, its office managing partner, could negotiate for our audit practice, but their tax division head had to negotiate the acquisition of our tax practice. Ultimately, our auditors went to KPMG, and our tax people went to different organizations. Our state and local tax practice went to Price Waterhouse, and other partners and managers went to D&T and E&Y. It was not our most desirable outcome, but we were not in a strong bargaining position. We did, however, succeed in getting KPMG to take as many of our admin personnel as possible.

Everyone was on pins and needles during the negotiations. I heard many heartbreaking stories. Administrative people came to my office concerned about how they were going to put food on the table. They had worked at Andersen all their lives and lived from paycheck to paycheck. How would they survive? What happened if the new firm didn't select them? How would they find another job?

Thank God for Steve Riek, who made the process as painless as possible. Steve was my right-hand man. He did all our financial analysis, helped control our back office costs, and tried to keep our office support people happy. He did an unbelievable job helping

KPMG through its due diligence process. Steve stayed to the very end, when we sold off our office furniture. Happily, he then was hired as the CFO of a local privately held company.

Negotiations with KPMG were not always smooth. Most of the shots were being called by its New York Office. Most of our face-to-face talks were with the local office. Sometimes commitments made locally were later reversed by the home office in New York. But this was to be expected on a transaction this large and complex. All this uncertainty increased everyone's anxiety. Not all partners would be selected to join KPMG, making it stressful on those who were on the bubble.

Concurrent with our negotiations, similar negotiations were taking place at each of the offices in our region. Most of our Milwaukee and Minneapolis offices went with Deloitte & Touche, while Kansas City and Omaha went with KPMG. In addition, our final terms with KPMG were dependent on how many clients would agree to be audited by KPMG. Typically, a client's decision was based on whether the Andersen partner was going to KPMG.

As a result, we participated on numerous KPMG audit proposals. It was ironic to work with a former competitor to try to convince our clients to go with them.

This whole period could be summarized in a simple phrase: "Working in Hell." Each day was full of surprises and stress. At risk were people's lives and careers, and our clients' futures. There were no good outcomes. It was a battle of survival. Everyone worked seven days a week to figure out a way to survive.

Little by little, our office shrunk as people started new careers with new employers. Since I had no place to go, I kept going to the office every day to make sure things were unraveling as smoothly as possible, although, I had ceased receiving any compensation. When my retirement finally did go into effect, I was not as fortunate as Tom Fischer. In my case, the firm froze all retirement benefits before I was entitled to receive any. My capital was replaced with a note that was nothing more than a piece of paper. There was still a question of whether the firm could pay off all its obligations, let alone guarantee retirement benefits for its employees. The firm elected four partners responsible for managing its financial affairs: Larry Gorrell from Chicago, Lou Salvatore from New York, Steve Rogers from Atlanta, and John Niemann from Houston. They were responsible for the final activities of the firm.

While all this was going on, I was approached by several individuals asking me to consider joining their organizations. They tried to convince me that it was time to start thinking about myself, but that was the furthest thing from my mind. I was exhausted. All my energies were devoted to the firm and getting our people and clients settled. I had no energy left to do anything else.

In May 2002, I was to be honored by Drake University with its Alumni of the Year Award. I felt embarrassed and didn't want to go to Des Moines to receive it. To me, I was not deserving of this recognition. If anything, my circumstances made me an embarrassment to my alma mater. I called David Maxwell, Chancellor, and encouraged him to name someone else.

David would not hear it. He said the award was not for Arthur Andersen; it was for Larry Katzen. What occurred with the firm had no bearing on my getting the honor. David would not accept no for an answer, so Susan and I flew to Des Moines.

At the dinner, I was one of three people receiving an award and the last to be introduced. The emcee was a local NBC news anchor. A video about the recipients preceded their remarks. The other clips focused mostly on careers. My video focused on my involvement at Drake. Because of recent events, there was virtually no mention of Arthur Andersen. As I was walked to the stage, I decided not to give my prepared speech. Instead, my remarks were to come from my heart.

I told the audience that I had spent 35 years at Arthur Andersen and despite recent events, I was proud that I had worked for the greatest accounting firm on the face of the earth. I told them how Drake University taught me to do the right thing, and that all through my life, I had been trying to do just that. I practiced this philosophy to the firm's bitter end.

I was proud of my career.

After my speech, many people congratulated me and expressed their respect and love for the firm. I was surprised by the reaction, but quite pleased. At least, Arthur Andersen still had a few supporters left.

Later, Susan and I journeyed to Drake to dedicate an "Arthur Andersen Time Element" that we donated to Drake with the help of a few other partners who also attended Drake. The timepiece is in the center of the campus. A plaque on the back of the timepiece is inscribed:

> *Arthur Andersen was founded in 1913 and for nearly nine decades was one of the largest and most respected professional services firms in the world. This time element was made possible by the generosity and leadership of Larry R. Katzen, BS '67 and Susan Nieder Katzen, ED '68 and other partners of Arthur Andersen who attended Drake University.*

As the firm unwound, I met with various individuals. I decided I needed guidance on what to do once the firm finally collapsed. One of the people was Bert Walker, the first cousin of President George Herbert Walker Bush. Bert asked Susan and me to come to his house for cocktails and dinner. At first, I declined, as I was embarrassed to be with anyone. But Bert was insistent. When we arrived at his house, Bert was just returning from Houston, where he had visited former president George H. W. Bush. Bert wanted to be an ambassador and was seeking counsel from the former President. (Later, he would be our ambassador to Hungary.)

Sitting in his living room with family portraits of his mother and father at either end of the room, Bert shared his personal trials in life and what he had to endure. It was refreshing to hear his story and, for once, not have to talk about what I was going through. By the end of the evening, Bert had inspired me and given me courage to survive my crisis.

I also met with three other individuals, all former CEOs, who for one reason or another were no longer in charge of their respective organizations. I asked each of them what they did after they left their careers and what advice could they give me. Independently, each said that he did not know my personal financial situation, but challenged me to reconsider taking another job right away that would require 60 to 70 hours per week. They encouraged me to think about what other aspects of my life were important and how I could fulfill them. They recommended I get away and not make any important decisions at this time. I needed to cleanse my mind.

This was good advice.

It was time to move on. When I got home from my last day at the office, I told Susan to pack our bags. It was time to drive to our home out West.

Susan asked, "But what are you going to do?"

I replied, "I have no idea. I'll decide later." With that, we left to start a new life that was yet to be defined.

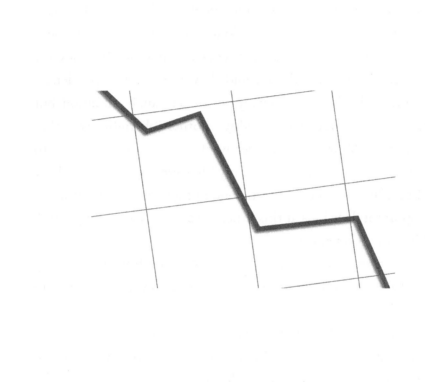

CHAPTER 26

No, I Am Not Crazy

No, my career at Arthur Andersen did not end as planned. With such a sour ending, accompanied by major financial losses, why would anyone deem their career a success? But I certainly wouldn't trade it for any other. I thoroughly enjoyed those 35 years. The firm gave me so many opportunities no other company would have.

First, where else could you receive so much responsibility at such an early age? When I was 25 years old, I was sent to Australia to run the audit of the largest retailing organization in the Southern Hemisphere. I had direct interface with the partner and senior management. By the age of 30, I was a partner, serving some of the largest companies in the world. Not many organizations could give you so much responsibility this quickly.

Second, I was involved in a profession where I had direct contact with some of the leading executives of some of the largest companies in the world. Just by observing them in action, I learned so much, including how to conduct myself in a mature and professional manner and how to think on my feet.

Third, I had an opportunity to work with some of the smartest co-professionals in the world. Those senior to me were constantly teaching and nurturing me. It was more than I could get from any MBA program.

Fourth, I got to travel the world and meet interesting people. I had the good fortune to travel to all continents and have natives available to introduce me to many fascinating people and share aspects of their culture.

Fifth, I made lasting, lifelong friends. The people I worked with and for eventually became some of my closest friends.

Sixth, I was part of an organization that believed in lifelong learning. Throughout my career, I attended exceptional educational courses at world-class facilities. I never became obsolete. Arthur Andersen made sure we were always on top of the learning curve.

Seventh, the firm was always there to assist. They were at my side when I was in greatest need with the birth of my quadruplets. This continued throughout my career as I went through other life-changing events. We also had the benefit of its investment counseling, income tax support, and other services for which we normally charged our clients.

Eighth, this profession did not make me among the wealthiest few, but it provided me with enough financial reward to raise a family in a nice house and to provide for all our family needs and many of its wants. It gave us enough financial security to make us better off than 98% of all Americans.

Ninth, if you like to help others succeed, this profession gives great satisfaction. During my career, I had clients call at all hours of the day, any day of the week. I never felt it was a nuisance. To the contrary, I always felt good that they had enough confidence in me to ask for my help at any hour.

Finally, the firm prepared me for whatever was to come. I knew that there would be life after Arthur Andersen, as the skills I'd learned at the firm would make me all the more desirable and effective.

So, no. I am not crazy. I would not change my path for anything. Arthur Andersen helped me become who I am today. It helped all of its employees become who they are today. It's no wonder, that post-Arthur Andersen, almost all our people landed on their feet. In many instances, these people have become leaders in their new organizations. I guess it's true. The cream really does rise to the top, and Arthur Andersen should still be on top.

Why Andersen?

In June 2002, I wrote a letter to the editor of the *St. Louis Post Dispatch*, which was later published. The letter described the injustice that cost more than 85,000 innocent and hardworking employees their jobs. I wrote that I hoped the government learned from the experience and that it would never happen again.

Since then, such prestigious firms as Bear Stearns and Lehman Brothers have disappeared. KPMG had a big scare of its own. In fact, some would say that if Arthur Andersen had not gone away, KPMG would not be around today. It reinforced my belief that every company is like a human being. There is a beginning and an end. After all, no tree grows to the sky.

During the 1990s, every major accounting firm was aggressively peddling various tax ideas to clients and non-clients and collecting fees based on a percentage of the savings. The most aggressive was Ernst & Young (E&Y). One time, I was invited to a CEO's office of one of my clients to listen to a phone conversation taking place with a marketing person of E&Y. E&Y claimed it had a great idea that could save my client millions of tax dollars. All my client had to do was sign a confidentiality agreement that made E&Y the exclusive provider for this service. If they ended up self-performing or using another firm, they would still have to pay a substantial fee to E&Y. They also committed to sign my client's tax returns, if we felt uncomfortable doing so. I was always astounded at what I was hearing. It was incredibly unprofessional.

When the IRS started to challenge these tax schemes, E&Y and others quickly settled and paid substantial fines. However, KPMG continued to challenge the IRS. This led to an investigation, which eventually resulted in large penalties and the resignation of a number of its tax partners, who were later threatened with prosecution. Some would say that if Andersen had still been around, KPMG would have been gone. The government saw the danger in having only three major accounting firms left on the playing field.

Following the demise of Arthur Andersen, the government passed the Sarbanes-Oxley Act, which required all publicly held companies to strengthen their internal controls and for the accounting firms to certify to their attestations. In addition, the Public Accounting Review Board was established to review the procedures of all accounting firms that audited publicly held companies. This put extra pressure on firms to change auditing processes and procedures. Since there were now only four large accounting firms left, with each needing to expand its procedures, the growth and profitability of the surviving firms increased significantly. In fact, billing rates more than doubled from where they were before Arthur Andersen went away.

So, what was the end result of Arthur Andersen's demise?

First, almost all of the Andersen audit and tax partners ended up at other firms, where, for the most part, they have advanced successful careers. In fact, many of these firms are led by former Andersen partners. Several former Andersen partners were hired by the Public Company Accounting Oversight Board to help police the profession. Further, former Andersen partners play leadership roles in many of mid-size accounting firms. How ironic that the government did not trust Arthur Andersen, and now that the firm is gone, its former partners are playing key roles elsewhere.

Second, there are now only four major accounting firms left. Since Sarbanes-Oxley expanded the definition of independence, it is now more difficult than ever to select an independent accounting firm. If by some chance you are dissatisfied with your firm, your alternatives are limited.

Third, the people most harmed by the demise of Andersen were not the partners and managers. Almost all have gone on to have successful careers. The ones who were hurt the most were the support staff. It is the secretaries and administrative personnel who had the most difficult time finding comparable jobs. These people were supporting their families paycheck to paycheck and needed jobs. The government destroyed many of their lives.

Finally, years after the Enron indictment, the firm appealed the decision to the U.S. Supreme Court. After hearing our case, the Supreme Court voted 9-0 in favor of our appeal. It was one of the quickest decisions ever made by the Supreme Court. However, for the people of Arthur Andersen, it was too late. Our people and clients were long gone.

It is also interesting to note that contrary to popular belief, to this date, no one has found any significant improprieties in the quality of our audit work at Enron. The two entities that had accounting irregularities were audited by two separate auditing firms, not Arthur Andersen.

So what is to be learned from this saga? From my perspective, the government should never destroy another firm. If there are improprieties, the government should go after the individuals directly responsible, not the firm. If it prosecuted those who were responsible for the crimes, it would have a chilling effect on the rest of the organization to perform in a more ethical and responsible manner. Why destroy the careers of so many innocent people?

I hope we never have another Arthur Andersen-like story. A great firm with great traditions and high ethical standards was destroyed. Along with it, the careers of many highly ethical and talented people were destroyed. Further, many hundreds of companies had to go through the cost and inconvenience of changing auditing firms. This shouldn't happen in a democratic country. In hindsight, perhaps Leonard Spacek, the former CEO of Arthur Andersen, was right. His idea in the 1960s to form an accounting court to police accounting firms may have been right on track.

My Lessons Learned

1. DO THE RIGHT THING

I was always taught by Drake University to do what was right. Professor Dilley told me I had to carry through on my commitment to interview Arthur Andersen. He was right. If I didn't do what was right, my life would have gone down a different path.

At the end of my career, I had to help our employees get placed and put all my effort in trying to make that happen, even if it was at my own expense. I did it because it was the right thing to do.

2. LISTEN TO YOUR HEART

Although Arthur Andersen gave me the lowest offer, I felt it was the place for me. My personality seemed to blend with their corporate culture. So I turned down higher and more attractive offers and went with my heart.

If Susan and I didn't approve her receiving the drug to prolong her labor, we probably would not have any children today. Even though the drug was not yet approved by the FDA, the risk was worth the reward.

3. BE PERSISTENT

I would not take "no" for an answer. My persistence with the U.S. Army Sergeant enabled me to take the CPA exam, as well as take my final examinations in order to be able to graduate.

4. INCREASES IN RESPONSIBILITY COME WITH PERSONAL SACRIFICE

Transferring from our roots to a strange city required a lot of personal sacrifice. But as it turned out, this short-term pain enabled us to later attain financial security and a better quality of life.

If you want to grow in an organization, success does not come without personal sacrifice. In my case, it later resulted in a fourth move, this time to St. Louis.

5. EXPERTISE AND CREATIVITY CREATE VALUE

In my case, it was retail industry expertise, which enhanced my personal value. Become an expert in your field and your services will be in great demand.

I showed creativity in figuring out how Zale Corporation could adopt the LIFO method of inventory pricing, when it was rarely, if ever used by a retail jewelry chain. When May Company needed a solution to deal with its real estate issue, I assembled a group to figure out a solution that was never used before. Clients relish creativity.

6. BEWARE OF THE POWER OF OUR GOVERNMENT

In my first substantive experience in dealing with the IRS, I quickly learned how coercive and powerful the agency can be. Even though the answer may be reasonable, you can't reason with the IRS. Don't think that you will always get a fair trial. They have the power and authority to do whatever they want to do. Later, in less than 90 days, our government put one of the world's most effective and profitable international accounting firms out of business.

7. LEARNING NEVER ENDS

No matter what your position or title, life is about continual learning. Take advantage of every opportunity. It will help you stay relevant.

8. A LEADER IN THE OFFICE SHOULD ALSO BE A LEADER IN THE COMMUNITY

It is important to leverage your office leadership skills to be a leader in the community. This not only helps develop your leadership skills, but also benefits the community. A healthy community enables you to have a healthy business.

9. A COMMON CULTURE IS THE GLUE THAT HOLDS THE ORGANIZATION TOGETHER

If your organization believes in your culture, do not change it. Culture is what bonds people together. Without a common culture, you face disaster.

10. COURAGE OF YOUR CONVICTIONS, WITHOUT PERSISTENCE PRODUCES LITTLE RESULT

I had the courage to tell our CEO, Jim Wadia, to settle the Andersen Consulting arbitration. I had the courage to tell my leadership partners to pursue a merger with another firm. But I took "NO" for an answer and dropped it. Perhaps if I was more persistent and got others involved, the result would have been different.

11. DON'T JUST COMPLAIN, TAKE OWNERSHIP OF THE PROBLEM

When our partners were frustrated about how our unit process was working, it was very easy for everyone to complain. Instead we focused on what we could do to make it better and took appropriate action. To settle our legal issue with AB, I could have easily complained how it was not fair, since it was not our fault. Instead, I took ownership of the problem and generated a solution that was good for all.

12. CELEBRATE SUCCESS

Celebrate the success of others and the office. Work should be fun and enjoyable by all. Professionals work hard and make many personal sacrifices. Don't forget to celebrate and enjoy your work. All work and no play is not good.

13. GOOD TEAMS ARE MORE EFFECTIVE THAN INDIVIDUAL STARS

No matter how many stars you have in the organization, effective teams can produce greater profitability than individual performers. This is true in business, just as it is in sports.

14. IN TIMES OF CRISIS, YOU FIND OUT WHO ARE YOUR REAL FRIENDS

When you are going through good times, it seems like everyone wants to be your friend. But in times of crisis, you know who your REAL friends are. It was comforting to have people like John Bachmann and Bert Walker rally and be my side. They showed their true friendship and support. Others, whom I thought were my friends, turned their back on me. We have spoken little since.

15. IN CRISIS, STAY POSITIVE AND FOCUSED

No one will be more positive than the person in charge. If that person thinks negatively, it will permeate the organization. Leaders must do everything possible to make sure that the organization can function and weather the storm. They need to give their people hope that they will end up well, whether it is with the organization or someplace else. The cream will rise to the top.

Exhibits

EXHIBIT 1

Partner Early Retirement Benefits

An Arthur Andersen partner had to retire by age 62. Each partner had the option of selecting "early retirement," starting at age 56. This was instituted for a variety of reasons. First, it enabled younger partners to have greater opportunities. Second, it enabled older partners to have more options outside the firm, since their value would be greater at age 56 than 62. Most partners selected early retirement at age 56.

A person who selected early retirement received three different forms of payment.

RETIREMENT PAYMENT

This was calculated based on the average of the two largest years of individual earnings. It was payable in either lump sum or in monthly payments, spread over 10 years at a fixed interest rate determined at the time of retirement. Most partners selected the 10-year option, as it provided a nice stream of earnings through age 65 and minimized the income tax burden.

CAPITAL PAYMENT

Upon joining the partnership, a partner bought into the firm by contributing a capital payment. Each year, they contributed a portion of their earnings to their capital account, so that the capital grew during the time you were a partner in the firm. The capital would be returned to the partner when he or she left the firm. This would be paid in lump sum and would not be subject to income tax, since the partner previously paid tax on those earnings.

OTHER BENEFITS

At the full retirement age, the partner received a monthly retirement payment for life, which was meant to be a supplement to his or her Social Security payments. If the partner died, his or her spouse continued to receive 50% of the payments for the rest of his or her life.

The partners continued to receive certain benefits that they also received during their careers. This included preparation of income tax returns, investment planning and counseling, health insurance, life insurance, etc.

When the firm was dissolved in 2002, all active partners lost most of these benefits.

EXHIBIT 2

Career Timeline for Larry R. Katzen

YEAR	ACTIVITY
1968	Joined Arthur Andersen Chicago Office upon graduating from Drake University, and after spending 6 months at Ft. Ord, married Susan Nieder
1971	Transferred to the Melbourne, Australia office
1973	Promoted to manager
1974	Quadruplets born
1977	Transferred to the Dallas office
1978	Promoted to Partner
1983	Investigated by the IRS criminal division—charges dropped 2 years later
1985	Assigned as the engagement partner for the May Co. audit while still in Dallas
1989	Participated on developing a vision for the firm
1992	Promoted to be the managing partner of the worldwide retail industry practice
1993	Transferred to the St. Louis office as office managing partner
1998	Appointed co-managing partner for developing the firm's strategy
1998	Promoted to regional managing partner for the Great Plains Region
2001	Elected early retirement to be effective February 19, 2002
2002	Firm is indicted and liquidated

Exhibits

EXHIBIT 3
ARTHUR ANDERSEN ORGANIZATION
U.S. OFFICE OPERATIONS
PRE ANDERSEN CONSULTING

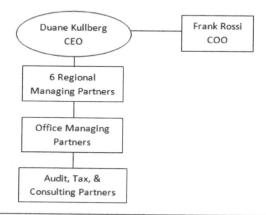

FUNCTIONAL ORGANIZATION
PRE ANDERSEN CONSULTING

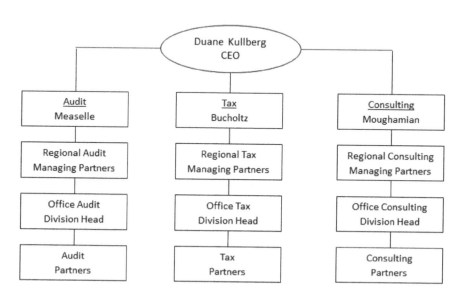

EXHIBIT 4
ARTHUR ANDERSEN ORGANIZATION
U.S. OFFICE OPERATIONS
POST ANDERSEN CONSULTING

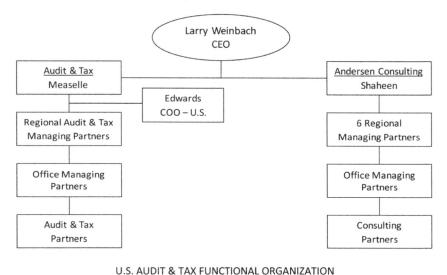

U.S. AUDIT & TAX FUNCTIONAL ORGANIZATION
POST ANDERSEN CONSULTING

Exhibits

EXHIBIT 5
ARTHUR ANDERSEN ORGANIZATION - U.S. OPERATIONS POST ACCENTURE

FUNCTIONAL ORGANIZATION – POST ACCENTURE

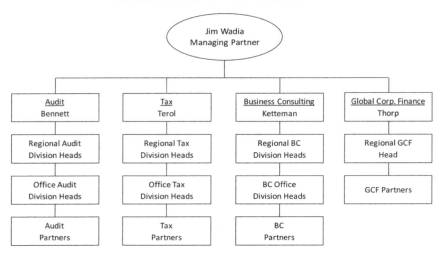

Index

CPSIA information can be obtained at www.ICGtesting.com
Printed in the USA
LVOW01*0259130614

389893LV00001B/1/P